Iranian cinema

a political history

Hamid Reza Sadr

in association with

 C

Prince Claus
Fund Library

Published in 2006 by
I.B.Tauris & Co. Ltd
6 Salem Rd, London W2 4BU
175 Fifth Avenue, New York NY 10010
www.ibtauris.com

In the United States and Canada distributed by Palgrave Macmillan,
a division of St. Martin's Press, 175 Fifth Avenue, New York, NY 10010

Published in association with the Prince Claus Fund Library, The Hague

ISBN 10 1 84511 146 X (Hb)
ISBN 10 1 84511 147 8 (Pb)
ISBN 13 978 1 84511 146 5 (Hb)
ISBN 13 978 1 84511 147 2 (Pb)

International Library of Iranian Studies 7

A full CIP record for this book is available from the British Library
A full CIP record for this book is available from the Library of Congress
Library of Congress catalog card: available

Typeset in Monotype Joanna by illuminati, Grosmont,
www.illuminatibooks.co.uk
Printed and bound in Great Britain by T.J. International Ltd,
Padstow, Cornwall

Contents

List of illustrations

To my loving sister, Mehrnaz, who brings joy to my life

Introduction

From its beginnings and until fairly recently, Iranian cinema has presented itself as a particularly legible form of escapism. Throughout most of its history, it has been characterised by bad scripts, poor performances and low production values. In form and content Iranian films have tended to be conservative, but reading between the lines we find a peculiar, sometimes contradictory, dynamic that provides the opportunity for examination of specific social and political problems. Behind a tale of happy childhood, for example, may lurk a subtext about disheartened adulthood; beneath the mask of a love story, one may often find a subtle explication of oppression.

It is no secret that Iranian film has had little direct influence on social attitudes and behaviour. For many years it could hardly be taken seriously, and rarely even took itself seriously until relatively recently – during the 1990s – when it began to be approached more thoughtfully by both film-makers and critics. But even the earlier films attempted to convince or teach audiences: how to conduct oneself in the public arena; how to act with the opposite sex; how to deal with dishonesty; how to protest and how to compromise; how to hate and how to love; how to make friends and how to take revenge; what to think about the rich and the poor; how to react against Westerners. These films instructed young men in their careers, and showed women the correct way to dress; they discussed right and wrong; sometimes they pointed up social problems and usually, though not always, suggested naive solutions. And they still do.

With its raw approach, Iranian film was perhaps particularly suited to the translation of political and social values into simple scenes that sometimes seemed as authentic as one's own childhood memories. When in *The Treasures of Gharun* (1965), the impoverished hero, Carefree Ali, came into conflict with the rich, arrogant Gharun, this could easily be read as lampooning a specific social class. When in *Gheisar* (1969) Behruz Vosughi's character vengefully killed his enemies, it was clear that he was standing outside, and questioning, the limits of the law. Although one might not agree with the messages of these films, or even recognise that they were counting on one's consent, one tended to process them in moral terms, intentionally or not. Whether good or bad films, they spoke the audience's language, and the audience learnt to speak theirs. It was clear that they presented a 'politics', an 'ideology', a 'doctrine', or at the very least a 'belief'. Even the weak scripts, repetitious messages, carbon-copy stories and ridiculous characters were charged with political meaning. The happy endings provided not only retribution for the characters, but a pat on the back for a society that supposedly made it possible to live life well.

With very few exceptions, mainstream Iranian film is uninteresting to anyone looking for imaginative expression. However, to those curious about the ways in which Iranian culture is or is not represented in films, it remains engaging and, occasionally, frightening. To understand the ideology behind these films, it is essential to look at who lives happily ever after and who dies; who falls by the wayside and who is rescued; who strikes it rich and who loses everything – and above all, why.

My inspiration to write a book on politics and Iranian cinema came around 1993, during a decade in which Iran produced one of the most ambitious groups of films in the world, films which were increasingly included in international festivals. Through its cinema, Iran was breaking out of a cultural cocoon. Following the successful films of Dariush Mehrjui, Masud Kimiai, Sohrab Shahid-Sales and Bahram Bayzai in the early 1970s, Iranian cinema had entered the 1980s in a state of almost total collapse. As far as the world at large was concerned, it was nonexistent, and its standing at home had sunk so low that during the days of the 1979 Revolution, half the cinemas were burned down in angry demonstrations. In recent years, however, many people have begun to show a renewed interest in Iranian film. With the emergence in the 1990s of Abbas Kiarostami, Mohsen Makhmalbaf, Majid Majidi and Rakhshan Bani-Etemad as directors of worldwide importance, Iranian cinema served notice that it had been reborn, after almost a decade of demise. Now, only a few years later, its leading directors are familiar names to cineastes internationally, and their films have reaped critical acclaim.

Behind this transformation lies a political background that occasionally threatens to overshadow the cinema itself in the eyes of the foreign audience. As a visitor to international film festivals, I continually face a harsh line of questioning, which essentially asks: Why are the portraits of society in Iranian films so different to our expectations? How come Iranian films contain humanitarian concepts, the opposite of the dark and negative image of your country in the West?

Gradually, I began to study and analyse Iranian films, their themes and characters, within the social and political context of their time, looking at such questions as why most Iranian films screened outside Iran in the late 1990s were rooted in the emotional framework of innocent, hardworking children. The truth is that these apparently non-political films were a reflection of the social situation in contemporary Iran. The children provided a tangible portrait of the Iranian people. The more we look at Iranian film, the more we learn about the ways in which film works upon an audience and the audience upon it.

The object of this book is to provide a comprehensive analysis of Iranian film and to challenge the marginalisation of political issues within it, exposing some of the prevalent conceptions about the role and place of politics in mainstream Iranian cinema. The intention is to look at the themes and characters in Iranian films since the turn of the twentieth century with respect to political, economic and social factors. The book deals both with cinema and with history, indicating the social and economic backgrounds out of which the key directors, films, themes and characters arose and, focusing on Iranian cinema's most persistent genres, offers a set of historical claims about Iran's popular cinema, which has always addressed – however indirectly – the wishes, fears and anxieties current in Iran at any given moment.[1] The final chapters survey some of the thematic concerns in New Iranian Cinema that have been disregarded, and introduce the lesser-known figures in this genre.

1 Early years: from 1900 to the 1920s

A crossroads between East and West

It all began with Mozzafar al-Din Shah (1853–1906), who was King of Iran from 1896 until his death, and his political machine. The visual arts in Iran at that time were restricted to sumptuous palaces and remained out of the reach of the common people. It is therefore legitimate to ask, if it were not for the Shah's many visits to Europe at the end of the nineteenth century and his enthusiasm for the new medium of film sweeping the West, when would the silver screen have finally lit up in Iran?

By virtue of its location, between the Caspian Sea and the Persian Gulf, Iran has always constituted a cultural crossroads between East and West. It has opened itself up to external influences in many different forms, but Western influences became especially pronounced during the Qajar dynasty (1796–1925), the last traditional dynasty before the Pahlavi dynasty (1925–79) came into power. Perhaps the essence of dependent development is that a nation has things done to it rather than doing them for itself, and this was the situation during much of the early period of modernisation in Iran, as foreign powers fought out their battles for control of resources, strategic locations and trade. Britain had long had a presence in the Persian Gulf, particularly in southern Iran due to its oilfields. Equally longstanding was the relationship with Russia, Iran's powerful northern neighbour, which seized many significant areas of Iran during the Qajar era. In the late 1800s Iran's government was weak, and the country was dependent on both Britain and Russia for money, arms and military training. In the process of modernisation, certain new technologies and developmental infrastructures were brought to the country, but always in such a way as to prioritise the needs of the foreign power over those of Iran.

FIG. 1 *Once Upon a Time, Cinema* (*Nasser al-Din Shah, Actor-e Cinema*), Mohsen Makhmalbaf, 1981.

Nasser al-Din Shah – Mozzafar's predecessor – had ascended the Qajar throne in 1848, and, as a great admirer of British telegraph technology, had in the 1850s ordered a line to be established between his Golestan Palace and Laleh-zar Garden, both in Tehran. In 1851–61, Britain tried laying undersea cables from the Red Sea past Muscat in Oman, to Karachi in Pakistan, but the operation failed. The alternative was overland cable, and in 1862 they negotiated an agreement with the Turks and the Iranians for the construction of a single-wire line. By the 1880s Iran was well equipped with telegraph lines that linked up its towns and connected it with various parts of the world.

It is an indication of the socially perceived power and influence of the telegraph – essentially, the people's notion that the lines ran straight to the Shah's palace – that telegraph offices were often chosen as places of protest, to the great embarrassment of both British and Iranian officials. The telegraph also aided the establishment of newspapers in Iran. The first daily was founded in 1898, and tapped into the foreign news coming in from Reuters en route to the Indian press. The Iranian elite – especially the Shahs – eagerly received other communications technologies. Nasser al-Din Shah was introduced to the telephone by his crown prince Kamran Khan, who in 1888 set up a line between the Shah's palaces.

The introduction of photography to Nasser al-Din Shah signalled the West's encroaching cultural influence. While the Iranian masses remained ignorant of contemporary technology, the Shah's fascination with all things scientific grew during his three visits to Europe in 1871, 1873 and 1889. He learned how to take pictures, and became an avid collector of photographs. Despite the clergy's antipathy, photography prospered within the court. Having established Dar al-Funun (the House of Arts and Sciences) the Shah even designated studios within his palace for the sole purpose of printing negatives. His love of photography was so great that sycophants would try to gain his grace by pretending to be interested in the subject. During his European trips, he posed for the camera on numerous occasions, leaving behind a plethora of photographs.

His enthusiasm offered an occasion for more foreigners to visit the country. In 1844, a Frenchman by the name of Jules Richard (1761–91) became the first Western photographer to work in the Persian court. He was fluent in a number of European languages, and was appointed to the faculty of Dar al-Funun in 1851. Soon, he began collecting and selling Iranian works of art. Luigi Pesce (1818–91) an Italian colonel who came to Iran in 1848 to train the army, became the first person to photograph ancient Persian buildings.

Other foreign photographers included the French brothers, Carlhiee and Henri de Blocqueville. The latter was so intimate with the Shah that he was appointed both court photographer and army officer, charged with making photographs and paintings of battle scenes recording the victories of the Iranian army. The famous photographer Luigi Montabone (d. 1877) accompanied the Italian commission that travelled to Iran in 1862 to take photographs to illustrate the scientific reports that the commission intended

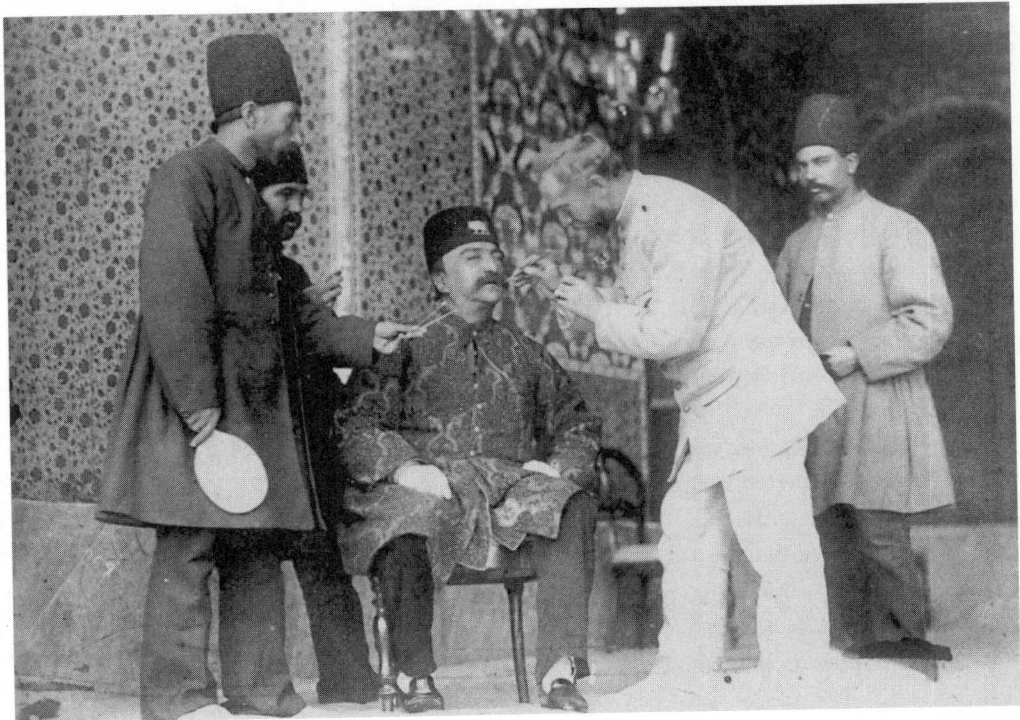

FIG. 2 Barber dyeing Nasser-al-Din Shah's moustache, c. 1880, photograph by Antoin Sevruguin.

to publish. Sixty-two albumen prints have been preserved, and are amongst some of the most striking depictions of the Qajar era.

From 1870, Western photographers in Iran pursued their work more systematically. Among them were noted researchers such as Franz Stolze (1830–1910), Jane Dieulafoy (1851–1916), Jacques de Morgan (1857–1924), and Friedrich Sarre (1865–1945). Photographs were also taken by well-known travellers such as Isabella Lucy Bishop Bird (1831–1904), Albert P.H. Hotz (1855–1930), and Gertrude Bell (1868–1926), and by commercial photographers including Ernst Holtzer (1835–1911). The best-known Iranian photographer of this period, Abdullah Qajar (1849–1909), taught at Dar al-Funun.

In 1896, two years after the birth of cinema in the West, Nasser al-Din Shah was assassinated by a man called Mirza Reza Kermani. His successor, Mozzafar al-Din Shah, was a sick old man who had waited far too long for his chance to reign. In the following years, Iranian national assets were mortgaged to Britain and Russia in order to fund the garrulous king's extravagant visits to Europe, ostensibly for medical care.

By 1906, when Mozzafar al-Din Shah died, government mismanagement and foreign influence had reduced Iran to a buffer state. The long-standing discontent that characterised this period – merchants and manufacturers had been protesting against the rising tide of European imports as early as the 1830s – forced the incoming political administration to undertake major reform. The Constitutional Revolution of 1905–11, brought about by a major alliance of clerics, liberal reformers, merchants, traders, students and workers who fought against the foreign political and economic influence and the weak and dependent government, aimed to reform the arbitrary nature of the monarch's power.

Movies come to Iran: the Western touch

At the time of cinema's first appearance in Iran, however, the country was still led by an autocratic monarchy scarcely out of the feudal period, headed by Mozzafar al-Din Shah, who believed that he ruled by divine edict. His journeys were instrumental in introducing cinema, via the magic lantern, to Iran.

In the summer of 1900, accompanied on his travels by Mirza-Ebrahim Khan Akkasbashi (*akkas-bashi* literally means 'cameraman'), the old king was mesmerised by the moving images he saw dancing across the screen. He attended several screenings, and about a month after his first visit to the cinema, travelled to Belgium. Akkasbashi was the son of Mirza Ahmad Zia ul-Saltaneh, the court photographer during Nasser al-Din's reign, and had accompanied his father on a ten-year trip to Europe. As part of Mozzafar al-Din's entourage, by order of the Shah, he purchased a camera to shoot the official visit to Belgium. Thus, Mozzafar al-Din Shah can lay claim to being the first Iranian cinephile, as well as the first Iranian to be captured on celluloid, while Akkasbashi was the first Iranian cinematographer. He did not, of course, use his art to narrate the story of the people, but instead left us disjointed footage of royal palaces and the houses of dignitaries. He remained the court cinematographer until the end of Mozzafar al-Din's reign.

On his return to Iran, the Shah brought cinematography with him. In *The Travels of His Grace, Mozzafar al-Din Shah* (1900), he would recall: 'In the evening I instructed Akkasbashi to prepare the cinematography and magic lantern that we had purchased from Paris.'[2] Until then, the only kind of public spectacle in Iran had been the traditional *taziyeh*, the earliest form of Iranian theatrical performance. Still a popular tradition in villages even now during some religious ceremonies, *taziyeh* comprises elegies and poetry about the lives of the martyrs, and has its origins in what is considered an exemplar of Shi'ite martyrdom, that of Imam Hossein in 680, the third Shi'ite Imam, and grandson of the Prophet Muhammad.[3] The new arrival, film, cautiously challenged the tradition of *taziyeh*.

When Akkasbashi shot the first Iranian moving images, then, the new lantern came to a very traditional Iran. The first films were screened at the royal court in front of a gender-partitioned audience. Like photography, the history of Iranian cinema began with an audience drawn exclusively from the court and the aristocracy.

It was yet another courtier, Mirza-Ebrahim-Khan Sahaf-bashi, who established the first public commercial cinema. His father had also been one of the privileged few who had been sent abroad by Nasser al-Din Shah to study. In 1904, with the permission of the Shah, he opened an ill-fated commercial cinema in Tehran, specialising in short films. Certain religious authorities denounced the venture as an act of Satan, and the Shah was forced to close it.[4] Sahaf-bashi's property was seized, and he and his family were exiled abroad. This period is characterised not only by the state's direct intervention in the film industry but also by the 'casting vote' of the clergy. With public disaffection growing against the 'ungodly' abomination of cinema, a leading cleric of the day, Sheikh Fazlollah Nuri, issued a *fatwa* against it. This was to be the recurring motif of Iranian cinema.

The Revolution of 1905–11 established a constitutional monarchy and a limited form of parliamentary democracy. In August 1907, Russia and Britain divided Iran into three regions, without bothering to consult the sovereign government. The north belonged to Russia, the south came under Britain's sphere of influence, and a buffer zone was created in the middle, which included the great city of Isfahan. In the midst of such tumultuous political events, the nascent film industry struggled for survival.

In 1908, a contemporary journal observed that: 'The newly imported cinema screens are now showing world events in all their glory on Nasseri Avenue, at a merchant's store.'[5] The merchant, named Tajer-bashi, a man who was at this time forging a strong bond with government officials, had a commercial rival however in the shape of Mehdi Ivanov, known as Russi Khan, an apprentice to the court photographer. The fact that Russi Khan, who in the same year was also attempting to show moving images publicly, was neither an Iranian nor a Muslim was to become a characteristic of the industry. The gulf dividing cinema from orthodox clerics acted as a spur for ethnic/religious minorities, in particular Armenians, who played a vital role in developing cinema.

Russi Khan's inaugural film was originally entitled *The War Between Russia and Japan*, but due to his pro-Russian sentiments, he altered the title to the more triumphant *Long Live Russians!* Religious opposition to the reopening of commercial cinema continued apace, although this time the pro-royalist Russi Khan found a powerful ally in the shape of the Shah. The antagonism between Russi Khan and Tajer-bashi, who were initially opposed due to their close relationships with Russia and Britain respectively, became politicised along the royalist versus constitutionalist axis, leading to street battles in 1909. After the sacking of his theatre, Russi Khan was forced to flee the country. Eighty years later, Hassan Hedayat would make the film *Grand Cinema* (1989), which presented a satirical portrait of this earliest period in the history of the film-screening business in Iran.

In 1910, the 12-year-old Ahmad Shah was enthroned. The same year saw the opening of another cinema, this time by an Armenian, Artashes Patmagrian. The following year, George Ismailov established a cinema facing it. They showed extracts from Lumière, Gaumont and Pathé productions. The conflict between cinema and *taziyeh* reached its peak during this period, with the latter extending its programmes from two in the afternoon until two after midnight in an attempt to undermine the popularity of commercial cinema. By 1911, the young Ahmad Shah was increasingly frittering away his time in Europe, while his country sank into chaos. As the protest of the people increased, unaided by an impotent government, the Qajar dynasty neared its demise.

2 The 1920s to the 1940s

The rise of Iranian modernism

With the beginning of the First World War, cinema demonstrated for the first time its function as a disseminator of news. Through newsreels screening in the cinemas, Iranian people could see what was happening in the rest of the world. Soon, however, political manoeuvrings delivered a new body blow to the film industry. At the peak of turmoil in the country, with politicians trying to seize power from the declining government and with Russian and British political activities within Iran also causing disorder, Reza Khan Mir-Panj of Mazandaran, a military officer, took the moment to establish a centralised state. He rose to power through a coup d'état in 1920, three years after the October Revolution had shaken Iran's neighbouring giant, Russia. He swiftly built a strong army to put down socialist revolts in Gilan and Azerbaijan. Tribal rebellions, too, were brought under control. Public gatherings were restricted, and for a short period cinema owners were forced to shut down their establishments before 9.30 p.m. every night. By 1921, Iran was bankrupt; its economic institutions were still primitive and it remained an overwhelmingly agricultural society. Modern industry was nonexistent. Iran was still at a pre-industrial stage, but the number of filmgoers was increasing.

The Afghan king's state visit in 1922 became an occasion for the first-ever gathering of unveiled women in the court. Piano recitals accompanied copious drinking bouts, the likes of which had never been seen in previous Persian dynasties. In the same year, Iranian graduates in Rome attended an Embassy feast in Italy. For the first time girls posed for cameras unveiled, and the young prince, Muhammad Reza, Reza Khan's son, was photographed in sports gear. It seemed that Iran was shedding its old skin.

Around 1924 a successful merchant named Ali Vakili, thanks to his government contacts, opened the Grand Cinema in Tehran, the distinguishing feature of which was the designation of a special space for female audiences. Although traditionalists frowned upon this limited innovative gesture, it represented a real gain. Between film screenings, the audience was treated to live music, another Western-inspired experiment.

In October 1925, Ahmad Shah officially handed over the reins of power to Reza Khan, who established the Pahlavi dynasty (Reza Khan took the name 'Pahlavi' some years after he came to power) with the aid of the British Consulate. Six days later, the government, addressing the peasantry, issued a decree: 'Henceforth, the new cinemas will screen the latest European methods of agriculture in the evenings.' This gesture was an indication that the rulers were acutely aware of the new medium's powers of persuasion. For a full transition into capitalist development it would be necessary to overcome the medieval feudal system of partition, which had proved difficult in the hands of the Qajar aristocracy.

Reza Khan's political outlook was secular and pro-military, and his programme focused on the creation of a strong modern centralised state in Iran. Although he was not a member of the aristocracy, his extreme brand of patriotism, which propagated a self-confident chauvinism, meant that throughout his reign there was no realistic cinematic portrayal of ordinary people. Iranian cinema was branded for many decades by this paternalistic stigma.

As Reza Khan's power became absolute and arbitrary – employing the tired excuse of national security – argument and criticism, even independent thought and action, ceased to exist. He increasingly fell prisoner, it seems, to the gutless and self-seeking 'lackeys' around him, and became a victim of his own propaganda. He seemed to be deceived by his own crude public image – in his trademark military gown, boots and hat – into regarding himself as a god incarnate. An over-emphasis on ancient Persian greatness, dished out in clichéd eulogies, permeated culture, and a society vacillating between monarchy and republicanism fell into the trap of authoritarianism. Cinema's potential role as an agent of socialisation was clear. It could reach the entire population; the illiteracy rate at the time was over 80 per cent, and cinema was the only book that even the illiterate could read. It would be a powerful tool with which to forge a 'new Iranian state' committed to the king.

A servant to the king and government, Reza Khan's brand of cinema also indulged in the plagiarism of foreign features in order to celebrate and legitimise the Pahlavi regime. Sometimes the attempt resulted in pure farce. In December 1926, a film entitled *Cyrus the Great and the Conquest of Babylon* was screened at the Grand Cinema. A newspaper waxed lyrical about it over a number of issues: 'Those familiar with Persian history are fully cognisant with Cyrus the Great's contribution to our society and his esteemed standing in world history. Come to the Grand Cinema to see this great king, his victories, the fall of Babylon, the Chaldean civilisation and life in those days of antiquity.'[6]

The title of the film, and all the panegyrics that passed for reviews, were calculated to draw comparisons between Cyrus the Great, King of ancient Persia (d. 529 BC) and Reza Khan. The irony is that *Cyrus the Great and the Conquest of Babylon* did not really exist. Shown at the Grand Cinema was an extract from a prestigious American film entitled *Intolerance*, directed by D.W. Griffith in 1916. The ancient Babylon episode pitted the scholarly, peace-loving Prince Belshazar against the rigid High Priest of Bel, who conspires with the Persian King Cyrus to destroy Belshazar's regime.

Early films, new tendencies

In May 1928 the first part of the Civil Code, comprising 955 articles, was submitted to Parliament for approval. These articles embraced laws relating to property, contracts, estates, wills and inheritance and were modelled on the Napoleonic Code and Western principles of law, while observing the fundamentals of Shi'a jurisprudence and Islamic legal precepts. Also in May, Reza Khan announced the abrogation of the capitulation rights of all foreign powers in Iran. It was now argued, in effect, that Iran boasted a judicial system as well as a body of law on a par with any European country.

In 1929, Ahmad Shah died quietly in Paris, and a year later the first Iranian feature, entitled *Abi va Rabi* (*Abi and Rabi*, 1930), was made by Avanes Ohanian.

This sixty-minute silent slapstick comedy hit the screens amidst a great deal of publicity. The reaction of the press was based on political rather than artistic criteria and responses revolved around an understanding of the film as proof of society's renaissance. The government's policies were lauded with a mixture of aplomb and self-serving platitudes. One writer pointed out that 'The film displayed images of old Tehran and compared them with the new buildings and avenues springing up all around us today.'[7] Another eulogy masquerading as a review stated that 'The film ably charted the progress Iran has made in recent years, depicting our customs, traditions, and everyday living habits.'[8] The two leading stars, Muhammad Zarabi and Gholam-Ali Sohrabifard, formed a comic pairing in imitation of their more prominent Western counterparts such as the Danish duo Fyrtaanet and Bivognen, who won worldwide success long before Laurel and Hardy. According to surviving photographs, they were dressed in impeccable Western attire, and came to be perceived as symbols of the new Iran.

Gradually, as the state opened music schools (ignoring the Islamic laws that banned music), and automobiles began to replace horse-drawn carriages, cinema revealed a new world to the Iranians. Various opposition tendencies not withstanding, film began to make real inroads into cultural life. Yet a significant section of the populace considered censorship indispensable. Three months after the publication of an article, in June 1930, in the leading newspaper *Aiene Iran*, complaining about the lack of censorship of foreign films on moral as opposed to only political grounds, the government presented the following bill for ratification:

> As the town council is responsible for improving public morals and combating corruption, and as the direct control and regulation of all theatres, clubs, public musical recitals, garden parties, etc., is not practical, the government recommends the following bill for ratification: cinema managers are obliged to seek a screening permit prior to the film being shown … Any part of the film that the council deems contrary to public decency and modesty will be edited out.[9]

Nine feature films were made between 1930 and 1937, signifying the emergence of the nascent film industry. They were made mostly for entertainment purposes, and in so far as they dealt with historical events, tended brazenly to censor and distort reality. Predictably, ordinary people were conspicuous only by their absence from these films.

One of the most important aspects of the years after Reza Khan's ascension to absolute power was the obsessive rate at which religion and traditions were rejected. Many Orientalist commentators, such as Said Amir Arjomand and Dilip Hiro, have suggested that contemporary Iranian history is characterised by the rapid passage from a medieval world-view to a modern one, a simplistic story that was repeated ad nauseam by Reza Khan and his son, Muhammad Reza Shah, in later years. What went by the name of 'modernism' in Iran and neighbouring Turkey, and was used as a template by Reza Khan, far from renewing society ended up simply mimicking the West. Modernism in this context meant dressing, behaving and even speaking like Europeans, a process that left an indelible mark on the films produced during this period.

The rebuilding of the capital into new Tehran was representative of Reza Khan's kneejerk reaction to the past. The ancient city gates belonging to the Qajar period were demolished one by one, and in imitation of Western capital cities a number of wide boulevards were built. This might have been partially justifiable as part of the city's regeneration programme. However, it soon became apparent that every project had a hidden agenda. The performance of Western-style plays and the setting up of a modern orchestra based on tonality, which could have opened a new chapter in Iranian art, became, instead, vehicles for Reza Khan's political drive towards *gharb-zadegi* (an invented word best described as 'westoxication'). When Ghamar ul-Molok Vaziri became the first female singer to give a recital in public, it sent shockwaves through the traditionalist community.

Reza Khan's visit to Turkey in 1934 represented the zenith of the state's alliance with modernity. He became fascinated by the reforms of Turkey's head of state, Mustafa Kemal Pasha (also known as Kemal Atatürk), who had instructed Turkish men to wear Western clothes, and women to remove their *hejab* (Islamic veil). He had replaced the Arabic with the Latin script, and the last day of the week had been changed from Friday to Sunday, in imitation of the Western calendar. All these superficial transformations acted as catalysts on Reza Khan.

Yet there were important differences between the two states. Iran possessed a weaker bureaucratic tradition than Turkey, and its central government remained heavily dependent on the support of the large landowners and tribal sheikhs who dominated the rural areas. Perhaps more importantly, since the Turkish state was founded on the ruins of the Ottoman Empire, it defined itself, in contradistinction to Iran, as secular; it remains the only secular state in the Middle East.

A few comparative dates relating to the modernisation of women's lives in the two countries give an indication of the scale of the gap in reform. While the first modern school for girls was established in Istanbul in 1858, there was none in Tehran until 1907. A teacher training college for women was opened in 1863 in Istanbul, but Tehran had to wait until 1918. In the Turkish capital women gained access to university in 1914, but this would not take place in Tehran until 1936.

While the Iranian reforms were more limited in content, they were carried out with greater brutality. What strikes us today, with the benefit of hindsight, is the tragicomic nature of these enforced 'reforms'. As reports of Reza Khan's historic visit to Turkey began filtering through, the government suddenly ordered the compulsory wearing of the Pahlavi hat, which closely resembled the French military cap. This came to replace the traditional Qajar hats that were prevalent at the time, just as Western suits took over from traditional clothes. In order to inaugurate this change, the government initiated a 'hat-changing' ceremony in 1934. Participants at the ceremony heard how the new hat, far from representing a superficial change of image, signalled a profound symbolic watershed for society. A circular was issued to government branches detailing the correct use of hats and ties for bureaucrats and politicians. Likewise, the wearing of European suits, jackets and trousers, already common in higher social circles, was made compulsory for civil servants, and was also encouraged among other social strata. A few years later, however, Reza Khan decided that the Pahlavi hat was not sufficiently modern. Orders were sent out for everyone to wear the 'French' *chapeau*, currently fashionable in Europe and America, known in Iran as the 'basin hat'. This incessant government pressure proved too much for the people and clergy of the religious town of Mashad, who finally staged demonstrations against the 'foreign hat'. In an attempt to quell the unrest, Reza Khan's army shot and killed scores of demonstrators outside the Goharshad mosque.

Reza Khan's modernising zeal reached a peak on 7 January 1936 when Iranian women were indiscriminately and forcibly – yet ceremoniously – 'unveiled'. On this day, Reza Khan, flanked by his unveiled wife and daughters, announced the new policy at a girls' college. Subsequently, numerous lectures were organised by the Women's Society on this topic. Young women and girls took part in theatrical and musical events, even a ballet performance. From then on, the wearing of the Iranian *chador* (a long overdress covering the woman's head and body) was forbidden, as was the use of any form of headscarf or headdress, except of course for European hats.

Since the appearance of veiled women in public was now illegal, many resistant women became prisoners in their own homes, so as not to fall foul of the 'government nannies' whose task it was forcibly to remove the offending garment. The screaming and cursing of angry women became endemic, as did farcical police chases in pursuit of women who refused to go out unveiled. They were forced to venture out only at night, sometimes making their way across the rooftops.

This process of dragging women away from tradition by a lock of their hair (these changes were generally only welcomed by middle-class city women) continued unabated and reached its peak the following year. In Parliament, a special section was designated for women; the first mixed kindergartens were opened; a bill was passed sanctioning the marriage of foreigners to Iranian women; a female delegate participated in the World Women's Congress in Istanbul and the works of Parvin Etesami, a famed poet, were published to great acclaim. A sumptuous masque was held at the Grand Hotel as an excuse to display these new liberated women publicly, side by side with men.

Six decades later, Ali-Reza Davudnezhad would make the film *Khaleh Selah* (*The Disarmament*, 1995) on the subject of women's treatment during the Reza Khan era. In it, the wife of the deputy governor of a small town in the province of Gilan takes refuge in a distant village to avoid the obligatory lifting of the veil. Meanwhile, the deputy governor himself is drawn to the women's liberation movement, but the outbreak of war changes everything and the government fails to achieve its objectives.

Under Reza Khan, reformers of the constitution faced the realisation that they could achieve their projected reforms not through their original vision of a parliamentary system but through the construction of a militaristic state. Reza Khan began a stern regime of punishment, choosing to browbeat and control a captive Parliament by means of personal domination. To this end he exploited all the powers and patronage that accrued to him as ruler. The result was a type of dictatorship. But although he attacked the power of the religious establishment by expanding the sphere of the secular educational and legal systems, the clergy stayed in possession both of its large endowments and its influential system of religious education, which ensured that much of its power base remained intact.

Newsreels, pioneering and propaganda films

In the 1920s, armed with a Gaumont camera, Khan-Baba Motazedi, one of the pioneers of photography in Iran, had become Reza Khan's new cinematographer. He had filmed the Parliament as well as Reza Khan's swearing-in ceremony in 1925. Everything that has survived by this cinematographer has the whiff of propaganda about it, whether depicting the inauguration of the telegraph and railway industries, new bridges, roads and highways, or military marches.

Rushes of Khan-Baba Motazedi's films, accompanied by the national anthem, opened every feature film shown in cinemas at that time. The audience was expected to stand to attention – a ritual that lasted until the 1960s. By the end of the 1920s, Khan-Baba Motazedi was not the only cameraman accompanying Reza Khan's state visits. In 1928 the following report, whose reference to a technical merchant indicates the increasing symbiosis of cinema and entrepreneurship, appeared in a daily newspaper:

> The Iran Comedy Company, whose specialists were chosen to accompany his grace on the recent visit to Khuzestan and Khoram-abad, filmed the proceedings. Unfortunately, due to poor preparation and lack of film stock and other resources, only the trip to Khoram-abad was filmed completely. This is because the technical supplier, a certain Agha Atigheh-chi, a successful merchant who had long been resident in Turkey, has only recently returned to Iran and has not had time to organise his company efficiently. Consequently, the main part of this glorious Royal visit was not filmed. Nevertheless, we are still blessed with 400 metres of rushes.[10]

All extant celluloid images before 1924 are in the form of fragmented rushes. In that year the Americans Merian C. Cooper and Ernest B. Schoedsack (who later created *King Kong*, 1933) had made a film in Iran called *Grass*. Considered the oldest existing 'Iranian' documentary, it describes the migratory habits of the Baba Ahmadi tribe and the tribe's near impossible task of transporting thousands of sheep through treacherous mountain areas. Unusually for the time, it is fully supplied with subtitles as well as inter-titles. Cooper and Schoedsack, accompanied by Margarethe Harrison, spent forty-six days with the tribe, travelling with them across Zard Kuh (the Yellow Mountain) and the Karun river. The 'documentary' contains a number of constructed scenes, such as a staged dance, and at times is marred by the Orientalism of Western travellers, which imbues everything with a touch of mysterious exoticism. Nevertheless, unlike many later Western documentaries and newsreels depicting Iran, *Grass* does not belittle the Easterner. The life-and-death struggle of this brave tribe is portrayed realistically. *Grass* was distributed in America by Paramount Studios and became a commercial and critical success.

The subject matter of *Grass* – an epic battle with nature and the harsh realities of poverty – did not tally with Reza Khan's agenda, however. His favourite propaganda themes were urban progress and modernity. During this period, road tolls and taxes were abolished and, under a development plan, 14,000 miles of new roads were built. This, together with the rapid import of vehicles, meant that travelling time was cut, and inland freight rates fell. Improved communications linked the regions and opened up the country for internal trade and the shipping of imports and, via the transportation network, the government tried to integrate diverse communities and to overcome existing factionalism. *Grass*, which was distributed under two different titles, *Grass: A Nation's Battle for Life*, and, following Reza Khan's predictable criticism of the film's emphasis on poverty, *Grass: The Epic of a Lost Tribe*, broached none of these themes. It was banned from Iranian cinemas. Four decades later, in 1964, the film was finally shown in Iran, with additional commentary provided in an attempt to ameliorate its negative impact.

The real problem was that while Reza Khan was busy disarming and subjugating tribal landlords, *Grass* depicted these 'renegades' as free men, whose prowess with the gun allowed them publicly to flout the law. Ten years later, in 1934, newspapers would report the execution of the heads of the Bakhtiari, Qasqai, Boyer-Ahmadi and Mamsani tribes. Reza Khan's power base was secure.

Iran's destiny, torn between anti-authoritarianism and autocracy, was now coming to bear in all its complexity, as was the fate of cinema. The banning of *Grass* set a precedent for the future. Every film related to Iran would henceforth be judged politically and was expected to paint the country in a positive light. In 1930, the German Union of Railways made a film called *The Iranian Railway System*. It portrayed the insurmountable obstacles with which engineers had to contend, and portrayed the peasants and villagers who lived along the route of the railroads. Sadly, this film too was condemned as a misrepresentation of modern Iran. The pro-government newspaper *Etella'at* complained that, since its scenes were five years old, the documentary was obsolete, suggesting that the country had undergone dramatic changes since then.[11]

In 1935 another film about the railway system, this time made by a foreign engineering firm called Iran Kompsax, and entitled *Iran: The New Persia*, also elicited negative reactions. One review summed up the general opinion when it said: 'This film is an attempt by European filmmakers to portray us as uncivilised, and suggests that our land is unsuitable for living in'.[12] It is hardly worth pointing out that this kneejerk attitude, which became the stock response of critics in later years, betrays a certain inferiority complex.

The responses to such films became the perfect excuse for Reza Shah to tighten censorship laws governing filmmaking. In 1938 a bill was passed by Parliament, which included the following punitive measures:

> Article One: All those companies or individuals, be they foreign or native, who wish to film in Iran, must first apply for a permit to the relevant police authorities, and proceed to film under the direct supervision of the said authorities.
>
> Article Two: All technical film apparatus must be impounded by the Customs & Excise Department until the successful issue of the film permit . . .
>
> Article Four: After the completion of filming, all stock must be handed over to the Police authorities for inspection and the issue of the relevant export permits . . .

> Article Seven: It is strictly forbidden to film, paint or sketch the following sites without relevant permits from both the police department and the Ministry of Culture: historical and religious buildings, roads, national parks, ports, cruise liners, factories and landscapes …
>
> Article Ten: It is strictly forbidden to film, paint or sketch military installations and fortifications.
>
> Article Eleven: Filming, painting and sketching any subject deemed contrary to the interests and dignity of the nation is strictly forbidden.

What began as the depiction of ordinary Iranians in films was brought to an end with the introduction of draconian catch-all phrases such as 'the interests and dignity of the nation' which, needless to say, were attributes assessed and interpreted by the state. These regulations resulted in alienating people from the cinema and transformed the industry into the disseminator of either escapist fantasies or state propaganda. As Hamid Mowlana, a global communications specialist, has put it:

> Under the rigorous censorship of Reza Shah's regime, freedom of thought, of speech, and of the press was suspended. Any discussion of political topics, let alone criticism of the government, was unthinkable, dangerous even in private conversation … He followed an authoritarian theory of the press, something of an imitation of the fascist ministers of propaganda.[13]

Censorship was not a security matter, but was tied in with the desire to remove all obstacles impeding modernisation. This was also the impulse behind the spread of 'commissioned' films in Iran. A prime example was *The Iran Oil Industry*, commissioned by the Shah from the Anglo-Persian Oil Company in 1925, which showed the refinery facilities and living quarters of both foreign and Iranian workers. The film was so well received by the monarch that three years later an abridged version entitled *The Land of the Shah* was distributed throughout Britain. The title itself is indicative of the sycophantic nature of the project.

The regime's enthusiasm for panegyric filmmaking continued unabated. In 1931, *Etella'at* newspaper reported the inauguration of a new cinema with a documentary entitled *His Majesty's Trip to Mazandaran and the Opening of the Northern Railroads*. Two years later, Reza Shah's stone-laying ceremony at the

Bank-e Meli (National Bank) was brought to the screens, as well as scenes from the Constitution celebrations. In fact, most of the newsreels that saw the light of day in the 1930s were about state celebrations. The titles speak for themselves: *His Majesty's Visit to the Military Academy, The National Council's Celebration, Reza Shah's Visit to Khoramabad*. During this period the government also provided special facilities for Western companies, such as Shell, Citroën, the Anglo-Persian Oil Company and German Railways, to make newsreels about their activities.

In 1932, the first Persian-language sound newsreel was filmed by Khan-Baba Motazedi in Turkey. It was screened widely in Iran. Showing the Iranian Prime Minister, Muhammad-Ali Foroughi, conferring with Kemal Atatürk and delivering a brief speech in Persian, it astonished audiences unaccustomed to hearing Persian spoken on the screen.

In 1934, a number of Turkish filmmakers accompanied Reza Shah to Iran on his return from Turkey. The intention was to make a film combining rushes of Reza Khan in Turkey with shots from the four corners of Iran. In June 1935 the following announcement was published in *Etella'at*: 'A seminal chapter in Iranian History. Pars Cinema and Iran Cinema are proud to present the first-ever talkie of his Majesty's recent visit to Turkey.'[14]

Reza Khan had also recognised the potential of radio, the first truly popular medium in Iran, as an instrument of modernisation. Wireless telegraphy in Iran had initially been established by the Germans, in 1915, for military purposes. By 1935 broadcasts could be received from Berlin, Ankara, Moscow and London. On 24 April 1940, with calculated symbolic significance since the date was the twenty-first birthday of Mohammad Reza, the crown prince, Radio Iran was inaugurated with the first nationally broadcast message: the national anthem.

Haji Agha, Cinema Actor: between past and future

Haji Agha, Actor-e Cinema (*Haji Agha, Cinema Actor*, 1932), a silent film made by Avanes Ohanian, is one of the earliest surviving examples of Iranian film, and accurately records the changing sociopolitical conditions of the time. It is ironic that Ohanian, as one of the pioneering filmmakers, was not even

Iranian. An Armenian émigré, Ohanian could hardly speak any Persian when, almost 40 years old, he arrived in Iran from Russia.

Ohanian's allegorical tale is of a traditional man in conflict with the new art form. Haji Agha, the main character, is a deeply religious man whose son-in-law is a filmmaker, reflecting the antagonistic societal forces that came into play over the issue of cinema. It also mirrored wider social concerns, with the clash between past and present, tradition and progress, giving the film a dynamic relevance.

Early in the film, the contrast between the modern director, sitting in front of his typewriter, and the traditionalist Haji Agha, armed with his rosary and hookah, is sketched out. By the end of the film, their literal and cultural distance has been overcome by cinema. The son-in-law seals the debate with the following rhetorical question: 'In every other country, cinema plays a vital role in economic, ethical and literary development. Why shouldn't we have filmmakers of our own?' When the religious man becomes convinced of cinema's benefits, the audience is encouraged to applaud his transformation. His character embodies responses to the social and political turmoil at the end of the 1920s and the early 1930s in Iran, including that surrounding the coup, religious reactions to the new government, corruption, industrialisation and modernity.

As a cornerstone of Iranian cinema, *Haji Agha* traces a transformation from one kind of Iran to another. The aim of the state was to reorganise its existing relationship with the religious infrastructure. The Islamic establishment had throughout the post-constitutional period exerted tremendous influence on the affairs of the state, nation and individual. But it had lost control over education, with the establishment of a national system in 1918. The Pahlavi dynasty accelerated this loss of power when the Ministry of Justice took over the administration of the judiciary. Religious courts and judges were replaced by secular ones in all spheres of the law except that of the family. The religious establishment was also brought under control through the political repression and personal degradation of the clergy. A notable example was

the imprisonment in 1929 of Seyyed Hassan Modarres – a celebrated cleric and an ardent constitutionalist – and his execution in 1937. The emphasis laid on national culture as opposed to Islamic heritage resulted for the first time in a symbolic and ideological separation of Iranian nationalism and

FIG. 3 *Haji Agha, Cinema Actor* (*Haji Agha, Actor-e Cinema*), Avanes Ohanian, 1932.

Islam. One of the central elements of the transition to modernity was felt to be the development of affiliations with and attachments to communities larger than family, neighbourhood, tribe or religion.

Haji Agha was intended to guide the audience in negotiating these major changes in identity, and to carry it across a difficult period of political and cultural transition in such a way that a coherent national identity would remain in place, straddling the fissures that threatened to expose its contradictions. It stressed the futility of resistance by traditional forces, and presented the family as the site of struggle between traditionalists and modernists. Even the title contains a deliberate contradiction. The term *haji* refers to a believer who has made the pilgrimage to Mecca; 'cinema' and 'actor' are imported English terms denoting modernity. The title implies their compatibility at a time when religious forces were organising resistance against the corrupting influence of cinema. *Haji Agha* was a legitimisation of the medium of cinema and its roots in the West.

In this period, Iranian society was a hierarchical one, with a small circle of upper-class urban elite at the top of the social pyramid. The urban way of life was officially promoted, while tribal or ethnic lifestyles were considered a hindrance to progress. As we have seen, Reza Khan ordered the people to abandon their local costumes and turn to a uniform way of dressing in the style of the West. Uniformity of appearance was regarded as an important aspect of nationhood, and the government imported large quantities of European-type clothes, selling them cheaply. Viewers of *Haji Agha* could see in this film both traditional and modern styles of dress, different modes of behaviour, and varying notions of what it meant to be Iranian. Haji Agha, although opposed to the West, wears a *kolah Pahlavi*, the obligatory cap introduced by Reza Khan. The implications are clear: the religious man may dislike modern trends, but he is a faithful subject of the monarchy. His daughter is shown without a veil, dancing to jazz with bobbed hair, and openly seducing her husband. Her behaviour clearly undermines her father's strict beliefs, implying that women could successfully supersede orthodoxy under the wise leadership of their patriarch, Reza Khan. The film attacks the very notion of sex as a taboo. In the ensuing decades, this would become a constant strategy in the ideological battle waged by modernists against traditionalists.

It is worth noting that when Ohanian decided to set up a film school for the training of both male and female actors and filmmakers, the first advertisement he placed attracted 300 applicants, with not a single woman amongst them. Another advert was published, this time specifically inviting women applicants. The school also taught Western dance and music. In the highly charged political climate of the time, this cultural 'invasion' would be deeply controversial, despite the political and cultural tolerance preached by the regime, and by Ohanian himself.

Lor Girl: a Western perspective

The first-ever Iranian talkie, *Dokhtar-e Lor* (*Lor Girl*, 1933), by Abdul-Hossein Sepanta, represents a seminal moment in the evolution of the country's cinema. For the first time, film audiences could experience characters speaking in Persian. The son of a member of Mozzafar al-Din Shah's court, Sepanta's education, close ties with the court, and distance from the religious fabric of his native land made him a stranger amongst his compatriots. He made *Lor Girl* in India, with the aid of the director Ardeshir Irani and the Imperial Film Company. Thanks to the preservation of a relatively intact print of the film, *Lor Girl* acts as an important source of reference for film historians.

The plot of this adventure film, whose alternative title was *Iran: Yesterday, Today*, reads like a narrative of Reza Khan's reign. Sepenta himself plays the government agent, Jafar, seconded to Lorestan in the rural west of the country to deal with local bandits. There he meets and falls for Golnar, a beautiful girl whom they are holding captive. After defeating them, Jafar returns with Golnar to the modern city.

A reviewer of *Lor Girl* pointed out a glaring inconsistency in the film's setting, which was later cut out; the filmmakers had originally evidently made use of the Indian studio as a modern location:

> The film, apart from being the first Iranian talkie, aims to compare the past with present, within a sweet tale. The last scene shows Jafar and Golnar's successful return to the Imperial Film Company in Bombay, but it would have been far more appropriate if they had returned to an Iranian port instead.[15]

A few months later the same journal, *Iran*, made explicit reference to Reza Khan: 'One must be grateful for the efforts of such Iranophile companies, who attentively sketch Iran's progress under the wise leadership of his Majesty.'[16]

For Reza Khan, whose slogan was 'Everything for the army, and again for the army', and who appeared on all public occasions in Western military uniform, the new state depended above all on a modern army. When Jafar fights off the bandits in Lorestan, a province notable for its unyielding attitude to the government, he parallels Reza Khan's battle in the 1930s with the powerful tribes in southwest Iran. When he brings the rural girl to the city, he echoes Reza Khan's attempt to introduce modernity through secularisation, industrialisation, urbanisation and the nuclearisation of the family.

The first and foremost programme of the state at this time, however, was national unification. The aim was to turn multicultural Iran into a homogenous state with one nation, one language, one culture and one central political authority. This was attempted by means of social, cultural and political repression of the tribal and ethnic diversity that made up the old Iran. *Lor Girl* covered all these themes through its plot, locations and characters.

The state policy of national unification had far-reaching implications for women. An important contextualising aspect of *Lor Girl* was the fact that although the state was constructing and imposing a nationally binding legal and social position for women, its gender policies did not penetrate deep enough to make the transition easy for women themselves. The theoretical power of the state to intervene was challenged by traditional patriarchal, communal and religious elements of society. On returning to Iran, Rohangiz Saminejad, the first Iranian screen actress, who played Golnar in *Lor Girl*, was forced to change her family name to protect herself from public scorn, and was socially ostracised because of her involvement in cinema. She appeared in only one other film, and died years later exiled, in a sense, within her own country.

The Pahlavi rhetoric of national identity and modernisation was increasingly belied, in any case, by the fact that the state was highly dependent, both economically and culturally, on Western intervention. Though Iran was never directly colonised by any single foreign power, intervention from abroad had left behind a legacy of psychological dependency. This was based on a widespread myth of the power of colonial nations that was sometimes in excess of their actual, or even potential, role within the country.

The pernicious results of the Western colonisation of Eastern lands are widely known and need no elaboration here. Imperialism has been an integral part of global history for centuries, and the world is still grappling with its unfortunate consequences. In adventure films such as *Lor Girl*, a fictional world is constructed that bears little relation to the actual facts of imperialism. Rather than pointing out these obvious deviations from historical fact, it is more productive to map the various ways in which the genre depicts its multiple forms.

The central protagonists in colonial stories are usually Europeans or Americans, a nationality shared with their primary audience, which instantly creates a feeling of cultural and racial commonality between viewer and character. This emotional framework creates the context for a story in which the hero belongs to an advanced society that will offer a more progressive, hopeful future. Jafar, the hero of *Lor Girl*, borrows from these stories in terms of his appearance and behaviour. Due to his style of dress and his gun, he resembles a cross between a cowboy and an upper-class British adventurer.

Western cinema acted not only as a pattern for *Lor Girl*'s content and form but also retained monopolistic control of its distribution and exhibition in much of the East, including Iran. *Lor Girl* sees its characters through a modernist, urbanised perspective, ignoring ethnic, religious and national contexts. This approach reflects the indirect colonialism that predominated at the birth of cinema and the advent of World War One. The story of the film (a lonely rural girl is rescued by a brave urban man) is typical of early Iranian cinema, which borrows from colonialist imagery. It is also the story of the place of women in traditional Iran, as seen through the filter of Orientalism.

Orientalism in the Western approach to the Middle East has been pernicious, but it has, since the 1970s, been subjected to frequent and vigorous critiques.[17] Western domination of the Middle East in the nineteenth and early twentieth centuries took many forms: the mission to 'civilise' Islamic societies through Western influence constituted its moral dimension; direct and indirect colonisation constituted its political and economic dimensions, and Orientalism constituted its social and cultural dimension. At the core of Orientalism lies a particular conception of Islam and its place in Middle Eastern societies: it believes in the essentiality of these cultures, and sees Islam as the factor that distinguishes them from the West.

The Orientalist analysis of political change as it affects women is built upon such a premise and rests on at least three assumptions: the notion of Muslim women as oppressed; the construction of oppositional dichotomies of tradition and modernity to explain political change, and the essentialisation and reification of women's history. Orientalism propagates the notion of Muslim women as slaves, just as Golnar in *Lor Girl* is portrayed as a slave in the early sequences.

Such notions can be particularly well illustrated through the long history of Western obsession with the harem. At the turn of the twentieth century, an assortment of missionaries, travellers, scholars and artists set out to explore the conditions of Muslim societies and peoples. The fact that the term *harem* or *harim* refers to something that is banned to foreigners, outsiders and strangers, and that Western voyagers had no way of accessing the object of their fantasy, did not prevent these male commentators from describing the harem as, simultaneously, both fascinating and revolting. The following observation made by Christian missionaries is characteristic: 'No-one can study the tragic story of women under the Muslim faith without an earnest longing and prayer that something may be done by the united Church of Christ to meet this need. We think with pity and sorrow of the veiled women of Islam.'[18]

Having constructed a view of Muslim women as oppressed, and of Islam as their oppressor, Orientalist observers turned their attention to the possibility of changing their position – as did Reza Khan. The state's gender policies, such as dress codes for men and women, were based on unifying concepts, and modernisation was seen as a homogenous and coherent process, affecting the position of women in a uniform and consistent way.

In a film like *Lor Girl*, the Iranian woman is subordinate to the Western man, whilst also being in a position of dominance in respect to the non-Western audience (male and female), since she is used to influence them towards adopting the new modes of behaviour. As the story moves away from its urban setting, it revels in the characteristics of Reza Khan's Iran. When at the end of the film Golnar is shown playing the piano and wearing a Western suit, the perfect partner of the city man, it is difficult to believe that she was once a rural girl.

Golnar's look, her make-up and outfits, are remarkably similar to the image of Oriental women in American film epics such as D.W. Griffith's *Intolerance* (1916) and Cecil B. DeMille's *The Arab* (1916) and *The Ten Commandments* (1923). All these films are about the ancient world and suggest nostalgia for a pure civilisation prior to the Western presence. They represent a romantic search for the lost Eastern origins of Western civilisations. Thus, although *Lor Girl* is an Iranian film, it reproduces the colonialist mechanism by which the Orient is rendered void of any active historical role, becoming simply the object of exotic spectacle. Through a similar process, Reza Khan had helped to reduce Iran, a country with a rich and spectacular past, to its current undeveloped status.

The construction of a male/female opposition, along with a number of other dualities in *Lor Girl* – city/village, modernity/tradition, West/East – echoed the governmental programme. It also borrowed from the implicit structural metaphors of colonial discourse, where the representation of the 'other' serves to define the West itself. An examination of colonial discourse reveals the crucial role of gendered metaphors in constructing the colonial subaltern. Europe's 'civilising' mission in the Third World – like Reza Khan's in Iran – is projected in narratives of the Western penetration of inviting virgin land.

The metaphoric portrayal of the (non-urban, non-Western) land as a virgin coyly awaiting the touch of the coloniser is a dominant colonial image. In the same vein, the portrayal of Third World regions as undeveloped is reinforced by topographical reductionism, for example, the reduction of the Orient to desert, and metaphorically, to dreariness. The desert, a frequent reference both in the dialogue and visual imagery of Orientalist films, is presented as the essential unchanging motif in *Lor Girl*.

The colonial challenge was regarded as good for the native, but also as a worthwhile test of Western culture. The colonial hero, however, never completely loses the fear that the natives will return to the local traditions that the Empire has attempted to overcome. After the hero's search for liberty has led to the discovery of the new land, the colony is adopted as a second or even permanent home. The discourse of Pahlavi in Iran, like that of Empire, calls for the taming of primitive landscapes (such as the deserts and cliffs presented in *Lor Girl*). Shrewish people (bandits, natives and villagers such as Golnar, who speaks with a local accent) are domesticated, and a more 'cultivated' nature is made to bloom.

The cliffhanger sequence, in which the hero rescues the woman at the last moment, plays a significant role in representing postcolonial geopolitics, metaphorically renderering the colonised land as a female who must be saved from environmental disorder (from a native, usually Arab slayer/rapist, or African cannibal), which helps produce the ideological role of the Western liberator integral to the colonial rescue fantasy. It carries with it religious/theological overtones, with the inferiority of the Islamic world to the Christian world encapsulated by the monogamous couple.

Yet the relationship between adventure and colonial imagery is a complex one, whose analysis cannot be approached through easy generalisation. This is due to the paradoxical nature of the genre. While presenting many racist undercurrents in portraying Eastern characters, colonial adventure films have long satisfied a human desire for escape. They offer a window on to foreign cultures and distant lands to curious and receptive audiences. Both of these currents must be recognised: the genre is on the one hand guilty of perpetrating demeaning stereotypes, while manifesting on the other an enlightened eagerness to experience and learn about different cultures and ways of life.

The statement read by Ardeshir Irani before the first public screening of *Lor Girl*, far from being focused on the film, was a celebration of Reza Khan and his policies. Before it would issue the distribution permit, the regime, desperate to exploit every opportunity to strengthen its power base, 'suggested' that an explanation should be added to the end of the film to make clear that the lawlessness it depicted took place during the reign of the previous dynasty. It also insisted on adding a paragraph listing recent achievements, ranging from the coup in March 1920 to reform of the Justice department.

A new chapter

After *Lor Girl*, Sepanta made four more films related to Iranian historical and literary subjects: *Shirin va Farhad* (*Shirin and Farhad*, 1934), *Ferdowsi* (1934), *Cheshmhay-e Siah* (*Dark Eyes*, 1936, also known as *Nader Shah's Capture of Lahore*) and *Leili va Majnun* (*Leili and Majnun*, 1937). Whilst celebrating ancient Persian history, these films also promulgated Reza Khan's policies. Ironically, although they are considered to be Iranian, they were filmed entirely on location in

FIG. 4 The image of the actresses in the early Iranian films, epitomised by Fakhrol-Zaman Jabar-Vaziri. The make-up is inspired by prevailing Hollywood fashions and her ornamental appearance is straight out of the epic *The Thousand and One Nights.*

India, a land ruled by Britain; no one was likely to forget that Reza Khan's ascension to power would have been impossible without British backing.

Meanwhile, Reza Khan was initiating his own projects. One such was the millennium celebration of the great epic poet, Ferdowsi, held in 1934 with the participation of scholars from the four corners of the world. The VIP guests were taken to Ferdowsi's burial place in Tus, a small, ancient city in the northeast of Iran, where Reza Khan personally opened the celebrations. The regime commissioned Sepanta and Ardeshir Irani, the owner of Bombay's Imperial Film Studio at this time, to produce the film *Ferdowsi*, to mark the event. The state propaganda surrounding this event was exaggerated to a ridiculous level:

> And what are London, Paris, Berlin or even America compared to the glory of Tus? … A new chapter has been opened in the history of New Iran … adorned with the blessed name of his Majesty, Reza Shah Pahlavi.[19]

In the same year, Parliament passed a motion to the effect that, henceforth, Reza Khan's name would be suffixed with the title Kabir (Great).

Reza Khan personally ratified *Ferdowsi* after its completion and ordered that a number of scenes should be cut and others re-filmed. One of the deleted scenes involved an encounter between Ferdowsi and Sultan Mahmud Ghaznavi, played by Nosratollah Mohtasham (the Iranian *chargé d'affaires* in India). Reza Khan could not approve a scene in which a mere poet got the better of a king, and this would not be the last time that apparently stupid monarchs would be expunged from films shown in Iran. The initial intention was to show the film only during Ferdowsi's millennium celebrations, but it was eventually screened commercially. It ran for a mere three nights and was a total flop.

Sepanta's three other films were historical romances. Made under the political directives of the state, they clearly depicted Iranian men and women, not as they were, but as Westerners perceived them. These films are now lost, but what can be understood today from the few remaining stills is that they were saturated with Orientalist iconography. Having defined Islam as static, the changing position of women could only be explained in terms of the declining hold of Islam and the increasing impact of the West. The image of the actresses in these films, epitomised by Fakhrol-Zaman

FIG. 5 Hollywood's silent matinee idol Rudolf Valentino, in his famous Arab disguise.

FIG. 6 The Iranian filmmaker Abdul-Hussein Sepanta, as an Arab and at the same time as Rudolf Valentino.

Jabar-Vaziri's crown and fancy gown in *Shirin and Farhad*, is borrowed from Western depictions of Eastern royalty, while the make-up of Daftari and Saminejad in the same film is inspired by the prevailing Hollywood fashions. Vaziri's ornamental appearance in *Leili and Majnun* is straight out of the epic *The Thousand and One Nights*. She wears a veil that reveals elongated eyebrows, and eyes heavy with make-up, highly reminiscent of Claudette Colbert in *Cleopatra* (Cecil B. DeMille, 1934). The romanticism of *The Thousand and One Nights* is also conjured in the English promotional poster of *Leili and Majnun*, with its stereotypical minarets, mosques and brilliant moonlight shining through date trees.

In the photographs and pictures of this time, we again see the image of the harem from a Western viewpoint. Decades later, in the 1950s and 1960s, these images still remained unchanged in Iranian pseudo-historical films. This fascination with the fantasised harem was not just an imitation of the Western approach however; it also authorised the propagation of sexual images of women, in harmony with Reza Khan's policies. Modifying, changing, ignoring and of course eroticising the past history of Iran through cinema allowed the government to justify the dominance of the monarchical system and to confirm its sexual liberation. The Iranian audience was participating not so much in the Western gaze, but in a governmental plan.

The male lead, played by Sepanta himself, is also made to resemble a contemporary looking Westerner, whose Eastern characteristics are limited to a symbolic gown and headscarf. The only surviving photograph of Sepanta shows a blatant attempt to cash in on Rudolf Valentino's universally recognisable image in *The Sheik* (George Melford, 1921) and *Son of the Sheik* (George Fitzmaurice, 1926). The storylines of many early Iranian films were also heavily indebted to Valentino's romantic escapades. In *The Sheik*, a Western woman (Agnes Ayres) falls under the spell of desert chieftain Valentino, who remains dumb and passive until he is revealed to be the son of Europeans, when he is transformed into a man who risks his life to rescue women from their insane Arab torturers. Even decades later this plot was still being repeated in different forms in Western films.

3 The 1940s

A period of volatile mix

Between 1936 and 1948, Iranian cinema sank into a state of hibernation; no films were produced during this period. This was the result of a combination of factors, including the lack of production facilities and the inability of Iranian films to compete with foreign imports. With the advent of the Second World War in 1939, the world entered a tense and unpredictable phase. At first Iranians paid little attention to the war, but the combination of Communist Russia in the north, Britain in the south and an increasing German presence in Iran meant that the country was inevitably caught up in its web.

During Reza Khan's reign, Britain had maintained its position as the major Western power in Iran. Reza Khan also turned to the United States for technical advice and for the modernisation of the state's finances, loans and investments on the pretext of preventing the threat of Communism. Germany, too, took a leading role in Iran's foreign trade and eventually came to be favoured over the British because of historical bitterness against the latter. Reza Khan promoted Nazi ideology and, in return, the Germans declared Iran a pure Aryan country. Joseph Goebbels, the Nazi Propaganda Minister, referred to Iranians as Germany's 'Aryan brothers'.[20]

As the Nazi army extended its sphere of influence, the world's attention became focused on the oil reserves of the Middle East. Reza Khan had gradually established closer ties with Germany during his reign, as a result of which there were numerous German architects, pharmacists, medical and printing technicians working in the country. Significantly, Iran earned the bulk of the revenue.

This affinity with Germany did not pass unnoticed by Britain, which had strategic interests in the southern oilfields, nor by Russia, which despite its initial peace treaty with Germany, had found its land occupied by the Nazis. As the war escalated, Reza Khan flagrantly ignored Iran's supposed neutrality and Britain finally invaded in the summer of 1941. The first bulletin of the New Army announced the Allied invasion and warned of aerial bombardment. In the face of overwhelming superiority on the part of the Allied Forces the Iranian army collapsed within 48 hours and on 28 August Iran petitioned for an end to hostilities. The Allied occupation of Iran demonstrated the fragile nature of the country's sovereignty. Muhammad-Ali Foroughi, a previous Prime Minister, came out of retirement to head a new government and eventually, on 16 September, Reza Khan was forced to abdicate in favour of his son. He was drummed into exile, first to Mauritius and then to Johannesburg, where he died in July 1944.

Britain and the Soviet Union once again divided Iran into different zones of influence. This time, however, the United States also became a significant player. While the British and the Soviets concentrated on the south and the north respectively, the Americans placed advisers in key government departments and in the military. Each power attempted to influence the country's politics to its own advantage.

Despite the occasional air-raid siren, the war did not interrupt Iran's love affair with cinema. Western films, especially of the Hollywood variety, flooded the cinemas and mesmerised audiences during these hard times. Another innovation increased the appeal of foreign films during this period. For the first time, a group of Iranians resident in Egypt and Turkey began dubbing them. In a country with a high rate of illiteracy, this was a welcome breakthrough. By the end of the 1940s, out of 400 films screened, some 300 were American, with British, Russian and Egyptian films making up the remainder.

Rules governing film screenings

After the Allied invasion, the exhibition of films came under the jurisdiction of the Ministry of the Interior department, known as the Exhibition Office.

This was run by a British woman named Nilla Cram Cook, who was severely criticised for her lack of knowledge of local customs. One journal wrote:

> It is hardly surprising that a foreigner who accidentally gains a position of responsibility in a strange environment will either not have adequate knowledge of the terrain, or alternatively, after a couple of months of frustration and hassle, may delegate all responsibility to underlings, and become a mere figurehead…
>
> We do not blame Mrs Nilla Cook personally. Anyone who wishes to serve our people should live in this society for a considerable time, become acquainted with our customs and attitudes, before undertaking such a daunting task. The truth of it is that Iranians have never been very good at taking orders from foreigners, and if they seem to tolerate the situation without much complaint, this should be put down to good manners rather than anything else…
>
> In our view the issuing of film and play permits must be the sole responsibility of the Ministry of Culture, with the police authorities involved in an advisory capacity. After all, it is their duty to exercise any banning order the Ministry of Culture may deem necessary…
>
> We used to think the Iranians in charge of such matters were incompetent, but since Mrs Cook's appointment, the situation has deteriorated considerably, without any hope of improvement in sight.[21]

From this period on, two modes of film censorship would dominate Iranian cinema: state intervention at the point of production, distribution or exhibition and 'invisible', ideologically conditioned self-censorship.

Fierce competition among Western countries

The most important outcome of the Second World War for Iranian film was the proliferation of newsreels. Some of these were eulogies to the royal family and the state: *The Shah's Marriage Ceremony to Princess Fuzieh* (1939); *Inauguration Ceremony of a Cotton Factory* (1939); *Inauguration of Radio Iran* (1940) and *Inauguration of the Boy Scout Movement* (1940). The foreign output of short and feature presentations was by now a disputed terrain involving German, British, Russian and American competitors. Prior to the Allied invasion, the Germans had achieved a strong presence in Iranian cinemas, and during the 1930s German imports gained considerable popularity. Most of these had a military theme. The last German film was screened in August 1941; after the Allied invasion, all German imports were banned.

The publication of the Persian-language cinema journal *Hollywood* in the summer of 1943, co-financed by the British Council, when the Second World War and the Allied presence in Iran was at its peak, is indicative of the West's desire to pacify the populace through its 'dream factory'. As the name suggests, the journal's main agenda was to promote Hollywood actors and films, and the screening of Hollywood films was an integral part of the regime's Westernisation policies. Somewhat pretentiously, the editorial of the first issue stated:

> When the world is burning uncontrollably amidst raging fires, when the scythe of death is mowing down humanity's crop in their thousands, when tears of sorrow banish joy and laughter ... [suddenly you receive] a bunch of gorgeous roses to brighten up your day ... this sweet smelling bunch of flowers is called Hollywood.[22]

In another issue, *Hollywood* took up the question of the *hejab* and whilst pointing out the great changes occurring in the rest of the world, referred to Iranian women as backward and atavistic. Another issue carried an advertisement about the establishment of the Hollywood Society, whose aim was the promotion of acting, music, painting and the setting up of a film studio. During the winter of 1943, after Muhammad Reza Shah's ascension to power, *Hollywood* ran the following eulogy:

> Do you know your history? If you do, you must know that once five million Iranians ruled the world. The secret of their success was unity between populace and monarch. The close ties between them meant the Shah could rely on five million loyal soldiers for his expansion policies. That greatness and unity no longer exists. If we desire to be great again, we must re-learn the art of unity.[23]

Due to the length of their stay in Iran and the widespread activities of the Anglo-Persian Oil Company, the British made numerous newsreels, and the promotional department of the British Council set up a special cinema for their permanent screening. The same department had filmed the marriage of Muhammad Reza Shah and Fuzieh in 1941. After the Allied invasion, the

Americans too increased their activities through the Iran–America Cultural Society, which had been established in 1925.

The Russians also began screening their films in Tehran and in various provinces. Occasionally, in order to boost attendance, they would add Persian subtitles. In addition, they organised a number of ballet, theatre, opera and music recitals, most of which were free of charge. One of the main political developments of this period was the spread of socialist ideology amongst some Iranian reformers, which resulted from the radicalising effect of the Russian Revolution of 1917 and which peaked at this time. In 1920, the Communist and Socialist parties of Iran had been established and the first Congress of the Communist Party of Iran had taken place in the northern town of Anzali. Democratic rights in the context of a bourgeois state were rejected as superficial and inconsequential, and the rule of the proletariat was praised as the only system within which 'true rights' could be achieved. In the same year, the Jangali movement had announced the establishment of a socialist republic in Gilan province, in co-operation with the Communist Party and the Red Army.

Foreigners and propaganda films

The Allied invasion continued until 1947, the year in which the Russians were finally 'persuaded' to leave the province of Azerbaijan in the northwest of Iran. Among the myriad newsreels and documentaries produced during this time were films revolving around the themes of war, military manoeuvres and the shipment of armaments. They portrayed Iran as a passive subject, the site of conflict between the super powers.

The decade following Reza Khan's rule witnessed the proliferation of the pro-Soviet political tendency. In 1945, the newly established Democratic Party in Kurdistan province set up an autonomous Democratic republic. On 4 November, in Azerbaijan, the Democratic Party leader, Jafar Pishevari, seized power in a *coup d'état* and took up military positions in the province. Two battalions sent by the Tehran central government to regain control of Azerbaijan were halted by Soviet troops. On 13 December an 'autonomous government', the Azerbaijan Autonomous Provincial Assembly, was set up in

FIG. 7 The Tudeh (Communist Party) meeting in the film *On the Other Side of Araxes* (1947), a Russian documentary recording political tension in Azerbaijan.

Azerbaijan with Soviet support. The Democratic Party programme included the introduction of local Azeri Turkish into the schools and its adoption as the official language, the nationalisation of the banks and the distribution of land to the peasants.

The Soviet decision to engineer these revolts in Azerbaijan and Kurdistan stemmed from the events of 1944, when the Tudeh (Communist) Party launched 'Positive Equilibrium', a diplomatic offensive aimed at giving the Soviets an oil concession in Northern Iran. On 19 January 1945 the Iranian government appealed to the new UN Security Council to consider the matter of Soviet interference in Azerbaijan. The Security Council promptly set up direct negotiations between Iran and the Soviet Union. Qavam al-Saltaneh, the new Prime Minister, spent two months in Moscow negotiating with the Soviet premier Josef Stalin and the Foreign Minister Vyacheslav Molotov, principally over the Iranian refusal to accept Tudeh Party members in government or to recognise the autonomous Azerbaijan republic, which Iran considered merely a Soviet satellite.

On 24 March 1946, in the wake of the expiry of the Tripartite Treaty (an Iranian–Soviet treaty based on the Russian troops agreeing to leave Iran) and the ordered evacuation of British and US troops, the Soviets committed themselves to the withdrawal of all troops from Azerbaijan within five to six weeks. But they did not withdraw, and the Iranian government presented several documents protesting about this to the UN Security Council. In May, the Soviet Union finally fulfilled its promise to evacuate its troops from the northern province. The Azerbaijan Autonomous Provincial Assembly abandoned its resistance to Tehran as central government troops penetrated the province, taking its capital, Tabriz, on 13 December. After some resistance the rebel regime collapsed and Pishevari escaped to the Soviet Union. He was later reported to have been killed in a road accident.

Two years later, in 1947, the Russian government made a documentary based on this event. The film, *On the Other Side of Araxes* (a river on the Iran–Russia border), was never shown in Iran. However, it remains a highly important record of the political tensions of the period. An article in the Russian paper *Pravda* conveyed the political significance of the film:

> The film recalls the glorious tradition of the struggle for independence and lists the names of the people's heroes. The victory of freedom-loving peoples over Fascism, headed by the Soviet Union, spurring on the liberation movement of oppressed peoples throughout the world, inspired the Azerbaijanians of Northern Iran to a struggle for autonomy and democratic rights. On the screen pass the partisan detachments that forced the troops of the reactionary Tehran Government into capitulation in December of 1945 ... The struggle continues. The time will come when Iranian Azerbaijan will recover its freedom.[24]

The 1950s 4

Awakening from the big sleep

With the end of the Second World War and the resolution of the Azerbaijan crisis, it was assumed that a period of reconstruction and stability could begin. The young monarch, Muhammad Reza Shah, had inherited a shaky throne, and consequently spent the early part of his reign in a state of flux between hope and despair. Once the Shah had consolidated his power, he made a point of putting forward the idea that there would be important changes in the way the country was ruled, attempting to reveal a shift in the character of his rule from a dictatorship to a traditional monarchy who would accept parliamentary decisions.

The fourteen governments that came and went between 1945 and 1960, whose Prime Ministers either resigned voluntarily, were forced to do so, or had their contracts terminated by an assassin's bullet, reflected a crisis-ridden nation. When the hibernating Iranian cinema poked its head out of its cocoon, it found itself faced with a regime that, far from encouraging native filmmaking, was in fact hell-bent on hindering production in punitive ways.

Esmail Kushan, a director and producer, can be credited with initiating the post-war filmmaking movement, laying a firm foundation by establishing the Mitra Film Studio in 1948. The first film he produced was *Tufan-e Zendegi* (*Life's Tempest*, Ali Dariabeigi), screened as a royal occasion in the spring of 1948. In this love story, the events revolve around a young woman. Her father fails to understand her desire for independence and forces her to marry a rich old man but the woman reconciles with her true love at the end. This film challenged taboos by introducing for the first time a love-triangle plot into Iranian cinema. It was a film that not only compared the difference between marriage, with its taint of familiarity, and adultery, with its tingle of desire, but also looked at different ways of loving.

Zendani Amir/Dokhtar-e Kord (*Amir's Prisoner/Kurd Girl*), directed and produced by Kushan in the same year, is the story of a tribal conflict, during which a young woman is captured by an enemy tribe and sent to the harem of the Emir (or governor). A young man sets out to free her in a series of daring adventures. The film emphasised social and pedagogical issues and attempted to depict some of the injustice and discrimination that routinely afflicts society through envy and ignorance. The cinematic representation of these issues in a country with a high rate of illiteracy was of the utmost significance. The names of the lead actresses in these films, Mehraghdas Khajenouri and Zinat Moadeb, figure large in all reference books on Iranian cinema. It seems the revival of Iranian cinema was dependent on its female stars.

The importance of the role of women in these two films gives an indication of what was transpiring politically. The compulsory unveiling of women was accompanied by a series of measures to increase their role in society. The Ministry of Education required its female staff and that of other government organisations to enrol in physical education classes and schoolgirls marched en masse in public parades. The government also set up a national Girl Scouts organisation. The number of women entering the University of Tehran increased. The Civil Service (but not the judiciary) was also opened to women, though their employment was largely concentrated in teaching, and in midwifery, which was rationalised. A new teacher training college for women produced teachers for girls' schools. Some women gained access to the new middle-class professions. A handful who had been educated abroad returned home to practice medicine or lecture at the university. Foreign companies were among the first to employ women as clerks and typists, a trend that was taken up by other firms and government departments.

The existence of a radical nationalist atmosphere in the post-Reza Khan 1940s had led to a re-emergence of women's organisations, alongside the more independent but still pro-establishment Ladies Centre. The Ladies Centre later became a training institution for women who could not afford further education. Run by Iranian women, the journal *Zaban-e Zanan* (*Women's*

Voice), which had ceased publication during the war, relaunched in 1942. The second issue carried an editorial on 'Women and the Bread Shop', which protested against the shortage of bread and reported women's riots. The journal was temporarily banned by the government because of this article but later published a further ten issues. The next political article to appear in the journal invited the Allies to leave Iran, as a result of which the paper was closed down for good.[25]

The presence of women in the media, and in the cinema of the 1950s, signalled an attempt to challenge the past. The new wave of filmmaking emerged in an environment characterised by external tensions and permanent political feuding between clerics, leftists and nationalists, while the Shah desperately attempted to solidify his power base. The competition between Britain and America in Iran had peaked at the end of the 1940s. The Shah's first foreign visit after his inauguration was to London. Meanwhile, Ayatollah Kashani, an influential member of the clergy who had fought against the Shah and who had recently returned from exile, set up the Society of Militant Muslims.

In February 1946 the Iranian Parliament had revealed Iran's first economic plan, which had included a wide variety of development projects such as increasing production, expanding exports, developing agriculture and improving public health and education. These goals were to be achieved within seven years. The Shah had taken an oath of loyalty to the new Iranian constitution in May of that year, stating that the recent amendments would guarantee the proper functioning of a true democracy.

During the government's opening assembly in 1949, however, the public angrily heckled the incumbent Prime Minister, Gholam Hossein Hazhir. On the defensive, the Prime Minister, who was accused of harbouring secular beliefs, tried to placate his critics by banning the sale and production of alcohol in the religious centres of Mashad, Qom and Shahr-e Ray. But the demonstrations rapidly grew in intensity until, in November 1949, Hazhir was shot at a mosque ceremony and died the following day. Martial law, which had been lifted, was imposed again in Tehran and other towns. The Prime Minister was the victim of the Feda'iyan-e Islam (Devotees of Islam), a militant Islamic underground organisation founded in 1945. The Feda'iyan called for the implementation of the *Shari'a* (Islamic law) and the banning of alcohol, opium, cinema and other amusements, including gambling.

The Shah fared only slightly better. On 4 February 1949, during his visit to Tehran University to commemorate the anniversary of its founding, a press photographer named Naser Fakhrarar shot at the Shah. Three bullets went through his cap; the fourth entered his right cheek. Generals, officials and policemen ran for cover, nobody daring to help him until the assassin's gun jammed. The gunman was then mobbed to death by the crowd. His identity papers showed that he was working for the *Parcham-e Islam (Flag of Islam)*, a religious publication, and belonged to the journalists' union, then affiliated to a pro-Communist labour federation.

The Shah's wounds did not prove fatal. He even sent his bloodstained uniform to be displayed in a glass case in the Tehran Officers' Club. Martial law was declared and the communist Tudeh Party was banned. According to the new military governor, stamps bearing the words 'Iranian Republic' had been discovered at the Tudeh Party offices. The Shah called on the Constituent Assembly to revive an article that would allow him, at the government's request, to dissolve the Majlis (Parliament). His decision was intended to reflect the poor economic state of the country and the fact that Parliament had passed no budget for five years.

The military curfew that followed only made matters worse. Night-time shootings, daytime paranoia, the arrest of political suspects and a general atmosphere of terror helped the Shah consolidate his power. All publications, with the exception of the pro-government *Kayhan* and *Etella'at*, were banned. Ayatollah Kashani was once again exiled, this time to Lebanon, and opposition members of Parliament were reduced to a mere three. Despite the instability created by the assassination attempt, the 29-year-old Shah left Tehran the same year for a six-week visit to the United States. There he met President Harry Truman, whose Point-Four Programme promising economic and military assistance to Iran was to be of great benefit to the Shah. Meanwhile, Iran's northern neighbour, the USSR, was beginning to test its atomic bomb.

Amidst this turmoil, Ayatollah Kashani, from the clerical ranks, and Dr Muhammad Mossadeq, from the nationalist camp, began their opposition to the Shah. The political–economic struggle between Britain and the United

States in Iran exacerbated social chaos, economic stagnation, poverty and illness, due to a lack of doctors in rural areas, and illiteracy. When Mossadeq eventually became Prime Minister in the spring of 1952, Iranians found for the first time a politician willing to oppose Western interests.

In 1950, the commercial success of Kushan's *Sharmsar* (*Shameful*), starring the popular diva Esmat Delkash, had attracted the interest of investors, who discovered in filmmaking a relatively safe way of making a profit during uncertain times. The film's sentimental plot – girl and boy fall in love, then lose each other, only to be reunited in the end – was a reflection of the hopes and despair of a people who were the passive observers of political discontent. During 1951, as the political crisis reached its zenith, a record number of seven films were produced.

Reverence for tradition, praise for the past

With the beginning of a new era of filmmaking in Iran, response to Western influence became polarised between the portrayal of Iranians based on a Western point of view and a reaction against these values. At this time, descriptions of the cultural orientation, attitudes, values and psychology of Iranians were appearing in two different but closely related contexts. The first were based on the various accounts of historians, travellers, diplomats and other 'observers' of Persian society, culture and character. The second was the more modern work of social scientists, who described and analysed the cultural values and supposed psychological characteristics of Iranians through a discussion of the contemporary problems of Iranian society, policy and economy. Often they carried the implication that these characteristics had impeded Iran's political modernisation and economic development.

Arthur C. Millspaugh's first book, *The American Task in Persia*, had been published in 1925, primarily as an interim progress report on the work of the Second American Financial Mission. At this time, Millspaugh was convinced that the work of his mission was progressing satisfactorily and was highly optimistic about the country's future economic prospects:

> The patient [Persia], as I look back after two-and-a-half years of intimate observation, appears to me to be enjoying a fair expectation of survival … Persia, according to the diagnosis of the last doctor, was suffering from a case of arrested development with complications … [but now] seems likely, not merely to live, but to grow healthy and vigorous if left alone on a simple, nourishing financial diet with active economic exercise in the fresh air.[26]

The tone and substance of Millspaugh's analysis of the Persian national character, presented in a chapter entitled 'Persian Psychology', are correspondingly amiable and positive at this time. Deploring the 'tribal instinct' of those who consider any foreigner to be 'inferior' (although in pointing to the Aryan origins of the majority of the Persian population he makes a deeply problematic assumption of superiority on the part of the Aryan race), he argues against the stereotyping of Persians: 'One Persian differs in character from another precisely as Americans differ; but apart from the superficialities of dress and manner, they look, think, talk and act like the rest of us.'[27]

Fifteen years later, Millspaugh was invited back by the Persian government to set up another American Financial Mission aimed at checking the country's serious economic and financial crises, in part the results of the Allied occupation and the consequent abdication of Reza Shah. The Third Mission was beset by a host of problems, including dissension within its own ranks, misunderstandings with the American delegation in Tehran, conflicts with various government officials, and attacks by the press and some parliamentary deputies.

It was against this background that Millspaugh wrote his second book on Iran, *Americans in Persia*, in 1946. Under the title of 'Minds, Morals, and Government', he again devoted a chapter to an analysis of the Persian personality. However, in sharp contrast to his earlier views, his analysis now reflected a profound sense of bitterness, frustration and desperation. He states that the Persian 'is not a man of reason. He falls short of intellectual maturity. He generally lacks the apparatus that more advanced people have developed to solve problems and engineer progress.'[28] Whereas in his earlier book he had praised Persians for their democratic character, this time his appraisal seems to reflect not only a radical change in his perception of them but also a justification for the continued involvement of the West in the political and economic affairs of Iran: 'One may guess that this still primitive people has unconsciously yearned for a Great Father, in the form of a dictatorial Persian or a benevolent American, who would extend protection and work miracles to the vicarious satisfaction of Persians without calling for initiative or courage on their part.'[29]

This 'benevolent American' was not a metaphor. Convinced that Persia was 'a child forced prematurely to live the life of an adult', the doctor prescribed the appropriate cure: his well-known proposal advocating the tutelage of Iran by England, the United States and the Soviet Union.[30]

In his book *Iran* of 1946, William S. Hass based his central thesis regarding the nature of Iranians on three major issues: the advent of Islam, long periods of foreign rule with the consequent disintegration of the old institutions, and a succession of despotic governments.[31] He argues that throughout the 'fateful centuries' of Persian history, Iranians had stood on continually foundering ground and had come to believe that they could not depend upon a predictable, responsive societal order for their security. Having thus been 'thrown back' on themselves, they were forced to adopt a number of psychological strategies in order to ensure self-preservation and to cope with a hostile social order. They became masters in the art of deluding and frustrating the oppressor, increasingly individualistic and fatalistic, and so nostalgically attached to the past that the present became an illusion. There is in Hass an overwhelming emphasis on the psychic consequences of certain cataclysmic epochs in Persian history, and the belief that a formative impact on the Persian character had persisted from medieval times.

An anthropological inventory of supposed Iranian cultural traits and behaviours can also be found in the 'Country Survey Series' of the Human Relations Area Files of Yale University under the editorship of Herbert H. Vreeland, compiled in 1957, whose tone has the assumed authority and certitude of latterday anthropologists.

> The individual puts up a psychological 'wall' over which he reaches to play the game of life. This wall is his face. He must preserve a front for outsiders to see. He will fight to defend his honour if it is publicly assailed, but only according to his assessment of the probability of winning, for he must not

> lose, if he is to keep face … Highly emotional, the Persian is more open to persuasion by excitement than by logical argument.
>
> … A Persian admires dead heroes, but he ordinarily has no desire to become one immediately.
>
> … The Iranians' respect for strength and submission to superior forces is part of their respect for fate … acquiescence is an attribute of Iran's sense of time and history. Time being a steppe with episodes looming on the horizons, and the ideal future being the past regained, Iranians can readily accept a few centuries of rule by foreigners with the inner assurance that the present is but transitory while the past can never be destroyed.[32]

Whatever one makes of these stereotypes, it is certainly true that the films and literature of the time consistently reflected an extreme respect for and glorification of tradition. The concept of the future seems to have had little meaning except as a possible means of recapturing the past. Plans were apparently deemed unnecessary since the future was regarded as predetermined, though uncertain and precarious. Inscrutable forces shaped the hero's destiny and it was a foolish man who would attempt to alter fate.

The concept of *taghdIr* (fate) increasingly took the form of psychological determinism and directly influenced the way in which on-screen characters approached both their personal problems and those of the government. The theme of the individual stoically accepting the status quo due to impotence in the face of a force too powerful to be surmounted predominated in many Iranian films, perhaps due to Iran's history as a country which expected of its citizens unquestioning obedience to despotic leadership.

The coup in Iran and cinematic patriotism

The transformation of the era of nation-building into an era of nationalism, an inevitable phase in the discourse of modernism, brought about certain major events in the early 1950s. Firstly, it resulted in the separation of nationalism from the state with the rise of independent opposition nationalism. Blind faith in the modern state was also challenged. Under the influence of nationalism, the government announced on October 1949 that all diplomatic documents must refer to the country as 'Persia' in English, and 'Perse' in French, rather than Iran, which sounded too much like Iraq.

This reversed Reza Khan's decision of 1935 to change 'Persia' to 'Iran' on official documents.

In September 1950, the outbreak of a Kurdish revolt near the Iraqi border was reported. Tehran blamed the uprising on Soviet-propagated support for a separate Kurdish state. The following day Kurdish tribesman fought with Iranian soldiers after turning down an ultimatum to surrender their arms and ammunition under the government's policy of disarming all tribes.

At this time, the Iranian government was protesting against Soviet propaganda, which sought to undermine its power; it was also defending its improving relationship with the USA. However, the government showed leniency towards those who had tried to break away from Tehran's control with Soviet backing. Sensitivity to the feelings of its giant neighbour influenced the Iranian government in November 1950 to ban the state radio from broadcasting foreign programmes attacking the USSR, including those of the BBC and Voice of America. Iran's Head of Press and Propaganda was even sacked after broadcasting a programme that was criticised by the Soviet Ambassador, who had signed a new Iran–Soviet trade treaty.

In early 1951, the Shah proclaimed the sale of crown lands to the peasants, principally to gain popularity at a time when the country was becoming highly emotional on the question of the nationalisation of the oil industry. Ayatollah Kashani and other clerics issued a *fatwa* in favour of nationalisation. The Prime Minister, General Razmara, was assassinated by a member of Feda'iyan-e Islam, and a mass demonstration took place throughout Iran in favour of a nationalised oil industry. The replacement premier, Hossein Ala, who later resigned, announced a new cabinet and ordered the censorship of foreign news dispatches that appeared to be dangerous to the nation's security or violated rules of decency. The Shah eventually gave his assent to oil nationalisation and formalised the appointment of Muhammad Mossadeq as the new premier.

In these turbulent times, two films, *Royahai-ye Talaie* (*Golden Dreams*, Moezeddin Fekri, 1952) and *Sultan-e Yek Ruz-e* (*Sultan for a Day*, Parviz Khatibi, 1953), both based on the theme of 'the Prince and the Pauper' (which has its cultural equivalent in Persian mythology), were brought to the screen. Using satire as a cover, they commented on the conflict between the Shah and the government, and discussed the people's dreams for a brighter future. *Golden*

Dreams, based on the play *A Day in the Life of Shah Abbas* tells the story of an encounter between the Shah, on an anonymous walk, and a young peasant whose only wish is to become king for a day, so that he can win the girl of his dreams. When the peasant falls asleep, Shah Abbas transfers him to his palace. Waking up in rich garments surrounded by courtiers and servants, the peasant wins the affections of his sweetheart. Majid Mohseni, who starred as the peasant, turned this successful outing into a template, playing numerous stereotypical simple peasants in his film career. Using his popularity as a platform, he even managed to win a seat in Parliament.

Generally, however, and despite Esmail Kushan's *Dr Mossadeq's American Journey* (1951) – a documentary about Mossadeq's historic visit to the United Nations to challenge the Security Council's legal right to adjudicate on Britain's resolution regarding the Iranian oil industry – the turmoil of the early 1950s did not spur filmmakers to indulge in politics – not that the censorship laws would have allowed such transgressions.

Finally, the people became active participants in the political turmoil. When the Shah tried to replace the popular Mossadeq with the more pliable Ahmad Qavam, demonstrations ensued. Crowds bearing a fake coffin demanded vengeance against Qavam, and National Front leaders even called for his execution. The Shah was forced to backtrack. Mossadeq, strengthened by the episode, pursued the constitution with renewed authority and, albeit temporarily, reduced the powers of the Shah. Amongst all the features made during this period, only *Velgard* (*Loafer*, Mehdi Raisfiruz, 1952), a film which implied the impossibility of a peaceful existence under military dictatorship, alluded to these feverish street demonstrations.

In 1951, Iranian legislators, led by Mossadeq, nationalised the British-owned Anglo-Oil Company. Washington at first resisted London's calls for help in reversing the nationalisation beyond sponsoring their negotiations (which failed) and supporting a boycott of Iranian oil. The Truman administration was torn between loyalty to Britain and supporting greater Iranian self-determination. But Truman's successor, the conservative Dwight D. Eisenhower, was alarmed: Mossadeq *might* lead Iran towards Communism.

An elderly, aristocratic liberal, Mossadeq opposed Soviet interventionism, the British monarch and the young Shah. In early 1953, he demanded the ousting of the Shah; by then, however, even the Tudeh Party had turned against him. The moment had come: Eisenhower and the British Prime Minister Winston Churchill decided to strike. Yet the coup started badly: dismissed by the Shah, Mossadeq refused to leave; his followers rioted, and the Shah and his new queen, Soraya, fled to Rome in August 1953. Royalist forces commanded by General Zahedi overthrew Mossadeq. The CIA hired mobs and organised a military revolt. In a week of street fighting, 300 Iranians died. Finally Mossadeq was arrested and the Shah returned in triumph. Only years later, in 2000, would Madeleine Albright, the US Secretary of State, confess to the 1953 coup in Iran and apologise to the Iranian people.

The choice of Major General Zahedi as the new Prime Minister reflected the dawn of a new age of dictatorship. Iran fell under military rule and anti-Americanism became a powerful force in Iranian society. In December 1953, the Shah embarked on the creation of a new secret police force called Sazman-e Amniat va Etella'at Keshvar (Organisation of National Security and Intelligence), popularly known by its acronym SAVAK. A new era had begun.

As the Iranian government grew closer to the USA during the early 1950s, its relationship with the USSR deteriorated. Iranian Communists came to be seen as figures of fun. Parviz Khatibi, who had once been imprisoned for unauthorised travel to Communist countries, scripted and directed *Ghiam-e Pishevari* (*The Revolt of Pishevari*, 1954), about the Russian presence in Azerbaijan after the Second World War. The promotional material describes the film as 'The first ever political movie accompanied by music, song and dance, and containing exciting displays of war, romance and comedy.' The satirical arrow aimed at Iran's northern neighbour is unmistakable: a buffoon of a police officer, in charge of a group of raw cadets, takes on and defeats the combined might of the Red Army and the Iranian 'fifth columnists'.

In his *Mihanparast* (*Patriot*, 1953), Gholam-Hossein Naghshineh displayed such an exaggerated nationalism that the film became unintentionally surreal. Here, the hero, following his father's dying wish, joins the army to defend Iran during a regional war. After the conflict he retires with the rank of colonel. Years later, Iran is invaded again. The hero's son-in-law refuses to do his military duty, whilst his own son dies defending the country. Now

"God, King, Country."

an old man, he decides to volunteer for the army once more, this time accompanied, somewhat ludicrously, by his daughter. The film's fanatical patriotism captures the mood of the Shah's propaganda machine, which employed the slogan, 'God, King, Country', on every possible occasion. Moreover, when the hero and his daughter are temporarily arrested on the mistaken belief that they are spies, many saw in this a criticism of the pro-Moscow Tudeh Party, several of whose prominent members were actually arrested and put on trial around the same time.

The activities of Studio Artesh, which was financed by the military, reflected the importance that the army attached to propaganda. The prioritisation of message over artistry, however, meant that its feature films met with little success. In *Noghl Ali* (Parviz Khatibi, 1954), for example, the transformation of an overweight and clumsy peasant boy into a competent, obedient solider is somewhat eclipsed by the comic overacting of Asghar Tafakkori.

During this period, the Shah forcefully recruited a large number of peasants for his modern army. This was reflected in *Khun va Sharaf* (*Blood and Honour*, Samuel Khachikian, 1955), made with private finance and Armenian expertise. Depicting a mighty army fighting a fictive battle, it begins: 'We were nine youths from different social backgrounds ready to lay down our lives to defend our land.' It then cuts to a group of soldiers on horseback ascending a sand dune in a stingingly cold desert wind, as they reflect on the uncertain fate awaiting them. The plot traces the kidnapping of a young village girl. With the aid of local officers, her brother tries to rescue her, but the brigands decimate their forces. When all seems lost, the cavalry (soldiers from the central government) arrive in the nick of time to save the day. Newspapers announced that the Shah would attend the opening of *Blood and Honour*, but the royal visit did not materialise. As a film journal pointed out, the film's primary function was to catalyse patriotic virtues:

> The aim of *Blood and Honour* is to show, a) the sacrifices the soldiers make in order to impose the rule of law, b) that their ranks are swelled by patriots from all walks of life, c) that rebels and brigands will always receive their just desserts. Based on these three principles, the military authorities agreed to furnish Diana Studios with all the material and manpower they could muster. 120 soldiers armed with real bullets, guns, light machine-guns, helmets, etc. took part as extras.[33]

The dependence of the characters in this story on an invincible army was somewhat bizarre, since the memory of the army's humiliating capitulation to the allied forces only a decade earlier was still fresh in the collective psyche.

A dream of splendour and kingdom

From the second half of the 1950s, pseudo-historical adventure films became all the rage in Iran. This trend would continue, encouraged and financed by the government, until the end of the following decade. Trashy plots, cardboard sets, awful performances and ludicrous outfits characterise these films. But for a post-coup regime, and a government that was hanging on to its authority with the aid of foreign powers, alluding to a distant golden past that would make Iranians proud of their heritage was a sound survival stratagem.

Oriental swashbuckler films were still popular in Hollywood and films such as *Desert Hawk* (1950), *The Golden Horde* (1951), *Thief of Damascus* (1952), *The Veils of Baghdad* (1953), *The Adventures of Haji Baba* (1954), *Son of Sinbad/Nights of the Harem* (1955) and *Omar Khayyam* (1957) were familiar to Iranian audiences. Iranian filmmakers therefore attempted to imitate their plots and characters.

Yet Iranian cinema's amateurish attempts to mimic Hollywood failed to reproduce the obligatory Orientalism and the imitation of Western film stars was frequently ridiculous. When *Yusef va Zoleikha* (*Yusef and Zoleikha*), by Siamak Yasami, went on general release in 1956, audiences were treated to the depiction of a famous ancient literary character, played by Mohsen Mahdavi, dressed like a cross between a Western cowboy and an American Indian. A journal wrote scornfully: 'Mahdavi's gestures remind one of Gregory Peck's performance in *David and Bathsheba* … and Shohreh as Zoleikha tries to impose a contrived sex appeal by wearing a wedding dress based in its design on foreign swimsuits.'[34]

The most productive period for Iranian pseudo-historical adventure came between 1956 and 1969, when some twenty films in this genre were churned

FIG. 8 Iranian cinema's amateurish attempt to mimic Hollywood during the 1950s was frequently ridiculous: Mohsen Mahdavi in *Yusef and Zoleikha*, 1956, dressed as Gregory Peck in *David and Bathsheba*, 1955.

out. Most were produced at Pars Film Studio, owned by Esmail Kushan, while a few were made at the Studio Asr-e Talai. Pars Studio already possessed ready-made sets, costumes and props, which it had retained after the success of *Amirarsalan-e Namdar* (Shapur Yasami, 1955). This did not go unnoticed by the press, with a review of *Yaghub Lais Saffar* (Ali Kasmai, 1957) noting that 'the actors wear the same outfits seen in previous films'.[35]

These hyper-formalistic and excessive epics are either despised or completely ignored by most scholars of Iranian cinema. Since their function is seen as essentially in bad taste and their historical depictions anachronistic, the genre is generally regarded as a suspect form of cinematic representation. Indeed, at first sight, their purpose seems significant only as a perverse and inflated display of autocratic power – a tumescent Iranian cinema, institutionally full of itself, swollen with its own generative power to mobilise labour and money. They seem neither subtle nor substantial enough to invite much in the way of semiological and cultural analysis, even from scholars interested in exploring the nature and function of various forms of historical representation. But adventure films give a clear perspective on political issues, communicated through the actions of the hero. This character is not only the narrative centrepiece but also enunciates the film's political views, and – following a standard code – provides a moral compass. Personal and political events become intertwined and inseparable. The genre's ideology emanates from the adventurer's strenuous moral stand – he is usually an ally of the king; a hero shaping society, rather than being shaped by it.

Tradition is revered in these films as part of a glorious past but they also imply a willingness to grow with the times. The hero is a fundamentally constructive person, building for the future, capable both of a social vision and of having the practical ability to implement it. The dream of freedom and justice is never an intangible utopia. The adventurer's life is incomplete unless it extends beyond the personal to encompass larger interests, maintaining a political responsibility to the king. He becomes a 'great' individual because his goals coincide with historical imperatives; he is the standard-bearer of the popular will. Such heroes appear at the moment when the fictional nation is facing a crisis, providing the spark for rebellion.

FIG. 9 *Hossein Kurd*, directed by Esmail Kushan in 1971, a pseudo-epic formula of a hero with pro-King/Shah beliefs.

By means of these historical productions, or productions of history, the regime was emphasising a glorious past based on monarchical rule. The code followed by these films dictates the basic formula of a hero with pro-king/Shah beliefs. Frequently he is descended from noble blood, but his family has lost its position and he must restore its former prestige. Before this has been achieved, however, he never hesitates literally to leap into the palace, bypassing guards and the social barriers they represent, to provide a warning against or provoke confrontation with the king's enemies. This reflects a subsumed longing to transcend rigid class relationships. However, the common element in these pseudo-historical films is their implicit legitimisation of the monarchy and their encouragement of absolute subservience to the leader.

Coincidences and chance events are rife in these films and song-and-dance routines spring up out of context. Moreover, Persian chauvinism becomes so exaggerated that reality is either ignored or greatly distorted. Thus the youth depicted in *Shaheen-e Tus* (*Hawk of Tus*, Karim Fakour, 1954) manages to defend his village from the mighty Arab army, and in *Arus-e Dejle* (*The Bride of Tigris*, Nosratollah Mohtasham, 1955), in imitation of swashbuckling films, Jafar Barmaki, an Iranian warrior, similarly defeats the Arab Caliph Harun al-Rashid.

Paradoxically, the Iranian pseudo-epics were not so much accounts of specific historical events, as narrative constructions of fictional events loosely based on old Persian stories. Film epics are usually made, and best received, at a time when a country still believes in its national myths but feels itself slipping into decline, which produces a spate of nostalgic evocations of those myths. During these periods, to articulate the past is to seize hold of a fond memory as it flashes up at the moment of danger. History emerges in popular consciousness not with any particular accuracy or specificity of detail or event but through the concept of a particular theme, in this case, king and land. All these films, despite their superficial exoticism, take for granted the transparency of the past, believing in the continuity of humanity over time rather than the differences. Past human events are shown to be relevant and significant, and these films always return to the same central question: how to comprehend ourselves across time. If the opaque work of academic histories is an objective projection of 'ourselves-now' as 'other-then', the transparent work of epic histories is a subjective projection of 'ourselves-now' as 'us-then'.

The Bride of Tigris, which was not officially commissioned by the government though its making was encouraged, was billed as an historical epic, yet one journal criticised it thus: 'it is as if the camera has been let loose on Haroun's palace to take random snap-shots of Barmaki's court intrigues, with a plethora of repetitive and unattractive song-and-dance routines thrown in for good measure.'[36] Given such distortions, other government-commissioned films based on historical or mythological characters could hardly fare any better.

Complex, three-dimensional literary characters are reduced to pale imitations in films like *Yusef and Zoleikha*, *Rostam va Sohrab* (*Rostam and Sohrab*, Shahrukh Rafiei, 1957), and *Bijan va Manijeh* (*Bijan and Manijeh*, Manuchehr Zamani, 1958), *Pesar-e Darya* (*Sea Boy*, Shapur Yasami, 1959) took such misrepresentation to its logical conclusion by plagiarising the story of Moses – replacing him with a Persian prince.

Pars Film Studio went as far as promoting its feature *Rahzan* (*Brigand*, Siamak Yasami, 1954) as a seminal cinematic event, claiming that the film realistically displayed the customs of local tribes. Perhaps the most interesting feature is the description of the two dances featured in the film – one is allegedly a traditional Kurdish dance, the other, 'a special brigand's dance', whatever that might be. The narrative of *Bohlul* (Sadeq Bahrami, 1957) revolves around the reign of Harun al-Rashid and how the eponymous Bohlul, with the support of other patriots, stands up to injustice. Strangely, a Spanish dancer frequently accompanies the other court dancers in scenes that are completely devoid of historical validity.

At the end of the 1950s, with typical over-the-top fanfare, Pars Film Studio announced the filming of *Cyrus the Great*, billing the film not only as 'the greatest film ever produced in Iran, comparable in scope to foreign epics' but indeed as 'one of the greatest films produced in the Middle East in recent years.'[37] In fact the film, about the birth of the Persian monarchy, was never made, but this minor detail did not prevent Pars Film Studio from continuing with its pro-royal promotion.

Ironically, although the genre did not narrate and dramatise historical events accurately, its interpretation of history was the direct result of the current situation. Not only did these films strengthen the sovereignty of a king who was trying to prove his legitimacy; they often depicted a rebellion against his power by a figure such as the treacherous Prime Minister who gets between the monarch and his people. That this character became a cliché in these films is unsurprising in a period in which the Shah was replacing his Prime Ministers one by one.

The ethics of the adventurer's code and its relationship to patriotism and chivalry also strengthened the handling of political issues in Iranian cinema. While the stories were wide-ranging in their subject matter, most concentrated on the adventurer's interaction with the government, the law and the authorities. From the outset, the principal motivation for conflict was political, revolving around oppression and injustice, as the hero battled to attain and preserve the social ideals of the Shah's code. Emphasising the union of the people with the national interests, these adventures demanded a just Iranian society in which individual rights were respected and class differences were minimised.

Kushan would go on to make several such films in the second half of the 1960s, including *Amirarsalan-e Namdar* (1967), a remake of his previous adventure film *Gohar-e Shab Cheragh* (*Gem of the Night*, 1957) and *Nasl-e Shojan* (*Breed of Bravados*, 1969), in which the loyal hero defends the monarch against villains. In Amin Amini's *Ali Baba va Chehel Dozd-e Baghdad* (*Ali Baba and the Forty Thieves of Baghdad*, 1967) the protagonist fights with the devilish army and goes on to marry the King's daughter, as does one of the characters fighting against traitors in his *Pesaran-e Aladdin* (*Sons of Aladdin*, 1967).

Patriotism, a generally conservative belief, becomes in the adventure genre a rationale for leading insurgencies against any unjust force. Since patriotism is expected and assumed, the hero must serve the legitimate needs of the state in the way the king believes best. True loyalty, and the obligations it imposes, is owed less to the country than to the people, promoting the ideal of the Iranian nation as one in which the needs of its people will be met. In these films the hero – as the representative of the people – is largely selfless in his motives, never desiring power or a kingdom that does not rightly belong to him. Enemies are punished but the king remains aloof from any vicious reprisals that would bring him down to the villain's level.

Politics in these films is expressed through a recurring motif, an accepted formula that need only be mentioned rather than explained. The stories are full of the rhetoric and romanticism of justice, honour and liberation, with the hero instinctively enunciating a view that becomes the film's rallying cry. Since the genre is organised around the issue of political legitimacy, authority must constantly demonstrate its values. Tyranny is given a historical background so that the adventurer's response becomes morally necessary and justified. The overthrow of authority moves beyond personal or vengeful conflicts to encompass a broader clash of social forces over issues of class and economic justice. To be accepted, rebellion must be justified on an intellectual and political basis, offering not only an end to injustice but also a positive alternative for the future.

Consequently, the Iranian adventure films of this period demonstrate empathy with the less fortunate; their primary concern is always for the lower classes, chivalrously caring for the weak and defenceless. The actions of the hero both illustrate the obligations of the upper class and make clear that the people's needs are just. Elitism has no place in the behaviour of the hero, who prefers to associate with common folk for friendship, companionship, and sometimes love, reflecting a political movement that believed in creating unity across all social strata, the Shah's familiar slogan.

The Iranian historical adventure film can be characterised by the cultural values identified with bourgeois patriarchy, with colonialism and imperialism, and with entrepreneurial and corporate capitalism, values which in the 1950s, for a variety of reasons – the emergence of militant Islamic groups, Mossadeq's nationalism, Soviet threat – were in crisis. The peak period of the pseudo-historical epic in Iran coincided with the culturally homogenising politics of the Cold War, and the genre began to decline in the mid-1960s. This era witnessed a substantial consolidation of the Shah's personal power and of his modernising policies, including constitutional and economic changes, political repression and pro-American and anti-Communist legislation. Consequently, as a major political challenge to the state, there was a rise in cultural nationalism.

Censorship codes

It is evident that the real obstacle in the path of decent historical features was not a lack of capital or equipment but the dominance of censorship. Iranian history is so enmeshed with the presence of charismatic leaders, sultans and monarchs that the smallest deviation from the norm in their depiction has been perceived as an implicit critique of leadership. The historical features of this period were therefore subjected both to state censorship and, just as ominously, to self-censorship.

A prime example is *Agha Muhammad Khan* (1955), based on the life of the monarch who established the Qajar dynasty and starring the film's director

Nosratollah Mohtasham in the title role. In the first version of the film, which runs for 150 minutes, the hero is castrated by Karim Khan Zand, and after a series of adventures, manages to secure power, only to be killed by foreign agents at the end. Ironically, by the time the film was sent for inspection, Mohtasham had become the head of the Exhibition Department at the Ministry of the Interior. In an unintentional parody of the censorship laws, he cut twenty-five minutes of his own film, completely changing it in the process. In the new version, the king's death is edited out, showing instead a heroic Agha Muhammad Khan who leaves his palace empty-handed to fight his foes.

One film critic commented wryly:

> The plot does not tally with reality. The film claims Agha Muhammad Khan was castrated by Karim Khan Zand, whereas history teaches us that this was done by the Afshar dynasty ... In the movie [Karim Khan] is killed by his servant and at the behest of foreign powers, in reality his chef murdered him when he was sleeping. The film depicts Karim Khan as cruel and Agha Muhammad Khan as brave, whereas history's verdict is the exact opposite. History shows Qajar women to have been obese, with eyebrows that met in the middle, and 'tulip' lips. The film represents the harem women, such as Amineh and Salimeh, as tall and delicate, usually striking a European pose. In short, neither the fundamentals nor the temporal dimensions of history have been respected. Why on earth should we eulogise the Qajar dynasty and pretend they were a breed apart?[38]

Another critic, Hushang Kavusi, could barely contain his derision:

> Those wishing to make historical movies, especially if it is their first time, should consult experts in the field in order to counteract their ignorance. *Agha Muhammad Khan* ... contains horrendous historical inconsistencies. For one thing, Agha Muhammad Khan was highly respected by Karim Khan and it is not true that the latter dethroned the former. For another, Agha Muhammad Khan is shown carrying the current tricolour of the Iranian regime. This flag, as every school child knows, was the product of the Constitutional Revolution, and prior to that, the flag was white, with green margins plus the present lion and sun insignia in the middle.[39]

In June 1950, the Ministry of the Interior had set out a rigid code of conduct for exhibition halls, film scripts, plays and film production. This made a number of unusual stipulations, outlawing:

Films in conflict with the foundations of Islam and the twelve Imam versions of Shi'ism.

Films in opposition to the constitutional monarchy, his Grace and his immediate family.

Depictions of political turmoil in any country leading to the dethronement of the monarch.

Films that encourage political revolution with a view to changing the regime.

Films that promote beliefs and practices contrary to the law.

Any film where the criminal characters do not get punished.

Any prison riot leading to defeat of the military authorities.

Films that encourage workers, peasants, students and other classes to oppose the military, or engage in sabotage of factories or schools.

Films opposed to the nation's customs and traditions.

Films that create disgust and despair in audiences.

Films depicting female nudity (defined as the presentation of naked breasts and private parts).

Films containing foul language or derision of local accents (especially during dubbing).

Films depicting a 'naked' couple in bed prior to the act of lovemaking.

Films corrupting public morals and those containing 'gangster' vocabulary.

Films that intensify ethnic and religious tensions within society.

The joint forces of the Ministry of the Interior, the Ministry of Culture, the Department of Media and Radio, the police authorities, as well as the security apparatus, were responsible for overseeing the correct adherence to these laws. It is important to note that the scope of these regulations was not limited to native films. The following article from *Jahan-e Cinema* in 1952 illustrates the approach to the censorship of foreign films:

> Since the first foundations of the film industry were laid in this country, the Ministry of the Interior has attempted to limit and censor film imports using severe measures. Over the last two or three years, you may have seen the following films: *Monsieur Beaucaire, The Bride Wore Boots, Unconquered, Joan of Arc, Desert Hawk, Christopher Columbus, Samson and Delilah, Silver Queen* … and *The Accused*.[40] But have you noticed any incomplete scene, any discontinuity? In

> all probability, the thought of sequences being ripped out of these films did not even occur to you. Yet it happens all the time. For instance, in *Monsieur Beaucaire*, starring Bob Hope and Joan Caulfield, there is a scene where the King calls for his court barber to shave his beard. The scene lasts for some six minutes but you do not see any of this. Likewise, there is an interesting romantic scene in *The Bride Wore Boots*, starring Barbara Stanwyck and Robert Cummings, which is censored. The fascinating historical film *Unconquered*, starring Gary Cooper and Paulette Goddard, was missing some twenty minutes. Ironically, the censor boasts that he has done his job so smoothly that nobody will notice the missing segments! … The second trial of *Joan of Arc*, which lasts some thirty minutes, was mysteriously deleted.
>
> The movie *Desert Hawk* was subjected to incredible distortion, the like of which has probably never been seen before. The story unfolds in the Tehran of two thousand years ago, although every utterance of the word 'Tehran' is deleted from the subtitles. Using a 'Leighton' machine technicians first marked the exact spot where the word 'Tehran' appeared in the subtitles. Then the offending word was blacked out to prevent light from projecting it onto the screen.

The article continues in a similar vein, citing further distortion to *Desert Hawk*, and to *Christopher Columbus*, *Samson and Delilah*, *The Silver Queen* and *The Accused*. The censorship of *Martyr* is, it goes on,

> arguably the most ingenious of all. Here the physical similarity of two of the characters was used to change the ending. Towards the end of the film Prince Ramon and one of his soldiers engage Carlos, the film's hero, in a sword fight, in a palace where King Lorenzo is being held captive. In the middle of the duel, Ramon notices Lorenzo and engages him in a fight. Then the two are shown in front of a column, engaged in debate. The audience expects one of them to kill the other. However, the conversation is abruptly halted and the scene shifts back to the duel between Ramon and Carlos, which is won by the latter. Now Carlos walks towards the column, only to find Lorenzo badly wounded … a few words are exchanged and, suddenly, Lorenzo is shown well and healthy in the next segment.
>
> Needless to say, this was not the way the film was put together. In reality, Ramon fatally wounds the king with his sword, and then engages Carlos in a duel, which Carlos wins. Carlos then goes to the dying king who thanks him for his loyal service and encourages Carlos to take over the reigns, with the aid of the trusted Prime Minister, once he is gone. He then dies and Carlos becomes the new ruler. Another interesting aspect of this film was the deliberate mistranslation of 'king' as 'governor'.[41]

With the invention of dubbing came a new chapter in Iranian censorship. First employed on the Italian film, *Le Meravigliose Avventure de Guerri Meschino*, shown under the Iranian title of *Feridun-e Binava (Fereidon the Impoverished)* in 1951, in which Iranian names were substituted for the Italian, the technique met with a positive audience response, but it also set in motion a trend that eventually led to dubbing being used as a mechanism for censorship. In future films, unfaithful fiancées would replace unfaithful wives, and, with a little help from the dubbing editor, thieves and criminals would piously repent.

After the 1953 coup, the Pahlavi state was still having difficulty in rallying the support of the new middle class. Barred from the freedom of political activity, many writers, teachers, lawyers, physicians, engineers and students were opposed to or highly ambivalent about the regime. From the beginning of 1954, the issue of censorship became even more acute, with the government setting up a special commission – peopled by military and government men – for the censorship of foreign and domestic historical films. This move was put down to the incessant complaints of film producers regarding the unwarranted editing of their products. Perhaps unsurprisingly, the campaign quickly got bogged down in marshy terrain, creating even more chaos than before.

In 1957 the Department of Public Buildings issued a breathtaking new circular. Part of the decree, which was severely criticised by some publications, accusing the government of ignoring business interests and freedom of choice, read:

> As morning screenings during non-holiday periods have encouraged truancy amongst civil servants, students and pupils, the Prime Minister has instructed that henceforth, films will only be shown after the noon deadline, during work days. This applies to all film festivals and other similar events.

The following year saw the production of Samuel Khachikian's *Ghased-e Behesht (Heaven's Emissary)*. Its run was interrupted five times by the censor's increasingly arbitrary objections. These ranged from the absurd criticism that a comic character had belittled the Boy Scouts by dressing in their uniform to the equally bizarre complaint that the judge character lacked the grandeur and dignity one would expect from the judiciary.

When censorship laws were permanently altered to disbar under-sixteens from 'corrupt' films, one journal considered the move atavistic:

> We do not deny the endemic corruption from which Iranian society has been suffering for some time, but why should cinema bear the entire blame? Is anyone seriously suggesting that the manufacturers of unhealthy food stuffs, rebel tribes defying central authorities, government bureaucrats accepting bribes, prostitutes ensnaring our youth on street corners, etc. … have all been corrupted by cinema? Our youth has no other entertainment, so if they were denied access to films as well, they would gravitate towards more harmful influences. Surely this is not the government's intention.[42]

From 1958 onwards, the chaos surrounding censorship became so embarrassing that government officials were constantly forced to justify themselves. Dr Muhammad Ali Sami'i, who had recently returned from the United States to take up his post as head of the Exhibition Bureau at the Ministry of the Interior, was up-front about the rationale behind censorship:

> As Iranians are still a very immature people, and as most cannot discern cinematic subtleties, there is no alternative to censorship for the time being. This is especially true of internally produced movies, given our nation's obsession with imitating foreigners … In any case, censorship exists everywhere and if producers followed the guidelines, there would be no need for censorship.[43]

In early 1959, the Exhibition Department circulated a stern directive to all film studios to the effect that any transgression of the censorship guidelines would result in immediate prohibition. Despite such threats, gangsters, murderers and criminals began to permeate an ever-larger number of films. The lives of ordinary people remained as far from the screens as ever.

Sudden wealth and the modern bourgeoisie

In the 1940s, Iran had received a $26 million loan from the USA to equip the army and the police. Less than two weeks after the Shah returned on 22 August 1953 from his short exile, making a triumphant entry into

Tehran following the coup against Mossadeq, the United States announced a $23.4 million grant for continued technical and military projects in Iran. This was the biggest sum ever paid out to one country under the Point-Four Programme by the United States. On 5 September, President Eisenhower granted another $45 million to Iran as emergency economic aid under the Mutual Security Act. Two months later, it announced a further $42.3 million grant and an $85 million loan to sustain Iran's economy until its revived oil industry began to bring in revenue again. It seemed the Pahlavi state was now rich and powerful enough to follow its dreams.

In 1954 the USA and Iran exchanged ambassadors. The resumption of relations demonstrated that the nationalistic Mossadeq era was over and that Iran would now be increasingly aligned with the West. Richard Nixon's visit to Iran, however, became an occasion for the most widespread anti-American demonstrations ever seen in the country. The political temperature was raised further when three student demonstrators were killed at Tehran University. The winter of the same year saw the trial of Mossadeq. In the next year, Navab Safavi, an Islamic fundamentalist who had fought with the Shah, and a group of his disciples from the Feda'iyan-e Islam were executed; Ayatollah Kashani was imprisoned. Iran received a further $45 million loan from the United States, but this financial generosity did nothing to kick-start manufacturing, and inflation remained the defining feature of the economy. In order to attract foreign investment, the government passed a law enabling foreign businesses to transfer as much of their annual profit outside Iran as they wished. In a very short time, this 'open-door' policy led to the formation of some 500 foreign and mixed-nationality companies, mostly concentrating on currency dealings and the importation of foreign goods. By the end of Prime Minister Hossein Ala's term in 1959, Iran had become a fully fledged satellite of the West.

A sustained period of growth for the Iranian bourgeoisie began in this decade, when the government started providing low-interest loans. Subsidised loans were initially allocated by the state-owned Industrial Credit Bank, established in 1956. In the first three years of its operation, 82 loans totalling $10.5 million were made to 70 projects. The Revaluation Loan Fund, administered by the National Bank from 1957 on, was much larger, providing $64 million in 1,541 loans over a three-and-a-half year period. The injection of capital and the establishment of foreign firms transformed the look of the big cities, especially Tehran, which could now boast its very own nouveaux riches. In this context, a great number of films telling miraculous 'rags-to-riches' stories began to appear, which more often than not employed humour as a mechanism for dealing with the increasing gulf between the social classes.

This sudden fictional wealth might materialise in the form of an inheritance, as in *Agha-ye Eskenas* (*Mr Currency*, Amin Amini, 1956), where the protagonist's relationships with his friends are transformed as a result of his new-found riches, or *Heaven's Emissary*, previously discussed, in which a windfall saves a man from bankruptcy. Sometimes, as in *Rozan-e Omid* (*Light of Hope*, Sardar Sagar, 1958), a winning lottery ticket is the cause of jubilation. In *Chek-e Yek Million Toomani* (*One Million Tooman Cheque*, Salaar Eshghi, 1959), two wealthy men amuse themselves by betting on a young simpleton's reaction to becoming rich overnight. Magic and the occult became a useful vehicle for expressing this form of narrative. In *Kolah-e Gheibi* (*The Invisible Hat*, Salaar Eshghi, 1956) and *Halgeh-ye Jadouie* (*The Magic Ring*, Mehdi Besharati, 1958), for example, the eponymous enchanted items lead to fortunes. If these formulaic films were successful, it was due to their ability to offer the illusion of happiness through miraculous fortune.

Films dealing with the same theme, but with ambiguous endings, did not fare as well commercially. In *Dozdan-e Ma'dan* (*The Mine Thieves*, Hossein Amir Fazli, 1956), two friends discover a mine full of diamonds, but after being attacked by brigands are forced to come clean to the authorities. More depressingly, in *Mardi ke Ranj Mibord* (*Melancholic Man*, Muhammad Ali Ja'fari, 1957), the hero ends up in jail on embezzlement charges. Perhaps predictably, both films flopped.

The political changes of the 1950s led to further socio-cultural transformation and to the emergence of new occupations, with the stereotypical middle-class male urban intellectual – usually an architect or engineer – permeating a large number of films. These included *Afsungar* (*Seductress*, Esmail Kushan, 1953), *Laghzesh* (*Blunder*, Mehdi Rais Firuz, 1953), and *Khab va Khial* (*Dream and Fantasy*, Majid Mohseni, 1955). Doctors were also common. The benefits of education were extolled in *Dast-e Taghdir* (*Hand of Fate*, Gorji

FIG. 10 Film stars were a new phenomenon in a country whose undeniable stars had been the Shah and his queens. Indeed Soraya Bakhtiari, after separation from the Shah, even appeared in the Italian film *Three Faces* (*I Tre Volti*), 1965.

Obadiah, 1959), in which a peasant girl enters law school, and in *Eteham* (*Accusation*, Shapur Yasemi, 1956). Some of the occupations, such as an English language teacher in *Doshman-e Zan* (*Women's Foe*, Parviz Khatibi, 1958), spoke of the need to learn foreign languages, but others, such as music teachers or lyricists, were Western forms of employment imposed artificially and having no cultural equivalent in a traditionalist society. Along the same lines, *Omr-e Dobareh* (*Second Life*, Parviz Khatibi, 1952) is about a private detective working for an insurance company, while *Jedal ba Sheitan* (*Challenge with the Devil*, Hossein Madani, 1952) follows the escapades of an adventurous investigative journalist. *Akharin Shab* (*The Last Night*, Hossein Daneshvar, 1955) evolves around a lawyer, while *Mr Currency* tells the story of a cabaret owner.

These films encouraged the desire to emulate Western modes and attitudes. The look and behaviour of the actors were copied from Western cinema; they wore Western clothes, smoked, and even threw punches and drew revolvers like Western performers. The government actively encouraged this brand of filmmaking. In fact, after the new censorship laws of 1958, it became even harder to go against the grain.

The few films that alluded to poverty and showed the lives of the lower classes were heavily edited lest they brought the country into disrepute. In *Light of Hope*, a country bumpkin who has won the lottery gets lost in Tehran, finds work at a slaughterhouse, then in a cabaret, and is eventually thrown into jail. Many of the sequences depicting the poor people of southern Tehran were censored. A poignant scene from *Ham-e Gonahkareem* (*We Are All Guilty*, Aziz Rafi'i, 1958), in which a burglar feels so sorry for his dirt-poor intended victims that instead of stealing from them he actually leaves them some money, was deemed too critical. Similarly *Jonub-e Shahr* (*South of the City*, Farrokh Ghaffari, 1958), a gritty, realistic portrayal of the harshness of life in southern Tehran, was banned by the government and all copies confiscated. When, many years later, the film was finally returned to the director, huge chunks of it were missing. These sequences have never been recovered.

The politics of Iranian melodrama

If in France, it was costume drama and the historical novel, in Germany, ballads and street songs, and in Italy, opera, in which the melodramatic form reached the highest degree of sophistication, in Iran the strongest melodramatic tradition is to be found in its literature. The earliest Iranian film melodramas were love stories such as *Shirin and Farhad* (1935) and *Leili and Majnun* (1937). Based on literary sources, they borrowed their traditional moralistic model, their emotional shock tactics and their blatant play on the audience's sympathies and antipathies.

In the 1950s, this melodramatic turn was also evident in foreign films. Indian melodramas, for instance, were extremely well received in Iran at this time. (The differing situations in British and American melodramas meant that these, by contrast, were not of interest to Iranian audiences.) In 1956, 21 Indian films went on general release there, with India's most famous actor Raj Kapoor appearing in 8 of them. In 1957, the New Year was celebrated with three Indian films, and a total of 49 Indian films was shown that year. The next year, Raj Kapoor and the legendary actress Nargess were warmly received in Iran.

Two main currents come together to make up the genealogy of Iranian melodrama in the 1950s: the morality tale and the idea of the doomed protagonist. Even *Bolhavas* (*Sensual*, Esmail Kushan), made as early as 1934, in which a feckless husband leaves his native wife for a city woman, had adhered to this pattern. Following on from this film, what particularly defined Iranian melodramas was the moralistic primary subject matter (sacrifice in the realm of the family, domestic crises, faithless husbands or wives, lost children, crimes of passion), and a subtext dealing with the distance between rich and poor, past and present.

Subsequently several films were made with similar plots based on sentimental stories, whose emphasis was on private feelings and inner (puritanical or pious) codes of morality and conscience. Historically, the popularity of this genre has tended to coincide with periods of intense social, ideological and political crisis, such as the brief period from the coup in 1953 to the shooting of the Shah in 1958.

These films derived their dramatic force from the conflict between the extreme and highly individualised moral idealism of the rural protagonists and the corruption of the town dwellers (despite being aimed at urban audiences, since there were no cinemas in rural areas), representing issues of land ownership and the invasion of modernism. They depicted a seemingly omnipotent urban upper class, and the extreme constraints and pressures, the quasi-totalitarian violence, perpetuated by the system or its agents.

Most 1950s Iranian films made use of rudimentary forms of the melodramatic–emotional plot but the definitive films of the genre have an element of interiorisation, or personalisation of what were primarily political and ideological conflicts, together with a metaphorical presentation of class conflict. The family melodrama deals largely with the theme of moral identity through family crisis: the absent father, murderous spouses and rebellious children. Titles like *Love's Intoxication* and *Thief of Love*, unimaginative though they might now seem, are indicative of the thirst for melodrama at this time.

Post-war Iranian cinema was rejuvenated by these melodramas. Imitating their Indian and Egyptian counterparts, Iranian filmmakers offered, with the aid of tacky song-and-dance routines, a mixture of tears and laughter. What made these films popular was the way in which they purported to look sympathetically at ordinary people in something resembling their true social circumstances – precisely what the political powers were endeavouring to resist.

While post-war policies failed to bring tranquillity to society, films based on the themes of forced marriage, rape, guilt, injustice and adultery produced a new form of social drama in Iran. Most of the films of the 1950s focused on suffering and victimisation and last-minute rescues, sudden reversals of fortune, the intrusion of chance and coincidence, all pointed to the haphazard life of the individual unprotected by the law in an absolutist society. The system stood accused of greed, wilfulness and irrationality and this was portrayed through the suffering of selfless heroes or pure virgins in the midst of intrigue and callous indifference. The 'woman as victim' was a central theme in these melodramas. In both *Gonahkar* (*The Sinner*, Mehdi Garami, 1953) and *The Familiar Face*, the heroines are raped, and even the

more solemn examples of this model, such as *Baray-e To* (*For You*, Jamshid Sheibani and Sadeq Bahrami, 1955), fall prey to this absurd victimisation and objectification of women.

Following Mitra Film Studio's inaugural *Life's Tempest* seven more films were made between 1948 and 1952, either produced or directed by Kushan. In content, form and style they became models for future productions. The most noteworthy were *Madar* (*Mother*, 1952), *Thief of Love*, *Amir's Prisoner*, *Shameful* (1950) and *Seductress* (1952). Although the financial disaster of *Life's Tempest* led to Kushan's first company being declared bankrupt and despite the fact that the critics dismissed *Shameful* as too commercial, the totality of his films cemented the templates, clichés and approaches that were to dominate Iranian melodrama for years to come. Thinly disguised morality tales thematically arranged around hatred, jealousy, rape and unrequited love became his stock-in-trade. The more outlandish and fanciful the stories became, the more audiences flocked to the cinemas.

Song and dance as a new phenomenon

The resumption of filmmaking in the early 1950s saw a predominance of song-and-dance sequences along the lines of Egyptian and Turkish patterns. Throughout the world there have been historical periods in which entertainers have been held in low esteem. In Muslim countries, they have consistently been treated as outcasts and completely rejected by the clergy. Observations on the status of Iranian entertainers should be carefully contextualised, however. An important element of the Iranian attitude is related to Islamic views on music, singing and dancing. During the Middle Ages, several occupations were considered disreputable: money-lending, slave-dealing, wine- and pork-selling, and prostitution. Dancers and other entertainers such as wrestlers, actors, storytellers and female singers were suspected of questionable morality and associated with vice and begging.[44] In the eyes of the religious authorities, entertainers were outside the community of believers, regarded as leading immoral and dissolute lives. As a result of their mobility, they were both spatially and socially marginal to the community and usually marginal too in economic terms – spending money on amusement was also deemed a vice. With these films a discussion on the lawfulness of music ensued, which cast doubt not only on the permissibility of its performance, but also on whether one could legally listen to it. Although most law schools deemed it unlawful, this did not prevent forbidden pleasures from flourishing in the palaces.

The gender of the performer was crucial in the debate: women were generally perceived as more enticing than men and the excitement aroused by looking was considered more powerful than that provoked by listening. Many forms and contexts of entertainment were thus either controversial or completely forbidden to women as both performers and audience. But in nineteenth-century Egypt, female entertainers had constituted a major tourist attraction, on a par with the pyramids and the Nile. In the first decades of the twentieth century, nightclubs and variety shows sprang up in Egypt to meet the demands of the colonial rulers and Western tourists. They put on 'Oriental' shows, featuring the *danse du ventre*, or belly dance, and elements imported from the West. Egypt and Turkey, who had both liberated themselves from strict religious rules in their films, inspired a host of Iranian imitators and song and dance were introduced into both shows and at the cinema. The development of cabarets, cafés and nightclubs, which combined food, drink and entertainment, were among the striking changes in Tehran. For many common people in urban areas who couldn't afford to attend these establishments, the only access to music was through watching films or listening to radio shows. Music blared out of every theatre, flowing into the mind like balm on the wounds inflicted by the daily battles of existence, and representing a shared experience for the otherwise divided populace.

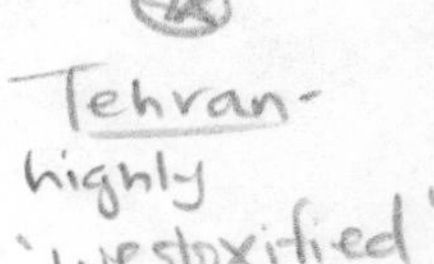

The manner in which song was treated in Iranian films reinforced their power to ignore the demands of realism. The ubiquitous film song went way beyond the bounds of the action on screen and took on an autonomous presence, suddenly coming to the fore completely out of the context of the film. Sometimes the song was in direct contradiction to the prevailing emotion on the scene, or to the apparent sexual modesty of the character. The convention was that there should be no tonal perspective – whether the person singing was close to or far from the camera made no difference to the volume and depth of the sound. The voices of the same playback singers emanated from characters in film after film in an attempt to provide a comforting sense of familiarity. Whenever a song came on, the projectionist immediately cranked up the volume to its loudest. The only concession to verisimilitude was in the allocation of different singing voices to different characters within the same film.

Just as film songs did not derive from traditional Iranian music, film dance depended on the imitation of Egyptian and Indian musicals, since there was no historical Iranian pattern for dance, and it never developed into a specifically Iranian form. The movement of the actors and actresses was childish and awkward when judged by the formal standards of classical and folk traditions, like a pantomime set to music. As a seductive spectacle of movement and fantasy, however, dance easily lent itself to film. Films featuring dance appealed particularly to women – a growing part of the Iranian middle-class film audience – and was undeniably associated with their new-found sexual freedom. The liberation of Iranian women on screen was crystallised in dance. From this period until the Revolution in 1978, Iranian cinema would continue to exploit the popularity of song and dance.

Women: from fallen angels to iconic mothers

The political tensions and spirit of anarchy one associates with the 1950s in Iran did not filter into films directly. It came through in the form of a questioning of conventional morality, particularly in the realm of marriage. The popularity of the family melodrama was connected in part to the fact that it set in opposition two different types of Iranian women – traditional and modern – reflecting a permanent tension between the Pahlavi state and the Shi'a establishment.

The state policy encouraging women's integration into society and participation in education and employment stopped short of the substantial reform of the family that would have been necessary to create the right conditions for their wider participation. As we have seen, the secularisation of the judiciary and the new laws drawn from French legislature that covered most other areas of social life did not include family law; the

Shari'a continued to be applied to the family. State policy regarding the family consisted of the codification of existing patriarchal laws. Only 100 of the 1,335 articles of the new Civil Code, which was completed in 1931, dealt with wills, marriage and divorce, legitimacy, custody, guardianship and child maintenance.

Most films of the 1950s were related to the theme of womanhood, and were increasingly focusing on the 'new woman'. Some encouraged her emergence, others satirised or exploited her. Esmat Delkash, one of the earliest female radio singers, became hugely popular as a film actress after her heart-rending performance as a cheated peasant girl in Kushan's *Shameful*, Iranian cinema's first box-office hit. She was arguably Iran's first cinema star, ironically famous for her masculine voice. Her on-screen character was the fallen but self-possessed woman who never hesitates to use her assets to get ahead and to gain control over her life, and her realistic performances signified the new values of the 1950s. Being a female singer, however, she was cast in the same role off screen.

Despite their low social standing outside the theatre, singers in Iranian cinema were seen as 'star' performers. The popularity of Delkash ensured that song-led tales remained dominant within the women's genre. After *Shameful*, she repeated the same 'fallen-woman' role for Kushan in two successive films. In *Mother*, she was a cheated woman taking care of her illegitimate daughter, and in *Seductress*, a woman who loses her lover and becomes a cabaret singer. Delkash was typical of the kind of powerful, vibrant and intense woman cast in these stories of the 1950s. As a result of unfortunate circumstances (abandonment by her lover, the death of her husband, the end of her marriage) her character inevitably becomes a cabaret singer or dancer. The new phenomenon of singing was thus shown to be the only weapon with which such a woman could fight against the odds.

The 'fallen woman' is frequently misunderstood and unjustly tormented by a male-dominated society (these films are chock-full of brutal fathers, loutish rapists and slimy seducers). When the hero finally meets her, he self-righteously spurns her until, through suffering and self-sacrifice, she redeems herself in his eyes. These melodramas demonstrated women's dependence on their bodies when they were left to fend for themselves. In the final analysis, however, it is difficult to avoid feeling in these films that the 'fallen' woman towers high above the man of whom she is purportedly so unworthy. Not too far beneath the apparent anti-feminism of the fallen-woman theme, one finds the frantic distress signals of waning masculine self-confidence and an implicit indictment of patriarchal society which, after all, was responsible for the political crisis at that time.

The question of redemption for the fallen women frequently occurred in these films. She was more a fallen angel than a fallen woman, a 'good-bad girl' – good, because she was naive and hardworking, and bad, because she was a singer. She was the reverse of the 'party girl', who initially takes in the hero in these films, but gradually or, sometimes, suddenly, falls from grace. The good-bad girl, on the other hand, is initially misjudged by the hero, but is sooner or later recognised for her virtues. Her major quality is self-sacrifice; she is prepared to let the hero misunderstand her motives because she is devoted to her mother or father, is protecting her child, or acting on behalf of her profession. By the end of the film, the good-bad girl ends up in the arms of the man she has always loved; the misunderstandings are explained away and the hero often reproaches himself for his short-sightedness.

The tendency to divide women into mutually exclusive categories was largely a habit of traditionalism. It was a favourite ploy to play one type off against the other: the predatory female against the innocent one; the party girl against the uptight wife; the girl who loves only men against the devoted mother. The party girl was the embodiment of a charged sexuality, often essentially a prostitute, but due to censorship laws she remained an ambiguous figure. Far from being forced into her actions against her will, unlike the fallen woman, she enjoys performing for men. Though economically independent, she is portrayed as yearning for male protection. Because the enforced ambiguity of this figure lent itself to a whole range of interpretations, it was richly invested with allegorical possibilities. Skirting the boundaries of the legitimate and the illegitimate, an ambivalent repository of Iranian womanhood and female power/vulnerability, the party girl served as a national palimpsest inscribed with contradictory social meanings. In the 1950s, the representation of the party girl/prostitute projected a view of women that was at once humiliating as well as tantalising, essential and active. An impersonator of Western actresses, the figure of the prostitute allowed the culture to probe some of its own assumptions regarding sexuality, femininity and social mores.

The party girl/prostitute or cabaret entertainer entered Iranian cinema in the 1950s with films such as *Parichehr* (Fazlollah Baigan, 1951), *Bazgasht be Zendegi* (*Return to Life*, Ataollah Zahed, 1957), *Gerdab* (*Whirlpool*, Hassan Kheradmand, 1953), *Blunder* (Mehdi Rais Firuz, 1954) and *Bee Setareha* (*Without Stars*, Khosrow Parvizi, 1959), and remained there for the next two decades. Nor was she of less significance in those films in which she did not occupy the primary role. As the 'other' woman, Parvin Ghaffari, with her blonde hair and cool eyes, established a kind of Iranian vamp a decade later, when glamour was exaggerated and dangerously overvalued in Iranian cinema. Her role sometimes superseded that of the heroine, whether as a poignant reflection of dependence on the values of a man's world, or as a searing metaphor for postcolonial political corruption and moral decay.

Party girls were no more real than reflections in a mirror. Indeed, mirror imagery was abundant in party-girl films, giving an added dimension to the parable of woman as split between virgin/whore, mother/lover, and as the looking glass held up to man. Her identity was as various and dispersed as the abrupt social changes that had brought about such a confused notion of women's place in society, generating an image of 'woman as enigma'. These films provided a space in which to raise certain concerns. Did the primacy of the female image, for example, whether or not deflected through a mirror, allow for or legitimise a female subjectivity? Did the representation of the party girl as both the subject of the film and as the product of cultural policies alter the terms of address of Iranian cinema? In the female universe signified by party-girl culture, at once apparently economically dependent on and yet distinct from the world of men, could women's values be nurtured, even though this universe was conceived by the government (and by men, since the films were made exclusively by male directors)? The party-girl was the outcome of conflicting social policies. She was a threatened and threatening figure of cultural difference, a 'bad' woman who facilitated an exploration of the psychosexual dimension of the on-screen imaginary.

The party girl film was a classic instance of female objectification in cinema. Here was the representation of woman as spectacle par excellence;

she was a body to be looked at, the site of sexuality, an object of desire – everything, in short, that the apparatus of cinema could purvey and that the misogynistic tendencies prevalent in Iranian culture could exploit. The 'invasion' of the new women had fuelled the fires of lust and turned romantic love into its antithesis. Themes of rape and revenge may have lent novelty to the old relish for violence but their implications went far beyond entertainment. Variations on the motif of prostitution were to be found in almost every commercial film from 1950 to 1978: the attempted rape scene; the cabaret dancer scene; descriptions of the misfortunes and ostracism of the unmarried mother; the Westernised vamp lurching, wine-glass in hand, towards sinister-looking men at a bar or club; the orphan girl trapped in a den of vice; the village woman assaulted by phallic glances (if not actually molested) in the corrupt city.

Apart from providing dramatic potential and voyeuristic material, these scenarios of libidinal excess reinforced the sense of female vulnerability in the face of male power and aggression. The rape fantasies were the internalisation of a patriarchal ideology that insisted on a masochistic female passivity and submission to male domination. In this way society toyed with forbidden sexuality, making it acceptable as punishment if not as pleasure, while urban women, as consumers of these films, were allying themselves to a 'sinful' world of extravagance and luxury linked to the new woman's culturally encouraged acquisition of consumer goods. Women's autonomy on screen, as a reflection of the dominant policies in Iran, was turning into a nightmare.

The negative, stereotypical portrayal of women, which cast them as either vamp or victim, led to a blanket public denunciation of women in Iranian cinema. And there was little hope of seeing women cross the barrier of good/bad clichés. Bad city women and good country girls were painted in bold outlines. The rivalry between these two types of woman in film represented the conflict between the values they represented and reflected Iran's self-directed ambivalence, its guilt and anxiety over the consequences of the sudden and enforced changes to the status of women.

The modernisation of the family was countered in the early 1950s by the emergence in a number of films, again often featuring Delkash, of the long-suffering mother as the central protective point around which the children's fortune revolves and presiding as the symbol of family unity. In these films her word is law, and her happiness is the audience's primary concern. As cinema audiences came to be largely composed of the less literate within the urban population, films began to reflect their fears regarding the break-up of the family and the erosion of the traditional values that had bonded family units together. How a woman's personality might be developed both inside and outside the home, without denying the needs of the family, also became a concern of the middle classes, to whom such changing roles were in reality confined. Hence the glorified mother figure became, in film, a monument to subterranean fears of lost identity and security that continued to trouble the minds of those who lived between tradition and modernity. Self-contained, closed communities were increasingly disrupted by urbanisation. With the expansion of large urban centres, many traditional professions were being displaced by mass production. The workplace became more secular and modern. The home, therefore, remained the refuge and repository for the safekeeping of tradition for the members of families increasingly dispersed geographically and occupationally. In the films of this period, the family is broken up early in the narrative and reunited at the end in order to provide hope and reassurance.

The emphasis on family values was strong enough in a film such as *Intrigue* even to justify murderous revenge on the part of the mother in order to redeem her family's honour. Mothers in these films represented the family; fathers, who stood for the state, were practically without significance, except in their violence towards their wives. The father here neither enjoys the respect of his children, nor wields a positive influence over them, since he is too busy making money or fraternising with his lover, while the mother keeps the family together through love, suffering and patience. Another factor behind this pattern was the sense of mistrust developing within a country under increasingly centralised direction. The unwritten laws of the smaller units of society, in the form of the family, were to be trusted more than those prescribed for the entire population by the state. The suggestion was that society as a whole was too distant and nebulous, and therefore a somewhat fearsome concept compared with the accessible and reassuring values of the family.

Through the combination of an increasingly moralistic audience and the allegorical tendency of melodramatic films, the woman as victim emerged in her purest form as the most sacred and crucial image of Iranian culture. The suffering virgin-heroine or mother-heroine was rooted in the spirit of reverence for traditional womanhood in a changing society. Delkash often took on the role of an urban peasant sanctified by her vocation for love and sacrifice, who survived by the miracle of her inner strength. In *Mother* her character had an illigitimate child, but the audience forgave her, both because she was cheated – and because she was a mother.

If the female stars of the 1950s – Delkash, Puran Shahpuri, Vida Ghahremani, Fakhri Khorwash, Shahin (Mahintaj Mogholkeisar), Jaleh Olov, Rufia (Mahjahan Soluki) – were more defined by type than the men, they were also more colourful and more central to the debate of the period. Action heroes like Iloosh Khoshabi and male comedians such as Asghar Tafakkori enjoyed flourishing careers but most of the successful films of the 1950s were romances and melodramas dominated by female stars. This was a decade in which actresses outnumbered their male counterparts, and one which saw the emergence of film stars in a country whose undeniable stars had been the Shah and his queens, Fuzieh, Soraya Bakhtiari and finally, Farah Diba.

Unlike previous public figures in Iran, these stars did not create resentment in the public and had no access to real political power; in a country with a monarchical system according to which the people could not elect their own ruler, the star system provided a welcome opportunity for the populace to choose their favourites from a list of 'candidates'. And they are still remembered today, like old photographs of people whose distinguishing traits have not yet disappeared; thus the images of the 1950s act as a bridge between past and present.

The question of women's emancipation

In the 1950s, women's actions were subject to political repression and governmental planning. The state paid special attention to the question of social welfare, and women's activities were channelled mainly into this area.

FIG. 11 The 'new' Iranian women in Western dress: Vida Ghahremani (right) and Hamideh Kheirabadi in *Fire and Ashes* (*Atash va Khakestat*), Khosrow Parvizi, 1951.

In 1956, the Ministry of Labour founded the Welfare Council for Women and Children and thirty-five female representatives were appointed to run it. Women's publications continued to be produced, but these were mainly pro-royalist journals, which followed the government line on the question of women's emancipation. *Etella'at Banovan* (*Women's News*) was published on a weekly basis and soon became the main officially approved women's magazine in Iran, enjoying a high circulation. *Neda-ye Zanan* (*Women's Call*), *Banu-ye Iran* (*Iran's Lady*) and *Zanan-e Iran* (*Women of Iran*) were less significant magazines, published in the late 1950s. Women's professional interests were represented by various associations, which were formed by female employees

and professionals including teachers, civil servants, doctors, nurses and other working women. In March 1957, a new legislation gave the vote to women for the first time.

The women's organisations that had been formed in the 1940s and which escaped the repression of the 1950s were gradually absorbed into a central organisation under the tutelage of Ashraf Pahlavi, the Shah's sister, who was infamous for being involved in various scandals. Initially, in 1956, a loose organisation for co-ordinating activities was formed by fourteen societies. Some of these were religious minority groups, such as the Society of Zoroastrian Women, the Society of Jewish Women and the Society of Armenian Women. Others included the Graduates of the American College, or were more broadly defined, such as Rah-e Now (The Society of the New Path). Within two years, this co-ordinating body was dissolved into a state-sponsored body, the High Council of Women's Organisations, still presided over by Ashraf Pahlavi.

Towards the end of the 1950s, with increasing centralisation and encroachment by the state into all areas of public life, the High Council was dissolved and replaced by the Women's Organisation of Iran. Some of the old societies kept up their activities informally, but instead of each being one amongst several roughly equal societies, they were now part of a single all-powerful organisation, with a significant budget. The upper-class women activists of the 1940s and 1950s were joined, outnumbered and in part displaced by a new breed of women whose style and appearance had been created by the changes of the late 1950s.

In the films of the later 1950s, women were still subjected to abuse but were able to pursue men and even to embody 'male' characteristics, like Delkash's character in *Zalem Bala* (*Naughty Woman*, Siamak Yasami, 1957), who disguises herself as a man without being stigmatised as 'unfeminine'. It was no coincidence that the comedian Ali Tabesh disguised himself as a woman in *Mademoiselle Khaleh* (*Mademoiselle Aunt*, Amin Amini) in the same year. Films in which characters cross-dress or disguise themselves sexually, despite the requisite heterosexual coupling at the end, were characteristic of a cinema that was trying to break with traditional societal codes. They offered Iranian spectators a momentary transgression of society's accepted boundaries regarding gender and sexual behaviour, yet audiences could confidently rely on the orderly demarcations reconstructed by the films' endings.

Political turmoil and loafers

By the turn of the decade the male hero was no longer competitive and domineering. It was as if, following the failure to preserve Mossadeq's nationalistic, autonomous government, Iranians no longer believed that the individual could overcome disaster through raw nerve and sheer determination. The political collapse that had befallen the nation was met in film by a weaker notion of masculinity. The irresponsible, urban male, neglecting his duty to his family, became firmly established as a new character.

Though the filmmakers of the 1950s did not ignore the social problems of the day, their conception of the hero was deeply influenced by the wishes of the government and the film industry, who did not want the audience to look too deeply into the causes of political collapse, let alone seek a remedy. The male image of the early 1950s was thus dictated by the fear of those wishing to uphold the official morality and laid stress on individual responsibility rather than social wrong. Naser Malak-Motii, playing a typical modern urban man in *Velgard* (*Loafer*, Mehdi Rais Firuz, 1952), established the character of the neglectful husband/father. He repeated this role both in *Whirlpool* and in *Gheflat* (*Neglect*, Ali Kasmai, 1953). In all three films he played a man who loses his family through gambling, drink and pleasure. Malak-Motii's films did not attempt to distract the audience from its troubles; they were intended as a moral message to warn of the dangers of individual neglect. In *Loafer* we are encouraged to approve of the eventual punishment of the man through his death. This kind of protagonist was not applauded, not only because he acts outside the bounds of official morality but because he is reluctant to deal directly with his own problems.

In the mid-1950s, Malak-Motii's screen persona shifted to that of the innocent man unjustly imprisoned for murder, a role he played both in *Accusation* and in *Herdah Ruz be Edam* (*Seventeen Days to Execution*, Hushang Kavusi, 1957). Again, the emphasis is on individual passivity. Following his arrest, however, he faces the law without self pity, and his fierce refusal to be beaten by the system invests him with a quiet dignity.

In these roles as a simple traditionalist, Majid Mohseni arms himself with honesty against the corruption that haunts the city. In *Dream and Fantasy* (1955) and *Zendegi Shirin Ast* (*Life is Sweet*, 1956), both of which he also directed, he features again as the ordinary urban man who values tenderness and love while knowing that the price for such purity is to remain an outsider. In *Dream and Fantasy* he exudes a wholesome virility that sharply contrasts with the ineffectuality of the conmen and 'sharpies' of the city, who attempt to prey upon him and his sweetheart. Though he is helpless against the odds in some of his films, Mohseni manages to retain this virility through the sympathy he shows to the weak – proof that masculinity has nothing to do with a domineering despotism. Mohseni consistently defined love as self-sacrifice, even donating one of his retinas in *Life is Sweet* to the blind husband of the woman he loves. His version of the hero triumphs against the dehumanisation of the social order in which he finds himself. He is the representative of the ordinary man struggling for survival in the crucial period of the early 1950s.

From happy endings to tragedies

Whereas traditional Iranian literary melodramas, such as love stories and poems, often ended tragically, those of Iranian cinema tended to have happy outcomes, averting catastrophe at the last moment. In the films, the suffering individual was reconciled to his or her social position, affirming an open society in which everything is possible. Yet these weak happy endings still conferred a negative identity on their heroes: they emerged as lesser human beings for having acquiesced to the way of life in the new world.

Over and again, the victory of the good citizen over evil aristocrats, lecherous men and conventional villains drawn from the lower classes was re-enacted in sentimental spectacles full of tears and moral posturing. Complex social processes were simplified either by blaming a general evil or through manipulative plots and conventions that allowed these films to reduce the actual tensions of society to simple clashes of personality. Though many of these films acted to reinforce fantasies of female submission, their structure nonetheless presented fundamental social evils in moral terms. The ideological message was transparent: the female character stood for innocent traditionalism while the odious rich man represented evil modernism.

Social changes were taking place at such a conservative pace that the range of retaliatory action taken by the protagonists of these films was limited to the tellingly impotent gesture, the social gaffe, the hysterical outburst, which replaced any more directly liberating or self-affirming acts. The violence of the chase or of physical abuse in these films was perhaps a cathartic outward sign of inner violence, impending change and transformation. For change was hovering at the edges of society. Following an abortive attempt at liberalisation in the early 1960s, many religious people and students would adopt revolutionary ideas and begin to form numerous political, revolutionary and guerrilla organisations, waiting for a chance to strike out against the regime. For this, Iran would have to wait until the end of the next decade.

5 The 1960s

Urban–rural conflict

During the 1960s the Iranian economy underwent sweeping changes. The relatively impressive growth rates of the economy in general, and of the manufacturing and oil sectors in particular, created the illusion that the country was undergoing a genuine process of industrialisation and development. However, a closer look reveals the contrary. In fact, while the oil sector accounted for about 28 per cent of the GNP by the end of the 1960s, it employed only around 0.5 per cent of the country's active population. Furthermore while industry grew, employment in agriculture waned.

Iran entered the 1960s ever more dependent on its oil revenues, at a time when some 70 per cent of the populace was still living in rural areas. Under pressure from and supervision by the USA under John F. Kennedy's presidency, the government introduced a programme of 'rural reforms', whose aims were the simultaneous reorganisation of agricultural work and transformation of the social relations of land ownership, in order to entice the rural community to enter the age of consumption. However, calculations that seemed quite sensible on paper turned out to be a mixed blessing when transported to the complex structure of rural Iran and the Shah was fully aware that a society that had not superseded feudalism (at the beginning of the 'land reforms', a mere 36 oligarchic families owned 34 per cent of all land) could not be successfully modernised.

The government executed the main planks of the rural reforms during 1961–62. An upper ceiling was introduced of 400 hectares for land ownership which meant, in practice, and thanks to new regulations, that any businessman with sufficient means or the right governmental connections was now able to purchase the arable farms on offer. The plan had been that the mechanisation of agriculture would free surplus labourers for employment in urban industries. However, these large industries were still a pipe dream and the reforms turned farmers from producers into consumers. Divided villages were gradually ruined. The state's problems were reflected in the resignation of three Prime Ministers during the 1960–62 period and the 'rural reforms' only added to the tensions. The clergy objected strongly to their content and peasants clashed with authorities in various regions.

Rapid population growth, from approximately 19 million in 1956 to more than 34 million in 1976, combined with rising incomes, also led to an increased demand for foodstuffs – a demand that outpaced the rate of increase in agricultural products in the period of 1960–75. A major factor in this was the urban bias of government agencies, which, by pricing agricultural products below their real market value, saw that they lagged far behind the rapidly increasing prices of industrial products and wages. Even before the 'land reforms' made any impact, therefore, population growth was already encouraging the mass migration of villagers to the cities.

The changing economic situation at the end of 1950s and beginning of the 1960s was characterised by a drastic decline in productivity and a rise in unemployment, which shook people's faith in competition, individualism and hard work and which forced certain shifts in the organisation of the traditional family structure. These conditions were reflected by cinema: in *The Sun Shines* (Sardar Sagar, 1956), for example, one of the box-office hits of the late 1950s, a peasant woman who has come to the capital with her husband in search of work, utters the memorable line: 'To be successful in this country, you must either be a charlatan or very lucky.'

In *The Sun Shines*, the husband, who has come to the city following the advice of a film director, is flabbergasted by the decadence and opulence of his new surroundings; so much so that he spends his first night at the foot of a statue in the centre of the capital. The film accurately depicted the perennial rural suspicion of city dwellers; its philosophy was based on petty-bourgeois dreams and fears. The message was: be satisfied with the fate you are handed; wealth is the source of all evil and in poverty lies the security of virtue. However the film touched a sensitive political nerve since it called for city men to make an alliance with 'the common folk'.

The cautious Iranian cinema always lagged behind socio-political events but the undercurrents of conflict were so intense that they were bound in some way to be reflected in its output. The juxtaposition of rustic peasant with city dweller was also captured in *Kola Makhmali* (*Velvet Hat*, Esmail Kushan, 1962) and *Khodadad* (Amin Amini, 1962). In both films, the peasant is a scapegoat for urban crimes and their chaotic aftermath. Another recurring filmic theme of the period suggested that rural men were really better off than their rich city counterparts since they were physically hardier, less spoilt and more adept at survival.

From a rural perspective, the city was becoming associated with the West. The influence of Western methods in designing agricultural programmes was cautiously broached in a few films, which were passed uncensored. The topics of land ownership and agricultural production became a kind of code for discussing the rural reforms that peaked around 1962. Two films in particular by Khosrow Parvizi, *Khak-e Talkh* (*Bitter Soil*, 1962) and *Akharin Gozargah* (*The Last Crossing*, 1962), are relevant here. In *Bitter Soil*, two men fight over disputed land but, strangely, do not resemble local peasants at all: clad in leather jackets and long boots, their posturing is straight out of Hollywood cowboy films. Likewise the villain in *The Last Crossing*, played by Akbar Hashemi, is inexplicably called George. His language is artificial and over-aggressive and he murders the real landowners in unrealistic circumstances. Land parcelling was also a source of physical conflict in *Arus-e Dehkade* (*The Village Bride*, Naser Malak-Motii, 1962), a film which implied that the source of rural tension lay neither with the state nor with feudalism, but with modernism and its cronies.

The agricultural minister at the time, Hassan Arsanjani, considered these measures such a seminal watershed that he would henceforth divide Iranian history into pre- and post-reform periods. He also suggested that the reforms were more momentous than the nationalisation of oil, a remark not altogether inaccurate. In the southern province of Fars however, which contained a number of wealthy and powerful tribal landlords, the measures met with such fierce opposition that in 1962 the government was forced to introduce an emergency military curfew. In November of that year the functionary in charge of implementing the reforms in Fars was assassinated. Radio Iran interrupted its normal programmes to announce a nationwide period of mourning and to blame the death explicitly on wealthy landlords and criminal elements. The newly appointed governor of Fars, Lieutenant General Sepahbod, threatened citizens with tanks and cannons. Arsanjani confidently predicted the demise of feudalism in the Fars province within 45 days, and a large number of opponents were promptly arrested.

In May 1963, the Shah severely criticised landowners in a major speech. Malicious, overbearing and loud-mouthed feudal landlords who stole the possessions of hard-working farmers became a popular cinematic cliché. Films in the first half of the 1960s belonged to these landowners. In *Kheshm va Fariat* (*Fury and Roar*, Reza Safai, 1963), a peasant couple choose the uncertainties of the city over their landlord's injustice. But the farmers of *Ghanoon-e Zendegi* (*Law of Life*, Jamshid Sheibani, 1964), whose patience is exhausted as a result of their landlord's cruelty, use legalistic means to win their entitlements. This film contained actual footage of the Shah handing out farm deeds to peasants.

The master in *Taraneha-ye Rustai* (*Rural Songs*, Saber Rahbar, 1964), who starts by usurping peasant holdings, is forcibly brought to his knees by the end of the film. The moral of the story is in tandem with the fluffy concept of the Shah's so-called *Engelab-e Sefid* (White Revolution), which was being peddled by propagandists at the time. The Shah announced the six main points of the White Revolution in the winter of 1963, during the Peasant Congress in Tehran: the abolition of feudal social relationships, the nationalisation of forests, the sale of state factories to private entrepreneurs in order to finance the reforms, profit-sharing for industrial workers, the reform of voting laws, and the establishment of the Science Corps (specially trained teachers who were sent to villages in order to raise educational and medical standards). Parliament adopted the resolutions enthusiastically, and the Shah milked the occasion for all it was worth.

However, only a month later, widespread demonstrations were organised, based on Ayatollah Khomeini's opposition to the reforms, which led to ugly scenes. Arsanjani simply declared that some 15,000 farmers had descended on the capital to support the reforms and oppose the demonstrators, and that having expressed their views, they had calmly returned to the country.

The rural-based films proved a resilient genre since the traditional past provided a superb setting for the free, ideal hero. His time and energy were at his own disposal. Competition could offer him self-realisation because the illusion of individual autonomy was still credible – there were no conglomerates to squeeze out the little man and the environment allowed him to feel like a big man. When things went wrong, he had the power to make them right. Wealth, too, was a danger eluded in this genre, since it might lead a man to accept the city's way of life and the erosion of his innocence. Thus the poor and less privileged in Iranian cinema's fantasy world become the truly manly rather than the 'happy few', represented as effete, on top.

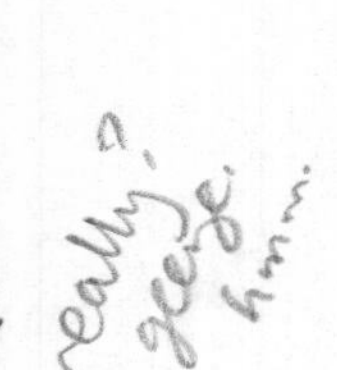

At the time of the land reforms, some films took as their task the sanctification of the Plan as a national ideal. In *Dehkadeh-ye Talai* (*The Golden Village*, Nezam Fatemi, 1963), Muhammad-Ali Fardin, who a few years down the line would emerge as a superstar of Iranian cinema, plays a Science Corps village teacher. During his 'missionary' work, he comes into conflict with the local geomancer, played by Taghi Zohuri, who stands for the greed and superstition of traditionalist elements in society. Fardin defeats the geomancer and by the end of the film turns him into a useful rural wage-worker. In reality, the land reforms resulted in increasing poverty for rural families and massive migration towards urban centres. Only five years after the implementation of the measures, three million residents had been added to the population of Tehran and half a million each to the population of Isfahan and Mashad.

Once upon a time, the family had represented a concept of agricultural kinship, bound by the common ownership of land and the labour upon it, untrammelled by geographical mobility or by the seduction of new professions and occupations. The happy man was defined as one who was not forced to live away from his small home – an ideal that had persisted for decades before the advent of asphalt roads and mass production. The image of the village, however, had ceased to be a reality in the life of the migrants of the 1960s. It lived more and more in the realm of the dream.

The extended family became impossible to sustain in the competitive atmosphere of the city. The protection of the rural family became the 1960s cinematic recipe, and revenge was wreaked upon the villain who harmed it. The frequent disappearance of the parent in the films of this period reflects the situation of the rural family whose migrant father leaves the children in the care of the mother, exposed to multiple dangers: the city divides, the village unites, was the message. The village is the fountainhead of security and identity in the psyche of the uprooted migrant, a lonely man harbouring in his heart a dream of return which he knows to be impossible. This pre-industrial dream haunted those souls imprisoned in the unfamiliar, impersonal conditions created by the divisive nature of production itself and the alienating anonymity imposed by urban conglomerations. The major part of the urban cinema audience was thus rural at heart.

In this decade two major reform attributes – populism and progressivism – shaped Iranian political thought. Both addressed the nation's anxieties over its cataclysmic transformation from an agrarian to a semi-industrial economy, from a nation of producers to a country of consumers, and from a community of individuals to a mass society. Iran had lived for years as a honeycomb of self-contained group identities at its grassroots, with shifting imperial boundaries but no concept of a national state. A secret fear of homogenisation haunted the national psyche. The rural population, the urban working class, the unemployed migrant, the petty trader and the slum-dweller remained a community set apart from those who had accepted city values.

The presiding deity of this world, the archetypal wandering farmer clinging to his traditional values in the big city, was represented by Majid Mohseni, who starred in and directed a series of big hits. His popularity was such that his election as a member of Parliament in the 1960s was a foregone conclusion – any urban villager could identify with him. During the height of Mohseni's fame, he starred in *Bolbol-e Mazraei* (*Canary Farm*, Majid Mohseni, 1957). It was typical of Mohseni's films, inviting the viewer to seek a compromise. He plays Shirzad, a farmer who pacifies his colleagues, encouraging them, through his inflated humanitarianism and boundless generosity of spirit, to make a deal with the boss. The opening scene, in which he says an Islamic prayer then suddenly bursts into song, which is prohibited by Islam, represents this compromise. In keeping with the standard pattern, Shirzad is in love with the boss's daughter, but the landlord will only agree to their marriage if Shirzad can prove his financial viability. By shifting Shirzad to the city, the film implicitly admits the impossibility of enrichment for rural peasants in their own environment. His naivety on arrival in the capital, where he is terrified by the cars and bustle, may be exaggerated, but no more so than the plot of a story that sees him gain a fortune there. His innocence is stressed by his childish desire to take a swim in a fountain, his chivalric conception of love and his utter inability to fathom the manners and attitudes of the city vultures with whom he comes into contact.

Shirzad manages to transcend his social class and with the help of a rich family becomes a wealthy man. What *Canary Farm* seems to say, then, is that the only thing implicitly wrong with Iran is the spoilt 'sissies' of the city. In some senses, Mohseni's films were overt 'message' films in an industry that generally believed interpretation should be left to the audience. These succeeded because Mohseni consistently used comedy to disarm his audience, making his moral thrust more palatable, and also because his vision appealed to a culture that hungered for an affirmation of these very values.

Canary Farm is in many ways the purest example of his approach to filmmaking. Though he holds strong convictions, the Mohseni hero is often untested; he has a childlike innocence of which more worldly and experienced people take advantage when he is placed, as he usually is, in a foreign environment. Though challenges to his social vision lead him to moments of self-doubt, his heroic side emerges. He is a man of unusual imagination, able successfully to articulate and defend his values against the greedy, cynical and spiritually corrupt.

However, placed in an alien environment, Mohseni is generally made to look foolish by the villains. These 'city types', who became increasingly powerful and threatening throughout the 1960s, are characterised by a lust for power and wealth. The ritual humiliation prepares for the final convention – the inevitable victory in which the Mohseni hero takes forceful action to overcome his self-doubt, affirm his values and emerge with his social vision intact.

Mohseni's peasant alter ego adapted itself throughout the decade to changing real-life circumstances. Yet his films repeatedly purveyed the message that Iran did not need real change; it simply required some restoration whilst returning to the values and beliefs of agrarian Iran. This kind of populism advocated honesty, morality and the unobtrusive central-government leadership of the Shah. To the frustrated rural population, the nation's fall from

FIG. 12 *Swallows Always Return Home (Parastuha be Laneh Barmigardand)*, 1963.

grace was seen as the result of a sustained conspiracy by a government obsessed with money and power. In other ways the populist spirit was undemocratic at its heart, since it tended toward a certain paranoia, especially in its treatment of groups with different social or economic interests.

Despite the growth of bureaucracy which led to an increased demand for technicians and managers, and the rapid expansion of a Western-style educational system resulting in the rise of a non-entrepreneurial modern middle class (including civil servants, military personnel, white-collar employees, technicians in private enterprise and an intelligentsia), these new social groups were not represented in the Iranian cinema of the early 1960s, which continued to be dominated by Mohseni. In *Parastuha be Laneh Barmigardand* (*Swallows Always Return Home*, 1963) he examines the usual battery of socio-political imperatives through his own sentimentalised prism. Having lost his second child due to lack of proper medical facilities, Mohseni's character sells his land and migrates to Tehran. In a reflection of the antagonism between labour and leisure in urban areas, he works as a builder and decorator whilst performing in his spare time as a *haji firuz* (people's clown). His zeal for Westernisation compels him to send his remaining son abroad for further studies (hinting at a new trend for middle-class Iranians).

In line with Mohseni's generally conformist outlook, however, the remainder of *Swallows Always Return Home* is devoted to fantasy. When his son refuses to come home, his father sends him a handful of Iranian soil. This had become a clichéd symbol of patriotism following reports that when Reza Khan had gone into exile, he had taken with him a fistful of dust to remind him of his homeland. As the film draws to a close, the son returns, amidst a joyful rustic festival. In these rural-based escapist films, Mohseni attempted to help his audience regain their self-respect, since for his characters it still seemed possible to 'stake a claim' within a rural situation, even as the individualist myth was becoming exhausted in real life.

The obligatory happy ending of *Swallows Always Return Home*, which encourages conformity and a return to one's social origins, was in tune with the state's farcical propaganda. On the celebration of New Year in 1964, hand-picked farmers dressed in immaculate ethnic skirts and feathered caps were invited to the palace, where they sat next to high-ranking government officials in tuxedos and military commanders with chests full of medals. The Shah then handed out gold coins and congratulated everyone on the sterling success of the land reforms. However, the evidence pointed to a less happy picture. Only a year after the implementation of the reforms, agricultural production was halved, forcing the government to import 60,000 tons of wheat from the Soviet Union, as well as 5,000 tons of corn and 140,000 tons of wheat from the United States. Peasants, unable to maintain their farms, were forced to migrate, resulting in sprawling squatter towns at the periphery of urban centres. By the end of the 1960s, the silver screen would be the only place where the dreams of the peasants were still fulfilled.

Law and disorder

Iran entered the 1960s with the police, military and security services busily dousing the flames of conflict, and with the expectation of even more turbulence. The political events that were unfolding were far more complex and sensational than anything that appeared on the screen. The stabbing of a police chief in Tehran by a brigand in the spring of 1959, and the similar murder of a university lecturer by a failed student the following year, were timely reminders that the destructive subterranean tensions within society were on the verge of breaking through. The first half of the 1960s also witnessed the emerging guerrilla conflict between various political groups and the security forces, at a time when the Shah's regime was trying to consolidate its power. The 1960s was a decade marred by violence and anxiety. Though politically neutered, Iranian cinema could not have avoided these occurrences even if it wanted to. In the event, it decided to use them to attract bigger audiences.

This treatment of social insurrection had a cinematic precursor in the Western crime genre, which had initiated Iranian viewers into the cabals of private eyes, good cops/bad cops and lovable rogues. In 1954, *Chahar-rah Havades* (*The Hazard Crossroad*, Samuel Khachikian), had become the first Iranian contribution to the burgeoning crime genre. The plot, about a youth on the run from the law who hooks up with an ailing girl and through her learns the error of his ways, did not escape the prevailing sentimentalism of Iranian melodrama. Nevertheless, the portrayal of the repentant gangster, played convincingly by Naser Malak-Motii, made it both a commercial and critical success. The next year saw the same actor playing an innocent convict in *Herdah Ruz be Edam* (*Seventeen Days to Execution*), directed by Hushang Kavusi, who had studied cinema in France. By eschewing melodrama, the film managed a neat synthesis of the mystery at the heart of the story and of the concept of justice.

Iranian audiences of the 1960s, faced with a wave of Western-style police and crime capers, could not help but draw comparisons with their own lives. The carrying of illegal arms, shootings in dark alleys, mountain chases and fights at the edge of the perennial precipice all seemed strangely familiar. Malicious conspirators and deceitful seductresses were the stock characters of these films and amateur imitators took full advantage of the vogue. The titles reflect the lurid content of these films: *Jad-e Marg* (*The Highway of Death*, Esmail Riahi, 1963), *Tars va Tariki* (*Terror and Darkness*, Muhammad Motevaselani, 1963), *Dam-e Sheitan* (*The Devil's Trap*, Nezam Fatemi, 1964), *Sheitan-e Sefid* (*The White Devil*, Ahmad Safai, 1965), *Mumiai* (*The Mummy*, Hamid Mojtahedi, 1966) and *Ghorbani-ye Sevom* (*The Third Victim*, Abolghasem Malakouti, 1967).

Amongst such potboilers, *Beem va Omid* (*Hope and Despair*, Gorji Ebadia, 1960) was unique, a sensitive portrayal of family loyalties without violence or over-the-top paraphernalia. In it, an 11-year-old girl (played by the future singer and superstar Googoosh) collects the wrong prescription from the pharmacist for her ailing father. As the medicine could easily kill him, the city police are mobilised to find her before she reaches home. The film was a commercial success, largely due to the young Googoosh, who could sing, dance and move the audience to tears or laughter without having to resort to sex or exaggerated performance, unlike the women actors playing older characters. But such success was rarely achieved by similar films that relied on sentimentalism rather than violence. The endless stories of suffering carried by the newspapers seemed far more titillating than the mundane problems of daily life.

Iranian crime films always concerned themselves with life in the city. One could see in this a socioeconomic logic based on the policies of the state, which was trying to create an 'urban class' as the social base for its regime. This was consistent with the Western liberal blueprint, providing the agents both for economic development and for liberal democracy. The real intention, however, was to bring about a degree of contentment among the educated and semi-educated urban community in order to forestall serious political opposition; to provide an alternative power-base for the rural landlords, who were economically too independent, and politically too powerful for the Shah, and to show Western countries that their financial and military support was obtaining results in combating Communism, by replacing 'backwardness' with imported refrigerators, motor cars and drive-in cinemas.

With this mechanism a boom in import–export business, and a related tide of consumption of modern products, was created. Iran began to display the signs of mass consumption, but only within certain sectors and social classes. Speculation in urban land became the most lucrative method of making money out of excess liquidity, at the expense of ordinary homebuyers and tenants. Bills of exchange began to circulate at a high velocity, often ending in default.

The films of Samuel Khachikian kept the crime genre bustling during the first half of the 1960s. At a time when the industry was still unable to produce colour films, *Fariad-e Nim-e Shab* (*Midnight Howl*) and *Yek Ghadam ta Marg* (*One Step to Death*), both made in 1961, overdosed on high-contrast black-and-white cinematography in an attempt to attract an audience used to direct lighting and low depth-of-focus images. Exaggerated displays of corpses, dark rooms, shadowy figures, brutal fights, screeches and howls became commonplace. Unlike other filmmakers, Khachikian did not insist on passing off his protagonists as natives. On the contrary, he delighted in caricatures, and his crime capers were made with implicit or explicit allusions to Western originals. *Ezterab* (*Anxiety*, 1962), about a victimised woman, was a combination of Henri-Georges Clouzot's *Diabolique* (1955) and George Cukor's *Gaslight* (1944), and became an immediate commercial and critical success.

His following two films, *Zarbat* (*Impact*, 1964) and *Sarsam* (*Delirium*, 1965), which relied on a highly Persian brand of comic buffoonery, were less successful. In Khachikian's films the villains are as fleshed out and significant as the heroes, sometimes even more so. With the exception of *Anxiety*, the police usually play a negligible part in driving the plot forward, often appearing only at the end of the film when the mystery is already solved. Even in *Anxiety*, the scheming husband, played by Abdollah Butimar, who is planning to murder his wife, is as important a character as the sharp investigator (played by Arman) who is trying to apprehend him. The central protagonist in *Impact*, again played by Arman, is a murderer who buries a corpse in the garden. The police investigator, played by Reza Beik-Imanverdi, who in *Delirium* had single-handedly tricked the 'baddies', only has a bit-part in this film. Sometimes the victim is the most significant character in his films. For instance, in *Anxiety*, Eiren plays the role of a woman who refuses to accept that those around her are scheming against her. One could say that in this sense she resembled her audience, which denied the connection between the socio-political realities of its existence and the images on the screen. Under the guise of entertainment, these films were an integral part of the delusional, escapist trajectory of the 1960s.

The increasingly Westernised woman was a by-product of the crime genre. Because of their distance from ordinary life, these films were able to justify showing women in Western dress and make-up. Vida Ghahremani, playing a traditionalist woman in *Farda Rushan Ast* (*Tomorrow Will be Bright*, Sardar Sagar, 1960), is forced to dye her hair, put on fashionable Western clothes, and wear make-up to keep her man (played by Fardin). In *Midnight Howl*, Parvin Ghaffari plays the blonde wife of a criminal, dressed in a revealing costume and employing alluring (Western) gestures in order to seduce a young man (again played by Fardin). By ordinary Iranian standards, her behaviour was so far-fetched that she could almost be perceived as foreign and ironically this allowed her more freedom on the screen. In many other films such as *Bonbast* (*Cul-de-sac*, Mehdi Mir-Samadzadeh, 1964), *Zan va Aroosakhayash* (*Woman and Her Dolls*, Esmail Riahi, 1965), and *Mutalai-ye Shahr-e Ma* (*The Blonde of Our Town*, Abbas Shabaviz, 1965), she re-enacted her role as a seductress. Filmmakers took full advantage of this constructed, devious Westernised female to display women ever more revealingly. The intermingling notions of female evil and sensuality – the femme fatale – fascinated the Iranian audience.

Throughout the 1960s, a mixture of explicit and implicit propaganda campaigns, and a build-up of official as well as unofficial gossip, gradually created a mythical image of the national security services, the infamous SAVAK. As we have seen, SAVAK was created out of a disparate collection of security officers seconded from the police force, the Ministry of the Interior and the army's counter-intelligence unit, with the aid of foreign specialists in the early 1950s. Rumours about the arrest and torture of dissidents by SAVAK abounded, and not all were exaggerated. The people became familiar with the methods of its leader, General Teimour Bakhtiar. It was claimed, for example, that he personally emptied a round of bullets into the body of Abdul-Hassan Vahedi, the second-in-command of the Feda'iyan-e Islam group. He was also the champion of the anti-Communist purges that saw a number of Tudeh Party members arrested. When Bakhtiar was assassinated in neighbouring Iraq by the very operatives he had once trained, the fear of SAVAK's long reach became entrenched in the collective psyche. This was perhaps the first time that people had followed the

FIG. 13 Jamsheed Mashayekhee (seated) and Naser Malak-Motii in *Gheisar*, Masud Kimiai, 1969.

minutiae of security operations with such consummate interest. It was against such a backdrop of security measures and counter-measures that the 1960s unfolded.

But despite the rhetoric of politicians, the whole 'regime of discipline' was under gradual erasure. Ayatollah Khomeini, who argued that the Shah had violated the constitution by failing to call new elections within a month of the dissolution of the Parliament in 1960, was expressing the radical view. The parliamentary elections in Tehran at the beginning of the 1960s had been systematically rigged. Oil workers went on strike in month 1960 and, over the following months, Tehranian furnace-workers, taxi-drivers, magnesium miners and cotton-spinners from Isfahan and Shiraz, and oil workers from the southern province of Khuzetsan joined them. Pro-National

Front students began publicly supporting Mossadeq, and in 1960/1961, Prime Minister Manuchehr Eghbal's car was set on fire, resulting in eight deaths. Eghbal's cabinet was forced to resign, but strikers and demonstrators besieged the next Prime Minister, Jafar Sharif-Emami, in the same way. In Tehran, teachers went on strike for better pay and were joined by sympathetic students. The Culture Minister warned the teachers of the severity of their actions but to no avail. Marching on Parliament, they were brutally assaulted by the police. One was killed, three severely injured. The demonstrations engulfed the universities and, finally, Sharif-Emami's cabinet too was forced to hand in its resignation.

The next Prime Minister, Ali Amini, lasted little longer. The years 1962–63, when the new Prime Minister Asadollah Alam was in power, witnessed the ruthless suppression of demonstrators. Following Ayatollah Khomeini's inflammatory speeches in 1963, the Shah's commandos attacked religious centres and a skirmish at the Faizieh School in 1963 resulted in the shutting down of the bazaar and universities. This period represented the pinnacle of the opposition movement. Tehran residents attacked radio stations, government buildings, buses, police outposts and dozens of other targets. The Iran–USA Cultural Society and the Pepsi-Cola factory were also targeted as manifestations of alien power. In all, some 5,000 people were injured during the hectic street battles that ensued.

Towards the end of the year a mass round-up took place throughout Iran of opposition politicians. In November 1964 Ayatollah Khomeini was arrested for 'provocation against the country's interests, security, independence and territorial integrity' and for his opposition to the Shah's new reform programmes. He was exiled to the holy Shi'a city of Najaf in Iraq. In January 1965, the current Prime Minister, Hassan-Ali Mansur, was fatally wounded when a young fundamentalist Muslim, Muhammad Bokharai, fired four shots at him outside Parliament. Two bullets hit him, one in the throat and one in the stomach. He died five days later. Bokharai was arrested on the spot and his two alleged accomplices were apprehended later in the day.

But the assassination of the Prime Minister was not the peak of the insurrection. In April of the same year, a soldier of the Imperial Guard fired at the Shah as he was stepping out of his car outside Marble Palace, killing two bodyguards. The Shah was unhurt, but the soldier was killed in an exchange of shots with the other guards. In November, 14 men were accused of complicity in the attempt and two were sentenced to death by firing squad. Every day, people would read about a new embarrassment for the security forces. Military and civil courts became busier than ever, and the files of both political and ordinary criminals grew thicker.

All these incidents sharpened the public appetite for the crime genre, yet in the early 1960s security officials and police were not just depicted as efficient, but as ever-dutiful, sacrificing all in order to enforce the law of the land. In a handful of films produced during 1963 a ubiquitous security apparatus was represented as fully in control: the observant police investigator in *Vahshat* (*Terror*, Siamak Yasami) could apprehend a criminal within 24 hours, and the very cool and couragous officers in such films as *Terror and Darkness* and *Tar-e Ankaboot* (*Spider's Web*, Mehdi Mir-Samadzadeh) were just as competent in enforcing the law. Ignoring family ties, the devoted officers in both *Panjeh* (*The Claw*, Amin Amini, 1962) and *Jahanam Zir-e Pai-ye Man* (*Hell Underneath My Feet*, Reza Safai, 1964) show no hesitation in killing their criminal brothers. The experienced investigator in *Dozd-e Shahr* (*The Town's Thief*, Hossein Madani, 1964) suppresses his feelings for a female burglar, condemning her to imprisonment. In real life, however, corruption was rife.

These films were reminders of the relationship between psychological factors and economic achievement, motivation and activity. No other psychological theme has featured so prominently in Iranian films as that of insecurity, fully developed in the crime films of the period. The chronic anxiety generated by the constant threat to politicians propelled a variety of intricate political reactions, both on the part of individual politicians and on a more general systematic level. It created an endemic mistrust, leading to interpersonal manipulation and betrayal, and the establishment of various networks of alliance and counter-alliance as coping mechanisms and self-protecting shields.

The power of the Iranian elite was not officially institutionalised within the formal structures of government. The Shah did what he wished regardless of the written laws, and his family was free of restrictions. Marvin Zonis, in his 1971 book, *The Political Elite of Iran*, analysed the social background as follows:

> The elite tended to be born in the capital in proportions greater than their fathers and than society as a whole. While the median age of the political elite bears no relation to the age distribution of the population at large, political power has begun to pass from the elders of the elite to younger men. Similarly, while the elite as a whole were born of families who claim disproportionately high social status and are extremely well educated, younger men of lower social status but with equally high education have found their way into elite ranks. The far-going foreign travel and language abilities of the elite reflect and foster the political ties of their country to Europe and the United States, frequently at the expense of Iran's immediate neighbours. Finally, the multiplicity and diversity of occupation pursued by the elite are central factors in the game of politics and in the ineffectiveness of the government's bureaucracy.

The characters of the crime films, however, were far removed from this elitist society. Their grittiness, their insecurity and cynicism, and the mistrust and exploitation that the films portrayed, gave them a populist, democratic appeal.

In the autumn of 1965, Terence Young, who had gained fame in Iran through the James Bond films *Dr No* (1962), *From Russia with Love* (1963) and *Thunderball* (1965), came to Iran to film *The Poppy is also a Flower* (aka *The Opium Connection*), creating considerable excitement. This film, partially financed by the United Nations, was about the drug trafficking business, and how part of the smugglers' route went through Iranian territory. Initially, the fact that prestigious celebrities such as Yul Brynner, Rita Hayworth and Trevor Howard were coming to Iran, and that Omar Sharif was to play the role of the Iranian delegate to the United Nations, met with universal approval. Even the Shah's brother and sister, Gholam-Reza and Ashraf, paid a much-publicised visit to the set and offered the filmmakers government assistance. But as the Hollywood publicity machinery went into full swing, a few dissenters began to voice concern about the depiction of Iran as a country of drug traffickers, with one journal commenting that, in light of Iran's real-life drug issues, 'a film that alludes to drug manufacturing must not be made.'[45]

Drug trafficking had been a long-standing social problem in Iran, affecting all the borders more or less equally. The three Iranian films related to this issue that were produced in 1962, however, showed repentant smugglers acknowledging the hegemony of the police authorities. In the first two,

The Last Crossing and *Tala-ye Sefid* (*White Gold*, Jamshid Sheibani), drugs were used as a mere backdrop for what were basically action films. Only the third film, *Sodagaran-e Marg* (*Merchants of Death*, Naser Malak-Motii), attempted a relatively realistic portrayal of smugglers and their precarious lifestyle. However, even this attempt was marred by the film's desire to dismiss the problem as alien to Iranian society. In its review of *Merchants of Death*, one journal argued not only that Iranian censorship laws discouraged directors from making films about important issues but that:

> these severe regulations are the perfect excuse for filmmakers who fail to engage with social reality. Blaming censorship deflects any criticism of their intellectual impoverishment ... Police stories are a favourite with censors, as they are both pedagogic and cautionary at the same time. After all, the criminals always get their just deserts in these films ... So, making crime movies becomes an unofficial form of bribing the censors ... Introducing drug smugglers into the plot, as *Merchants of Death* has done, seems the ideal way of guaranteeing success.[46]

The Shah, like his father before him, had staked the future of his regime on the army. Using oil money, he equipped the military with the latest and most expensive weapons available, and finally achieved his ambition of heading the mightiest army in the Middle East. With the 1961–3 armed uprising of the Fars tribes, this militaristic mentality became entrenched. In 1963, during a speech given in the city of Shiraz, the Shah warned that any further intransigence would result in the total annihilation of the rebels, and this bravado was soon backed up by real force when he dispatched his army to the Fars province. During one of the skirmishes, the head of the Boyer Ahmadi tribe, was killed: his corpse was hung in the city's main square as a salutary lesson to future rebels.

The 1965 diplomatic downturn in the Iran–Iraq relationship catalysed the militarisation of society. This period saw a marked increase in the army's attempts to impose obligatory national service on both urban and rural youths. In the mid-1960s numerous films with a military theme were produced, but the conformity and conservatism of filmmakers ensured that not a single one was worthy of serious attention. Bandits and drug smugglers thus became the army's only targets, limiting the opportunity to deal with real or imaginary foreign threats.

In this context of military activity, the James Bond genre became highly popular and encouraged a host of imitations. According to these films, the internal security forces had little trouble neutralising international conspiracies. The intelligence officer played by Behruz Vosughi in *Hashem Khan* (Muhammad Zarindast, 1966) exudes the cool sophistication of Sean Connery, successfully preventing the transfer of vital information regarding oil installations to foreign foes. Films such as *Mamur-e 114* (*Agent 114*, Esmail Pour-Said, 1966), *Almas-e 33* (*Diamond 33*, Dariush Mehrjui, 1967) and *Mamur-e 0008* (*Agent 0008*, Ebrahim Bagheri, 1967) were clumsy imitations of Western spy thrillers. Some chose the path of satire. In *Se Karagah-e Khosoosi* (*Three Private Eyes*, Muhammad Tavassolani, 1965), a trio of Iranian cinema's most famous comedians, Mansur Sepehr-Nia, Garsha Raoufee, and Muhammad Tavassolani, learn the art of crime investigation through watching films. In *Seh Nokhaleh Dar Japan* (*Three Tricksters in Japan*, Muhammad Tavassolani, 1966) they become more ambitious, going after international crooks, and finally, in *Seh Dynamite* (*Three Dynamites*, Amin Amini, 1966), they recapture gold stolen by Nazis in the Second World War.

Censorship: the usual suspects

The violent action scenes in the films of the 1960s gave rise to a renewed discussion of issues relating to censorship; the censor's blade was decimating foreign and native films alike. From 1963 onwards, a new breed of censors began supervising native and foreign films, but the prevailing chaos continued undisturbed. Under the critical heading, 'What has Censorship Wrought?' *Setare-ye Cinema* even attempted to recruit the Shah into its anti-censorship campaign. Despite such wishful thinking, the new censorship regulation, including 27 articles and two footnotes, passed in July 1965, had the end result of strengthening punitive regulatory measures against cinema. It is instructive to review this law in its entirety:

> Films containing one or more of the following features may be partially or totally banned:
>
> Insulting monotheism, people of the book, prophets or the Imams.

Offending the scared religion of Islam, and its Shi'a variety.

Casting aspersions on other religious minorities in Iran.

Insulting his Majesty the King and his glorious dynasty.

Encouraging rebellion and sedition against the government and the system of constitutional monarchy.

Offending civil or military authorities.

Offending friendly regimes, or casting aspersions on their national achievements, which may lead to diplomatic rows.

Promoting any belief system contrary to the law.

Scenes involving assassination attempts on heads of state with a view to encourage sedition.

Scenes containing revolt and uprising against military authorities, which end with the victory of rebels.

Scenes that belittle our proud and sacred history and lower our standing either in historical terms or amongst present-day nations.

Promotion of corrupt and inhuman acts such as: betrayal, murder, espionage, adultery, homosexuality, theft and bribery. This is especially so when no positive moral conclusions can be drawn from their depiction.

The victory of evil over good, inhumanity over humanity, immorality over morality, villainy over honour, in all its forms and manifestations whether explicit or implicit.

The depiction of sexual relations for the purpose of fulfilling cheap lustful desires and attracting audiences.

The naked display of parts of the body (male or female) that should remain veiled, in case public morality is compromised.

Films that encourage vulgarity.

Films that are misleading from a historical or geographical perspective, which no doubt leads to cultural deception.

Poor copies of original films that because of low audio-visual quality may cause frustration and irritation in the audience.[1]

Satirical insults directed towards local dialects or provincial ethnicities (includes both Farsi and dubbed films).

The usage of lewd and obscene language or the display of ruins, backward regions or ruffians in an attempt to lower our national prestige.

Scenes that may increase racial or ethnic tensions and whose purpose is to show one race as superior to others.

Scenes chronicling detailed murder or scenes where animals are killed sadistically and where their ill treatment may cause consternation in the audience.[2]

The use of valueless old film stock made with sulphur nitrate that could easily lead to accidental fire or the diffusion of poisonous gas during performances.

1. In the case of educational and medical documentaries, the Board of Censors is hereby permitted to exercise discretion for the exhibition of special films, at restricted cinemas, and for an exclusive audience.
2. Documentaries about slaughterhouses or laboratory experiments on vaccines or films related to hunting are entitled to special exhibition licence at the discretion of the Board of Censors.

These decrees resulted in the total deletion of nudity and violence from the screen and reduced the socio-political dimension of films to a bare minimum. Lack of state support for native filmmaking as well as the inability of Iranian films to compete with foreign output encouraged producers, who were already under great pressure, to become even more conservative in their outlook. This conservatism was masked under the guise of the new screen ideal: the loveable *luti*, or 'lumpen' rogue – a hero whose pseudo-rebelliousness became the perfect vehicle for preaching the virtues of passivity and submission.

Politics and masculine subjectivity

According to a parliamentary report, between 1955 and 1960 Iran had received $450 million of aid ($301 million from the United States alone). The 'open-door' policy catalysed the modernisation project. At the outset of his premiership in 1957, Manuchehr Eghbal had announced that government administration would henceforth be based on the American model. With increased foreign investment at the beginning of the 1960s, foreign-owned and mixed companies flourished, and a new class of mediators began to evolve. The import and distribution of foreign commodities became the most lucrative sector of the economy, displacing the internal production and distribution of goods.

The consumer trend reached dizzy heights. As the increase in oil exports and foreign loans swelled the volume of Western commodities, national production nosedived dramatically. A post-war future that had earlier been predicted as rosy gradually turned bleak. In 1961, the new Prime Minister, Ali Amini, declared the country bankrupt. The following year, the World Bank, the IMF and the USA offered loans of $550 million, $45 million and $17 million respectively.

Throughout the 1960s, relationships with the West were cemented. In 1960 the foundations for a branch of the Hilton Hotel were laid, and construction began on a new runway at Mehr-Abad airport. Tehran was rapidly metamorphosing, with the arrival of large hotels, conferences for international dealers, European and American banks concentrating mainly on currency exchange, boutiques, cabarets, discos, foreign cuisine, schools teaching dancing, ballet, piano and guitar. New magazines brought the latest fashion, decor and architecture to the attention of Iranians. Even streets were renamed in accordance with this wave of Westernisation: Kennedy Square, Eisenhower Avenue, and Elizabeth II Boulevard.

The most popular cinematic stereotype, however, seemed totally alienated from such influences. The 'lumpen rogue', who had entered Iranian cinema in the 1950s, became the seminal protagonist of the 1960s. This character should not be mistaken for a vagabond; he had more in common with the tradition of the *luti*, which has it origins in pre-Islamic Persia. After the advent of Islam, the *luti* became organised first around the brotherhood societies of *fotowat*, and later became known as *Ayyaran* (a class of warrior, traditional to Iran from the ninth to twelfth centuries and reminiscent, in its noble ancient values, of Japanese Samurai culture). Gradually they made a niche for themselves by combining chivalry and chicanery. They performed as wrestler-acrobats and professed a chauvinistic code of honour. (Some scholars believe the English term 'lout' is a derivative of the Persian *luti*.). The archetypal *luti* became the standard-bearer of tradition against the invading tentacles of modernity.

The *luti* also embodied a political struggle between ordinary lower-class people and the establishment. The political and cultural function of the *luti* genre was, like the *pahlevani* (heroic) myth, to resolve (or mask) conflicts between key Iranian values – conflicts, that is, between individualism and the social order, freedom and law, progress and past ideals. From this perspective, the genre has been read by audiences as presenting a 'foundation ritual' in which the hero's victory over the villain affirms order and social structure. The characteristics of the *luti* and the forces that structure him were consistently ambiguous. Though he stands for traditionalism, his distinguishing skills and strengths – toughness, machismo and optimism – are inextricably linked with urban modernism. And though the city – usually Tehran – stands in these films for the modern social order, it is characterised not simply by contemporary attributes such as cafés and automobiles but essentially by a lack of morality and law. These paradoxes reflected a wider societal anxiety. As domestic space increasingly became the site of male violence, it became obvious that the modern surface regularly masked a reaffirmation of older structures of power, and that the conflict between reconstructed outward behaviour and unchanged inner desires was generating anxieties and frustrations that could erupt with lethal consequences.

In *Lat-e Javanmard* (*The Honourable Scoundrel*, 1958), Majid Mohseni, as the film's director/star, cemented the *luti* as the most significant character in pre-revolutionary Iranian cinema. His role as an honourable man defending the daughter of a friend was a nostalgic dalliance with the romantic notion of chivalry. The distance between this old-fashioned ideal of masculinity and contemporary youth was explicitly alluded to in a review: 'The film's hero, unlike today's youth who are obsessed by wealth and profit, is a non-materialist who even refuses to reinvest his inheritance.'[47]

Abbas Mossadeq also established the *luti* figure in *Woman's Foe* (1958). In *Var-parideh* (Siamak Yasami, 1962), he rescues a young couple from the clutches of a profit-mongering merchant, while in *Mard-e Meidan* (*Braveheart*, Sardar Sagar, 1963) he guides a confused youngster back onto the straight and narrow. He saves a woman from infamy in *Madar-e Fadakar* (*The Devoted Mother*, Ebrahim Bagheri, 1963) and another just in the nick of time in *Jahel Mahal: Shabi dar Laleh-zar* (*The Local Luti: A Night in Laleh-zar*, Sardar Sagar, 1964). But perhaps the two films that he made with Hossein Madani embodied the quintessential *luti* reaction against modernity. In *Jahelha va Giguloha* (*Lutis and Gigolos*, Hossein Madani, 1964), Mossadeq and his henchmen give a group of Westernised youngsters fascinated by the American film *West Side Story* a good hiding. In the more pedagogical *Soghat-e Farang* (*Foreign Gift*, Hossein

FIG. 14 Three key male superstars of Iranian cinema from the 1950s to the 1970s (left to right): Naser Malak-Motii, Fardin and Behruz Vosughi.

Madani, 1967), he is forced to stand up to his Westernised brother and his foreign bride and acquaint them with traditional Iranian customs.

The scoundrels and rogues of Iranian cinema, who belonged to the lower classes, vigorously basked in their poverty, and used every opportunity to humiliate the affluent. For the *luti*, self-respect was defined in terms of fighting both tyrants and the Westernised rich, and giving aid to the needy. Their most characteristic feature was their populism. At a time when the state was promoting Westernisation, these protagonists distanced themselves from everything alien. The audience responded positively and the genre became entrenched. This hero was capable of fighting with his fists without recourse to that most foreign of instruments, the handgun. His attire was a loose, dark suit, white shirt, velvet hat, pointed leather boots, and silk handkerchief. He would never be caught wearing a Western tie, or using 'foreign-sounding' words.

Important here is the issue of the politics of masculine style and appearance, with its fundamental connections between the personal and the public. The *luti* dominating Iranian screens played a role in teaching men how they should display and position themselves in relation to their appearance. It was here that it became clear what was really at issue for men in this debate. What was involved was much more than simply a choice between dark or white, tight or baggy clothes, an undemonstrative style or street chic. Patriarchy had traditionally claimed its natural right to dominance on the basis of its permanence, unitary truth and resistance to change, its seriousness and no-nonsense rejection of the frivolous, superficial, ephemeral or trivial. For this character to play on his personal style did more than signify femininity, though that was what was pinpointed and ridiculed by those whom it disturbed. It projected a wholly new version of masculinity in Iran, a masculinity and power that had little to do with political and economic status. Thus a number of the most influential approaches to this cinematic character have viewed it as a form of mythic narrative dramatising themes of national identity.

The *luti*'s discourse of masculinity is linked with the growth of consumer economics in Iran and the close relationship with the West at this particular moment in history. This is not to deny that these films absorbed fragments of earlier historical formulations of masculinity, or that they drew on previous traditions of representation. While there were various sources for the *luti*'s attitude to male display and his assertion that masculine appearance was not a matter of pleasure but of power, these attitudes took on specific meanings in relation to the growth of consumer society. Social changes had set in motion a redefinition of gender that urged women to conceive of themselves as active consumers while at the same time situating a dominant model of masculine identity and activity distinctly apart from the consumer version of modernity.

Farrokh Ghaffari, a French-educated director, made a film similar to *The Honourable Scoundrel* in the same year, entitled *South of the City*. This production, however, was banned because it depicted the stark reality of poverty and destitution. Its script, by Jalal Moghaddam, differed from the usual clichéd offerings on a number of points. The story revolves around a woman, played by Fakhri Khorush, who is completely unaware that her friend leads a double life as a prostitute. Gradually, the truth dawns on her and, after a sobering encounter with the authorities, she gains first-hand experience of the seedy café in which her friend works.

In the hands of this critical filmmaker, the plot line became the perfect pretext for displaying the dark underbelly of society. The intense rivalry over the woman between two rogue-cum-pimps (played by Abdol-Ali Humayun and Ebrahim Bagheri) was perhaps a truer reflection of this subgroup of lumpenproletarians. The heroic glorification of the rogue in past films takes a battering here, when the central character admits to having human frailties: 'People have come to see us so-called rogues and *lutis* as unflappable … but we're no different from ordinary folks; we too have problems, we too have pain.' Ghaffari uncompromisingly sketches the residents of southern Tehran as lonely and pathetic. Unlike in *The Honourable Scoundrel*, his hero gets beaten up. The public response to this realistic streak in *South of the City* was an indication of the depths of machismo embedded in Iranian society. The promising young star of the film, Ebrahim Bagheri, was beaten up in real life by a group of disgruntled southern 'rogues', who objected to his portrayal of their 'profession'. To rub salt into the wound, the clichéd, safe performance of Majid Mohseni in *The Honourable Scoundrel* was concurrently winning both praise and prizes.[48]

The fate of *South of the City* was representative of that experienced by alternative cinema in general. Only a few days after its release, a group of high-ranking military dignitaries watched the film and promptly declared it banned. All copies were confiscated. It was reported that from now on the Minister for Home Affairs would personally supervise the censoring of native films. As a result, *South of the City* gained legendary status, being confiscated until 1963, when a mutilated version was allowed a permit under a new title, *Reghabat dar Shahr* (*Urban Rivalry*). Understandably, Ghaffari refused to acknowledge this as his work, and despite his efforts, the original version was never returned to him. The promotional campaign around *Urban Rivalry* once again hyped the film's *luti* culture: 'The most famous and controversial movie of Iranian cinema, preserving the traditional customs and beliefs of the honourable *lutis*.'

The metamorphosis of Naser Malak-Motii, one of Iranian cinema's first icons, from the Westernised gigolo of the 1950s to the fully-fledged 'lovable rogue' of the 1960s, was a reflection of the changing tastes of the audience. The Malak-Motii character of the 1950s was a smartly dressed urban man grappling with the problems of contemporary life. All this changed in 1962 when in *Velvet Hat* he donned the uniform of the *luti* and became an overnight hit, and the mould was set with his role as avenging angel in *Ba-ma'refatha* (*The Honourables*, Hossein Madani, 1963). His French detour in *Ebram dar Paris* (*Ebram in Paris*, Esmail Kushan, 1964) was an amateurish attempt to combine Persian traditionalism with a Westernised outlook. The promotional poster disingenuously described the film as an Iranian–French co-production and in what can only be understood as an unintentionally comic gesture, Malak-Motii is shown wearing swimming trunks, still in his trademark velvet hat, gazing lustfully at a woman sporting a tight swimming costume. As with other films in this genre, *Ebram in Paris* makes Iranian culture synonymous with the *luti* tradition. Having spent the better part of the film engaged in a titillating relationship with a Western girl, Malak-Motii eventually opts for his Iranian fiancée back home. This ending, however, does not deter from the gist of the film, which beckons the audience towards a promising relationship with the West, using seductive consumerism as bait.

The West came to constitute an implicit, and at times explicit, taboo in the films of this period. Filmmakers found it convenient to keep the forbidden at arm's length, using the mechanism of comedy and ridicule. In *Arus Farangi* (*The Foreign Bride*, 1964), Vahdat befriends a foreign girl, played by Puri Banai, only to remind the audience of the unbridgeable cultural differences that exist between 'them' and 'us'. Its simple morality encourages Iranian men to stick by 'their' women. These constant references to the West coincided with the Law of Capitulation (1963), which Prime Minister Hassan-Ali Mansur had presented to Parliament in order to legitimise Western presence in the country, and which led to his assassination in 1965. Cinematic rogues continued to ridicule foreigners and the trend remained dominant in Iranian films.

Sociologically, what is striking about the *luti* is that he did not have a fixed profession. He had become marginalised from the job market – a man without education or sufficient means for trade and business. His only ability seemed to be in fleecing bureaucrats and wealthy businessmen. The *lutis* of Iranian cinema were the antithesis of urban values. They became heroes in a period when city-centres were burgeoning with new immigrants and everyone appeared to have become slaves to consumerism. The country was facing recurrent budget deficits, which no number of tax increases were likely to overcome. The honourable and lovable rogues of the *luti* tradition stood for all the forgotten and alienated victims of urban growth: vagabonds, smugglers, extortionists, blackmailers, dealers, cut-throats, gamblers and pickpockets. The poverty and hopelessness of this subculture created a great deal of sympathy.

Iranian cinema was superficially acknowledging the unavoidable growth of a lumpenproletariat in an economy given to an artificial rate of development, bottlenecks and corruption. As the Shah's reforms were the result of decrees imposed from above, and not of organically determined changes from below, the society's potential wealth producers were increasingly marginalised. With the collapse of traditional agriculture and the advent of assembly-line factories, the inevitable migration towards urban centres became an exodus. Although Iran had in the past been considered a poor country, it had never been so dependent on its one successful export: oil. These economic imperatives, coupled with the state's obsessive drive towards the cultural imitation of all things Western, created a behavioural and linguistic subculture that was distanced from production and, consequently, a mentality that was antagonistic towards culture *per se*. Under pressure from unpredictable socioeconomic forces that they could neither control nor fathom, Iranian men became increasingly drawn to the safe haven of patriarchy; an extreme machismo tinged with a sentimental utopianism was the inevitable outcome.

An important locale in the films of the *luti* genre, providing a meeting place for the characters, was the traditional Iranian café, a uniquely proletarian venue totally unlike the French café, the English pub, or the American bar. Neither stylish nor exotic, the café was furnished with simple wooden chairs and tables and a stage, generally with a woman dancing on it, and could have been created for Iranian cinema. This was a masculine world of pleasure, adventure and disorder. The café posits a radically other culture – for the police, a place of social chaos; for respectable women, a forbidden zone, and beyond the understanding or acceptance of traditionalists.

The café's primary role lies in its relation to the film's hero, a man of the people, for whom it serves as a sheltering home. The confusing, maze-like spatial arrangement of the café – usually conveyed through extremely bad montages and a disorienting variety of camera zooms from the dancer to the hero to the villain and his henchmen – effectively foils the rectilinear agents of the law. Accordingly the café is inhabited by and protects a special fauna of social rejects and misfits. Some may think of themselves as traditionalists but they drink alcohol and pay money for cabaret girls. This contradiction invites them to compromise, to accept the new values of the city. In its impenetrability, the café becomes a powerfully suggestive metaphor for the inner psyche. To shelter in the world of the café is to live continually in the shadow of the dominant culture; here, one is forced to confront one's deepest fantasies and desires.

A popular hero with a heart of glass

Unwilling to challenge the prevailing political mood, which demanded obeisance to the status quo, Iranian cinema, like the culture at large, willfully turned its face away from official injustice. It created fantasy figures for its audience who could accomplish their exploits without having to deal with reality. Thus Muhammad-Ali Fardin, who specialised in playing destitute lutis, became the seminal character of Iranian cinema in the 1960s. As a successful wrestler by profession, in a country that loves its wrestlers, when he swapped a career in the ring for one on the screen his superstar status was preordained. The lutis that he played so convincingly attracted large audiences back to the cinemas and injected new blood into the film industry. On the screen, Fardin would come to articulate the unfulfilled dreams of the dispossessed. But to view his phenomenal rise as a mere sop to the poor would be to ignore wider social issues. Fardin's hold on the Iranian psyche transcends such explanations. The legend of the young wrestling champion who became a film star is still narrated by his admirers with awe. It is a legend that nourished the deep-seated yearning for self-improvement and success amongst the urban young. This myth, however, must be put into proper perspective.

As a star, Fardin was both the result and essence of the cinematic apparatus. On the one hand, he was a commodity constructed by an industry

whose primary motive was the pursuit of profit. On the other, he constituted the realisation of the dreams and unattainable fantasies of a people who lived vicariously through his screen personas. He was forever oscillating between a number of bipolar tendencies: an instrument (of profit) or a pretext (for happiness), an image or a real person, a manifestation of a social issue or an opiate.

Prior to Fardin's emergence, Iranian cinema was in dire need of a bankable product. Whatever his precursors – Majid Mohseni, Asghar Tafakkori, Muhammad Ali Ja'fari – might have been, they were not superstars, and they did not represent the same cinematic phenomenon. A certain, admittedly limited, performative formula came to be associated with Fardin's personas: supreme optimism plus fists of steel. Parviz Jalilvand expertly dubbed his dialogue, and his perfectly pitched melodies came courtesy of the popular singer Iraj. None of the stars before or after him, not even the great Malak-Motii or Behruz Vosughi, could quite match his knack of bursting into song whilst nonchalantly acquainting the villain's head with the pavement. The market dared not meddle with this piggy bank. It instinctively understood that Fardin belonged not to a few investors but to the cinema-going masses. He was the reflection of their tastes, dreams and modes of consumption.

Fardin did not achieve superstardom overnight and it was not until *Women Are Angels* (1963), with the addition of a religious dimension to his character, that his commercial appeal widened. The pushy investigative journalist in *Gorgha-ye Gorosneh* (*Hungry Wolves*, 1962), which he also directed, had no Iranian counterpart, and his melancholic and pessimistic performance in *Bitter Soil* was straight out of Western cinema. When he played a teacher working for the Science Corps in *Dehkadeh-ye Talai* (*The Golden Village*, Nezam Fatemi, 1964), no one could take him seriously. His pet project, *Hell Underneath My Foot*, which he also wrote and directed, found him heroically fighting a cruel tribal chief. Yet his favourite admixture of macho heroics, revenge and love interest failed to persuade the public to part with their cash. When his star eventually began to rise, it eclipsed that of all previous celebrities.

With *Agha-ye Gharn-e Bistom* (*Twentieth-Century Man*, Siamak Yasami, 1963) Fardin was only one step away from stardom. The film was produced at a time when the government was relentlessly breaking up strikes, attacking street demonstrators and squeezing the lower classes to the point of desperation. The aspect of social criticism certainly needs to be taken into consideration in an analysis of the Fardin phenomenon. All his characters were prisoners of their class and social circumstances, although this was masked to some extent by his happy face, which appeared to mitigate suffering. His character in this film is so appealing that when he manages to win the heart of a rich man's daughter, it seems convincing enough. He plays a hero whose charity towards the needy is boundless. The notion of bridging class differences was a major draw for Iranian audiences, a hopeful reminder that if chance smiled on them, they too could leave their disadvantages behind.

Throughout the 1960s, despite the increase in oil-generated wealth, the gap between rich and poor widened dramatically. Although political economists see the GDP as the true indicator of a nation's wealth, the unequal distribution of that wealth in Iran skewed the picture: the top 5 per cent owned more than 90 per cent of the wealth. Perhaps the most telling manifestation of this inequity was the unsanitary and crowded shantytowns that mushroomed around urban centres. This discrepancy was most apparent in Tehran, where downtown mud-huts fixed their accusatory gaze on uptown palaces, luxurious apartments and villas.

Films that hinted at such injustices, such as those starring Fardin, were bound to be popular with audiences. In this sense, he was more than a palliative, since he came to articulate real political, economic and social grievances that could not be aired directly. At the beginning of *Ensanha* (*Humans*, Mehdi Misaghi and Aramis Aghamalian, 1964), whose moral message is reminiscent of that in Charlie Chaplin's *City Lights* (1931), the narrator's voiceover, as the camera pans from luxury apartments to shantytown dwellings, is nothing short of a political manifesto:

> This is our city. Although the sun's rays have not yet reached the skyscrapers, its yawning majesty will soon witness the daily struggle of human beings. People of all walks of life. Some are burning with the inner fires of greed, cheating and conquering all before them, in the hope of amassing more wealth, more belongings. Others, who have no wealth, invest their hopes in their faith and God's benevolence. Their homes are humble. They have

no competitors who need conquering. Their one desire: to help others reach their dreams.

The subsequent juxtaposition of Fardin's kind face with that of a demonic-looking 'capitalist' was a caricatured device which portrayed the latter in the worst possible light.

The films that followed, *Ghahreman-e Ghahremanan* (*Champion of Champions*, Siamak Yasami, 1965), *Khoshgel-e Khoshgela* (*The Beautiful between Beautifuls*), directed by Fardin in 1964 and *Ganj-e Gharun* (*The Treasures of Gharun*, Siamak Yasami, 1965), were successful despite their structural weaknesses. This can be attributed to the fact that they alluded to class antagonism, pitting capitalists and the rich on one side of the social divide, against workers, peasants and lumpenproletarians on the other. Yet Fardin's character was always enchanting enough to be able to mingle with the rich. In *Champion of Champions*, the pretty rich girl, played by Azar Shiva, succumbs to his charms, implicitly acknowledging the superiority of the underprivileged. In a justly famous scene from *The Beautiful between Beautifuls*, Fardin seems to be articulating the frustrations of the audience when, on leaving a rich man's house, he delivers the following line: 'There isn't an ounce of integrity in any of you, not a shred of decency. Your be-all-and-end-all is money, wealth and prestige.' The simple formula of rich girl/poor boy was nearing perfection. Admittedly this was not a novel formula, but one that had maximum impact in the mid-1960s.

Fardin's character 'Carefree' Ali in *The Treasures of Gharun* is the child of an age in which Iranian society was rapidly shedding its old sociopolitical skin. After the brief premierships of Asadollah Alam and Hassan-Ali Mansur, a long spell of uninterrupted government began in 1964 with Amir Abbas Hoveyda at the helm and was sustained until the overthrow of the regime in 1979. Mehrdad Pahlbod served as the Minister of Culture over the same period. Oil was bartered for simple Western goods and the establishment of the national television service (with the Queen's uncle, Reza Ghotbi, in charge of its administration) coincided with increasingly chauvinistic propaganda in praise of the Shah, who after his coronation in 1967 had acquired the title *Aryamehr* (Light of the Aryans). With the establishment of national media, local cultures were marginalised and a homogenous culture came to dominate the urban masses. Cinema was enjoying a boom, and long queues in front of the ticket stall became a common sight. Carefree Ali was the perfect antithesis of the arrogance and egocentricity of the new age.

Audiences were now ready to embrace wholeheartedly the striking ex-wrestler who was also the champion of traditional values against the tempestuous rages of modernity. With *The Treasures of Gharun*, Fardin became one of the most saleable commodities of the mid-1960s. A film that clearly touched on the hopes and fears of the people, it speaks vividly of class anxieties and of the fantasy of a permeable class barrier. The wish to escape one's class is linked to an obsession with 'lifestyle' and more generally with social surfaces such as clothes and furnishings. These are particularly clearly portrayed through the *mise-en-scène* of this film. However, an explicit rejection of Western values is also articulated.

In the film, Gharun, a depressed and villainous tycoon, tries to drown himself but is saved by two impoverished young men, Ali Beegham (Carefree Ali) and his friend. Through them, he learns the pleasures of the simple life and finds new meaning in his own existence. In turn, he introduces Ali and his friend to wealth and luxury. The film marks a male-oriented, traditionalist assault on Westernised values, signalled through its symbolism. Ali and his friend, for instance, live in the most traditional neighbourhood of Isfahan, eking out a living guiding tourists through the ruins; the old city is their territory. Ali's initial battle against the Western-attired Gharun and his cronies takes place in the surroundings of the Hilton Hotel and he throws the enemy into the swimming pool – the Western rival to the Persian fountain. When Gharun attempts suicide, he chooses an ancient bridge from which to jump. This clash of cultures even extends to dinner etiquette, with Ali sitting on the floor eating a traditional broth whilst Gharun, waited on by servants, sits at a table and uses modern cutlery. The farcical song-and-dance routine of a bourgeois woman, played very poorly by Forouzan, and her increasingly desperate attempts to seduce our loveable rogue, are met with the traditional patriarchal reprimand: 'Be Iranian!' Most telling is the way in which Ali bridges the class divide. At the end of the film it is revealed that he is in fact the son of the wealthy Gharun. In effect, he has unwittingly saved his bourgeois father at the beginning of the story, only to pave the way for his own return to the bosom of patriarchal capitalism at the end. *The Treasures of Gharun* peddles the myth that class antagonisms are not as great as they may seem and that it is possible for social classes to overcome their differences and live harmoniously. This contradictory social status – having affinities with the lower class but belonging to the upper class – remained an essential feature of Fardin's persona.

The female protagonists in Fardin's later films also suggested ambivalence. In his first films Fardin was a cute, subdued youngster pitted against strong women. Later, however, they are worldly, modern women who nevertheless learn to accept the traditional path. Ali's mother in *The Treasures of Gharun* became the perfect embodiment of this contradiction: on the one hand she is the conventional, traditional mother who criticises her perfidious husband for leaving her; on the other she agrees to share his Westernised life.

At times Fardin represents an impish nonconformity; at others, he is merely a comic figure, and occasionally he takes a wild swing at authority. Violence is not central to the Fardin hero, although he is capable of it on occasion. Instead, the emphasis is on his moral and emotional message. His solitary individualism allows him to choose integrity freely, which for Fardin was the true mark of a man. According to his ethic, a man is a man only when he is true to himself. His deflating of capitalists, intellectuals and Westernised members of the elite met with huge approval from the masses. His film titles are evidence of this cult of heroism; titles such as *Champion of Champions* (1965), *Man of Tehran* (1966) and *Sultan of Hearts* (1968). The last became the phrase with which his mourners would eulogise him at his funeral in 2000.

Fardin's films shared elements in common with sentimental Indian cinema in that they were founded on a certain sermonising attitude towards the audience. The rhetorical cinematic repetition of themes of honour, kindness, sacrifice, integrity and charity ensured what amounted to a moral victory for the poor over their bourgeois exploiters. In truth Iranian cinema did not have a genuine reply to the Shah's reforms and his Westernising zeal. It therefore contented itself with sketching the broad outlines of social conflict whilst encouraging audiences to seek spiritual purification through charitable work. Fardin's films may have been simplistic, unsubtle and cliché-ridden (they were also full of inconsistencies, since they observed none of the conventions of logic) but to complain would have been to miss the point. For during those dark hours in the theatre, the shadowy screen created a magic world where, in the end, everything turned out right; where everyone was eloquent and beautiful; where prayers however feeble, were answered; where remarkable coincidences occurred on cue and where a harmonious natural order was finally re-established.

Fardin's repeated attempts to break free of his stereotyped Carefree Ali image met with negative audience response. His swashbuckling escapades in *Amirarsalan-e Namdar* were as ludicrous as his James Bond imitations in *Man of Tehran* (1966) and *Tempest over Patra* (1968), both directed by the Lebanese filmmaker Farugh Ajrameh. He fared no better when, abandoning the chauvinistic *luti* code of honour, he strapped a gunbelt round his waist, pinned on a sheriff's badge, and began shooting at cardboard cowboys in the pseudo western, *Mardan-e Bekosh (Kill Like a Man*, 1968), an Iranian–Italian film.

It is conceivable that Fardin's comedies, in the shape of *Baba Shamal* (Ali Hatami, 1971) and *Raz-e Derakht-e Senjed (The Secret of Senjed Tree*, Jalal Moghaddam, 1971), could have opened a new chapter in his acting career. Sadly, however, negative viewer response quickly put paid to this experimental phase. His appearance in Masud Kimiai's *Ghazal* (1976), which he hoped would introduce him to a new, more discerning audience, ended in disappointment. He was forced to accept that the expectations of his fans were more powerful than he had imagined.

In the end, films like *The Treasures of Gharun* and *Celestial Orb* remained stunted at the moral level of dissent, where their rebelliousness was seen simply as a personal rejection of consumerism and corruption. Obviously, censorship played a pivotal role in depoliticising characters such as Fardin's, but some built-in qualities of the *luti* genre also played their part. As the *luti* characters had no desire for gaining knowledge or improving themselves, they lacked both the conscience and consciousness to provide an all-embracing critique of the system. Though they cared about society at large, their concern was limited to their immediate surroundings. They ended up preaching conformity and submission by reducing the political to a mere personal problem and then even further to a simple moral dilemma.

By refusing to challenge injustice politically, these films invited their audiences simply to seek comfort in screen heroes who took their chances against evil. Longing for the self-confidence of Fardin, viewers contented themselves with its expression in film. Fearing that they could never be heroic themselves, they applauded heroes like Fardin, whom they knew they could never emulate, thus conspiring in their own impotence. The nostalgia that colours Fardin's films reflects a sorrow that ordinary lives do not permit one to stand as tall as this hero. The tragedy may well be the belief that it is only in films – and films of the past – that such men can exist.

A mirror on society

In the mid-1960s, with the luti genre at its height, the first sparks of a convincingly native Iranian cinema had been lit. Though the *luti* genre touched reality at some level, it was not a genuine reflection of the Iranian people. The first film to represent Iran through a full array of 'social types' was Farrokh Ghaffari's *Shab-e Ghuzi* (*The Night of the Hunchback*, 1964). Significantly, the plot revolves around the death of a *luti*-type character. The original script was based on a legend from *The Thousand and One Nights* and set at the time of the caliphates (the reign of the Abbasid Caliph Harun al-Rashid in Baghdad during the eightth century), but when it met with censorship restrictions, it was rewritten for contemporary times. The hunchback of the title is a member of a theatre troupe who accidentally chokes on his food and dies. The black comedy develops with the increasingly desperate attempts of his fellow actors to hide his corpse.

The Night of the Hunchback is an intellectual analysis of the social make-up of Iranian society. The hunchback represents the *luti* outsider, whilst his fellow actors represent the lower classes. The upper class was integrated into the plot through the inclusion of a rich woman, sensitively played by Pari Saberi, who having stumbled upon a group of smugglers entrusts the hunchback with a message containing their names and addresses. The smugglers represent the new bourgeois Iranians.

When the hunchback's friends discover the letter, they dump his corpse on the smugglers' doorstep. Coming face-to-face with the corpse, the two main smugglers, beautifully played as an 'odd couple' by Ghaffari himself and Muhammad-Ali Keshavarz, begin to crack up. After a series of tactical errors, they are arrested whilst attempting to leave the country. The depiction of the secretive lives of smugglers was unprecedented in Iranian cinema.

Traditionalism is also critiqued when the daughter of a traditional man commits suicide in order to avoid an arranged marriage. What connects all these disparate elements is fear: fear of being questioned, fear of a transformation in social relationships, fear of being unmasked. The policeman's summing up at the end of the film – 'The hunchback's death revealed many things' – was an indirect dig at the conservative, hidden nature of Iranian cinema up until that point, in which very little of value was ever revealed.

In the same year that *The Treasures of Gharun* found unprecedented commercial success, Ebrahim Golestan, who had previously made a handful of documentaries, achieved his first feature entitled *Khesht va Ayne* (*The Brick and the Mirror*, 1964). This film, too, represents a range of characters from different classes in an authentic picture of 1960s Iran. The two main characters are drawn with as much passion as they would be in a romantic melodrama. A taxi-driver, played by Zekaria Hashemi, finds a child in the back of his cab. In an echo of the treatment of the hunchback's corpse, the child is passed between a whole gamut of types. The taxi-driver's heated argument with his friends becomes an occasion for an absurd lampooning of intellectuals, and his girlfriend, wonderfully played by Taji Ahmadi, intelligently reveals the inherent weaknesses of this supposedly strong man. The taxi driver's fear of women, the chaos caused by a range of neighbours and a busybody landlord, and the continuing problem of returning the child to its parents, all bemoan an unstable society in which no one feels at ease. His visit to the police station, the courts and the nursery become subversive attacks on a weak and crisis-ridden government. The constant allusions to silly, superficial radio and television programmes emphasise the imbecility that passes for entertainment in the mass media. Hope for a better future is personified in the shape of a child who sells lottery tickets to a people desperate for a miracle.

Most Iranian films displayed people's personal lives as if they were taking place outside of history – as if history were just a dry document of political events. *The Brick and the Mirror* breaks down this comfortable separation in its presentation of Iran's everyday reality in the second half of the 1960s. It does

FIG. 15 *The Night of the Hunchback* (*Shab-e Ghuzi*), Farrokh Ghaffari, 1964.

not, as in so many Iranian films, reduce reality to a conflict between the lower and upper classes. Golestan provides rough sketches of contemporary life via the different characters and the various settings, such as the police station, the orphanage, the courts, and through the references to radio and television programmes. *The Brick and the Mirror* thus successfully combines melodrama with a developed sense of ironic social critique, emphasising the hollowness and artificiality of Iranian life in the 1960s. The end of the film, which shows the taxi driver who has been left by his girlfriend aimlessly wandering the streets, is a far cry from the happy resolution characteristic of Iranian cinema at the time. His directionless meandering is a symbolic illustration of a nation's plight on the verge of the heady 1970s. It was rare for politics to be shown as the substance of real life; *The Brick and the Mirror* achieved it. Golestan's radical politics were combined with formal inventiveness in a way that is still unique and inspiring to watch.

Another significant film that attempted to convey the 'true' national psyche was *Shohar-e Ahu Khanum* (*Ahu's Husband*, Davud Molapur, 1968), based on an award-winning novel by Muhammad-Ali Afghani. The film's structural deficiencies do not deter from its useful articulation of certain problems central to middle-class existence. The subject of marriage and divorce is narrated simply and effectively, and although the pedantic rhythm of the film can be irksome, it does manage to capture accurately the trials and tribulations of a typical family. The plot tells the story of a widow, forced through solitude to accept marriage to an older man who already has a wife and children. It constitutes an insightful peek at a traditional world in which men rule and women cook. At the end, when the woman realises that her presence is causing familial conflict, she decides to leave her new husband and his family.

This was the first film to locate a woman as the focus of the narrative whilst providing a serious analysis of her predicament in the context of prevailing social taboos. It showed a society that would not permit a widow to live alone, forcing on her a drastic 'solution' that in the end merely serves to exacerbate the problem. Common beliefs and religious convictions were juxtaposed in order to provide a more three-dimensional representation of Iranian women and the problems they faced. Without eroticising the woman, which was the only way in which previous films could engage with female characters, *Ahu's Husband* succeeded in broaching gender issues. Perhaps not surprisingly, the film collected dust for eight months while the authorities decided whether to grant it an exhibition permit. When it was finally shown, in only two cinemas, it met with an icy response. Nevertheless, the very fact that such a nonconformist film had been made was an indication of new times and new agendas.

A crucial turning point for Iranian cinema, however, had come two years before, with the release in 1966 of *Khaneh-ye Khoda* (*Home of God*, Jalal Moghaddam), the first feature documentary on the Muslim pilgrimage to Mecca. It persuaded the Iranian Muslim fundamentalists who were still against film to go to the theatres, or at least to accept the notion of cinema. Qom, Iran's most zealously religious city, did not even have a cinema until this point, but it opened one in order to screen *Home of God*. This was perhaps an unwise move, since it led a group of hardliners to attack the producer of the film, Abolghasem Rezai. He left Iran, never to return. Years later the same theatre was set on fire and forced to close.

6 The 1970s

From extreme optimism to beastly metamorphosis

During 1969, five cinemas were torched by revolutionaries in less than three months, with a fire at Shahsavar, a small city in the north of Iran, leaving 22 dead. Nevertheless, it remained an important year for Iranian filmmaking, with two seminal offerings, *Gav* (*The Cow*, Dariush Mehrjui) and *Gheisar* (Masud Kimiai), introducing a new mode of writing that was to leave an indelible mark on cinema in the 1970s. Both were politically oriented and both presented an alternative view of Iranian society, its people and their sensibilities. The bleak and bitter outlook of these films was in sharp contrast to the Shah's optimism: an organising committee had been set up to co-ordinate celebrations of the upcoming anniversary of 2500 years of Persian monarchy; oil prices were steadily rising and in his New Year's address he had urged his countrymen to take up the challenge of economic reconstruction. Yet the fabric of society was falling apart.

These oppositional films tried to undermine or subvert the mainstream values that the audience had absorbed from sources such as work, family and government and which had been reinforced by commercial films. They presented a strikingly different, dystopian picture of Iranian life. *The Cow* and *Gheisar* derided the alleged oil boom, the absolute power of the state, and its ritualistic bouts of self-congratulation, by portraying lower-class poverty and by rebelling against the status quo. Interpretations of the two films vacillated between a political reading around Iranian themes, and a more universal take, but whatever the mode of analysis, their influence shook Iranian cinema to its very roots and helped generate a new, more discerning, audience.

A thousand and one nights of trouble

The Cow, based on a famous novel entitled *Azadaran-e Bayal* (*Bayal's Mourners*, 1964), by Gholam-Hossein Saidi, a well-known political writer, was the first film to present an unflattering sketch of the countryside. It was such a bleak film that the Ministry of Culture and Arts, which was ironically also its producer, demanded major changes before it would issue an exhibition permit (the book had also suffered from censorship). The performers came from a theatrical background and had no connection with the Iranian commercial cinema of the day. In fact, they had enacted the work as a TV play before bringing it to the big screen.

Neither did Saidi, a leftish author, have roots in popular culture. He took a cynical and sociopolitical approach far removed from the protective romanticism of Iranian cinema. When certain filmmakers of the 1970s began to turn to the darker levels of the social strata, the political literary school was a ready-made source. The director of *The Cow*, Dariush Mehrjui, found the romantic treatment of colossal poverty in Iran, and any suggestion of its inevitability, utterly unacceptable. Poverty in *The Cow* was not depicted as dignified or innocent. It was shown as ugly, bitter and desperate. This was the first Iranian film to deal with the small-scale, the unredeemed and the unheroic.

The film's simplicity concealed a multilayered philosophical treatise. A peasant cherishes his cow to the point of obsession, since it is the village's sole source of wealth. He is constantly worried that the inhabitants of a rival village might steal or harm his precious animal. When he makes a short visit to the city, the cow dies of natural causes. The villagers bury the beast but cannot bring themselves to break the tragic news to its owner. On his return, he is initially told that his cow has run away. Unable to tolerate the gravity of this betrayal, the man has a nervous breakdown, gradually transforming in both body and spirit into his beloved cow. Exasperated by their inability to help him, the villagers decide to take the psychologically disturbed peasant to the city for therapy. Meeting fierce resistance from the peasant, the villagers tie him up and slowly come to treat him like a beast. Under severe physical and mental torment, the man perishes before reaching the city.

FIG. 16 *The Cow* (*Gav*), Dariush Mehrjui, 1969.

In *The Cow*, we find evidence that the upwardly mobile forces of the period have halted; optimism has turned to paranoia. *The Cow* emphasises loss, insecurity and lack of true friendship. It is a post-apocalyptic vision of life in which hope is as scarce a commodity as joy. At no time do we see peasants engaged in agricultural work, the bleakness of the environment militating against the very notion of growth. Apart from stark poverty, *The Cow* is saturated throughout by a suffocating sense of fear: the villagers' fear of cross-border raids by rival tribes, an invisible potential menace forever lurking beyond the boundaries. The conservative village in the story is a microcosm of Iranian society. Fragmentation holds sway amongst a people whose only collective act is the burial of the cow – the ritualistic interment of their one hope of breaking the cycle of poverty. The analogy with an economy that was over-dependent on only one saleable commodity could not be clearer. The fear of a future without oil permeated all discussion, just as the fear of losing the cow taxed the villagers' faith.

An interview with the Shah in 1973, regarding the proposed Arab embargo on the sale of oil to the West, revealed this over-dependence. The Shah constantly harked back to his one source of wealth – oil – while his fear of the neighbouring Arab threat was reminiscent of the villagers' fear of adjacent tribes. The Shah's constant allusions to oil (and the perennial use of the first person in his speech) paralleled the monomania and egocentricity of *The Cow*'s central protagonist.

The early banning of *The Cow* was sadly predictable. A government that intended to bask in the glory of its economic policies was not going to tolerate such a dystopian vision. The Censorship Office insisted on a note explaining the time-frame as being around four decades prior to Reza Khan's modernising project and his son's agricultural reforms. In reality, the cruel environment of the peasantry was an all-too-contemporary problem, in the face of which the central government seemed impotent. In April 1967, for instance, the Arras river had burst its banks, causing severe flooding in the surrounding villages. During the following months an earthquake in Azerbaijan and more flooding in Mehabad destroyed many hamlets. These had been followed by another earthquake and further floods in September and November of that year.

The Cow, whose ominous tone was enhanced by Feridun Ghovanlu's black-and-white cinematography and skilful lighting and camerawork, was entered for film competitions abroad, winning the prestigious critics' award at the Venice Film Festival. The film's central character, played by Ezatollah Entezami, also won the Best Actor prize at the Chicago Film Festival. This unprecedented international acclaim had two consequences. It led to the ban being lifted, giving Iranians the opportunity to view the film for the first time, and it helped to dispelled the inferiority complex plaguing Iranian cinema.

Mehrjui's next venture, *Agha-ye Halu* (*Mr Simpleton*, 1969), was a satire in which a naive, provincial civil servant, is swallowed up by the decadence of the city to which he has come in search of a wife. His escapades, from his first mishap when his suitcase is stolen on arrival to his inadvertent involvement in illegal land dealings, his sobering fisticuffs with local hoodlums and, finally, his intention to marry a woman who turns out to be a prostitute, chip away incrementally at his illusions, as well as his faith.  The golden pavements of the city are exposed as fakes, its ornaments and razzmatazz, skyscrapers and boutiques portrayed as the spectacular façade of a violent and dishonest monstrosity, and its alienated inhabitants are revealed as occupants of a spiritually barren landscape in which life has lost any purpose. Mehrjui's sociological analysis dissects society to find within it layers of disenchanted 'types', each pursuing their own self-interest: the ruffian landlord, the perfidious café owner, the shady dealer, the 'loose' woman and the simple-minded provincial bookworm, lost in his own world of fantasy.

The protagonist, who does not even have a name but gradually acquires the nickname Mr Simpleton, begins to question the value of tradition, so that even after discovering the hidden past of his intended, he still wants to marry her; somehow it no longer matters. On his return from the city at the end of the film, the experience is summed up in his understated quip: 'Travelling is good, it makes one worldly-wise.' Thus, despite Mehrjui's political bent, a social phenomenon is in this film reduced to a personal experience; the only solution offered is to escape the quagmire of urbanism.

Mehrjui's next film, *Postchi* (*The Postman*, 1972), based on Georg Büchner's play *Woyzeck* (1836), was an abstract, metaphorical work which was considered even more politicised than *The Cow*. A postman lives with his young and beautiful wife in rented accommodation belonging to the local landlord. He suffers from sexual impotency and is saddled with a vet for a doctor, who does not hold out much hope for his patient. When the landlord's relative returns from abroad to set up a pig farm, a liaison with the postman's sexually frustrated wife ensues.

Though the characters have little chemistry between them, and the actors turn in mostly lifeless performances, *The Postman* has been hailed as a clinical analysis of Third World societies, with their complex networks of bourgeois, bureaucratic and feudal relationships. The postman was seen by critics as a representative of the proletariat, while the pig stood for exploitation; the pig-farmer was the agent of capital, the woman the embodiment of sexual objectification. The return of the educated relative from abroad, and his decision to replace sheep farming with pig farming (pig meat is strictly banned under Islamic law), was a heavy-handed allusion to Western investment in Iran. The relative's Western wife is juxtaposed with the postman's Westernised wife, who, as his only remaining 'possession', is 'invaded'. His sexual impotence, therefore, comes to stand for society's inability to prevent assimilation and his dream of acquiring wealth and fortune through a lottery ticket encapsulates the overwhelming fantasy of the proletariat throughout the 1970s. Finally, when he discovers the affair, his reaction is to murder his wife and meekly await arrest by the authorities. Despite being screened at Cannes, *The Postman* was cold-shouldered by viewers when it finally made it to native screens. Due to its social commentary, however, it has since managed to gain for itself a place amongst Iranian classics.

Mehrjui's *Dayereh-ye Mina* (*The Cycle*, 1975–8), was based on a story co-written by himself and Saidi. The central character is a boy living in a poverty-stricken shantytown outside the capital. He has brought his sick father to the city for treatment, but not being able to afford the fees they squat on the pavement opposite the hospital. The boy gets to know a local pedlar who ekes out a living by selling the blood of poor people and addicts to the hospital. Gradually, the boy forgets his father's predicament and becomes a 'blood pedlar' himself.

The Cycle critiques a society in which everyone sooner or later becomes a dealer, selling themselves and others in an ever-increasing cycle of reified relationships. The use of colour cinematography accentuates the visual impact of the trade in blood. (Until 1980, about 98 per cent of Iranian films were made in black and white.) Mehrjui's documentary style sketches an unflattering portrait of societal relationships that are usually kept well out of sight. The haunting transformation of an innocent boy into a nauseating bloodsucker forces viewers to re-evaluate their own role in society. Even the junior doctor, who begins as society's conscience, is eventually trapped by material concerns. The journal *Ercan* commented: 'This movie was produced in a society where the term "freedom" is an imported concept … The originality of the filmmaker lies in choosing a young charismatic anti-hero … having gained our affection, the anti-hero is then transformed into the most horrendous monstrosity.'[49]

One of the toughest pictures of the decade, *The Cycle* was an uncompromising and sometimes frightening film that laid bare the inhuman conditions of the medical system in Iran. This powerful critique of a social institution led to a three-year ban.

The birth of the Iranian anti-hero

During the 1970s, Iran discovered film noir. In the post-White Revolution, post-Land Reform era, Iranian film noir spoke to a sense of cynicism and alienation that was circulating within society. It translated Western film noir not in terms of setting and theme but rather, more subtly, in terms of tone and mood. It was a politicised genre opposed to the optimistic commercial films of the period, and aimed to portray the dark side of urban life, with an emphasis on the theme of revenge.

For two decades, Iranian cinema had been struggling to compete with foreign films through crowd-pleasing escapist fantasies. Now, both audiences and filmmakers were ready for a less optimistic view of the world. The disillusionment felt by many ordinary people regarding the new economy, with the acute rise in oil prices sparking revolt among the lower classes, was directly mirrored in the sordidness of the urban crime film, which became increasingly dark as the political mood hardened.

The appearance of Iranian noir in 1969 coincided with an emphasis on monarchic ideologies following the Shah's formal coronation in 1967. At this time the ideology of national unity, which was under debate in the 1960s and which tended to gloss over and conceal class divisions, began to falter and decay, to lose credibility. The encounter with a boom economy, with its threat of inflation, began a process of general disillusionment which found its way into Iranian film noir through a series of complex transmutations. The feelings of loss and alienation expressed by the characters in these films could be seen as the product both of post-1960s depression and of the reorganisation of the economy.

With Masud Kimiai's *Gheisar* (1969), a huge box office and critical success, Iranian film was taken seriously as a subject of intellectual debate for the first time. It presents a decidedly dark vision of Iran. The country is portrayed as an inferno, inhabited by a disaffected populace that is plagued by crime. When a man returns home from a business trip to find his sister has been raped, he viciously turns on society itself. By ditching his previous lovable creations in favour of a vengeful male rebel, Kimiai injected a rancour into Iranian cinema that soon became an integral part of its modus operandi. The fascination with outsiders and with the genre of crime melodrama reflected the public's anger and inclination to step outside the norms of established society. The most striking feature of this new antihero was that he was a love–hate figure for audiences, who had lost their taste for fantasy and were preparing to embrace violence.

Kimiai was not a trained filmmaker, but his direct knowledge of the lower classes added an authenticity to his work. *Gheisar*'s precise use of camera angles and real locations, its punctuation of close-ups and occasional long shots, were all galvanised into a gruesome, gritty reality. A raw, factual look is shrewdly juxtaposed with an ironic lyricism, hinting at the hero's dangerous state of mind. Kimiai wrests a sour poetry out of traditional locations such as public baths and cemeteries. The best scenes depict Gheisar's lone preparatory arrangements, his total organisation of himself as a physical instrument of social justice.

Hatred, murder and revenge were recurring preoccupations in Kimiai's films. Revenge was usually dealt with as a fight against the law, which he saw as central to his work. Gheisar (played by Behruz Vosughi) expresses his rage through a spontaneous act of folly. Although he too is murdered at the end, death in a society that has no use for his values is a virtue and this explicit act of retribution, which represents an anarchic sense of justice, appealed to the sensibilities of 1970s audiences. Gheisar became the archetypal anti-hero of Iranian cinema and a manifestation of nonconformity. Even Vosughi's hairstyle in this film became popular amongst Iranian youths.

Gheisar's title sequence depicts a wrestler whose body is ornamented with calligraphy from *Shah-Nameh* (the *Book of Kings*), an epic poem by the nationalist poet Ferdowsi (935–1020). The soundtrack, a ringside bell and accompanying drums, leaves no doubt that we have entered the realm of Persian chivalry. As a symbol of anti-modernity, Gheisar has a great deal in common with past cinematic heroes. He too lives in southern Tehran amidst historical ruins, shunning the modern handgun for the more traditional weapon of

vengeance – the dagger. However, he does not sing or dance and hardly ever smiles. His only true possession is his self-respect. Even his pretty fiancée cannot soothe his rage. This hero is a vulnerable human being who can be incapacitated by failure, whose fist may be hard but whose heart is soft. The image is both somewhat lubricious and refreshingly unsentimental.

Vosughi's performance is largely an evocation of anger against an unjust world in which a moral existence is becoming an anachronism. It was this ubiquitous anger, visible in most of his films after *Gheisar* that branded Vosughi as the anti-hero. If he had chosen to abdicate his earlier suave roles for this rebellious image, it was because the nation needed an angry young hero as a repository for the predominant emotions in the 1970s.

Aside from increasing anger about class inequality and corruption, the rise of the rebel was also partly connected to the sense that the individual was in danger of disappearing into the urban industrial crowd. Iranian cinema was battling against this vanishing individual, and the social stress on conformity only served to bring to light the pressing need for autonomous action. The rebel's popularity was also connected to an opposite notion, however: that individualism – the rugged individualism of capitalism, free enterprise, and unregulated competition – was dangerous to society.

The rebel was a positive role model; anti-heroes were applauded because their daring and brashness demonstrated that survival was a matter of individual effort, even if it was outside the bounds of official morality, and even if they laid the groundwork for their own tragic demise. At the same time, however, since members of the audience could not possibly emulate the rash brutality of the anti-hero, they felt smaller, weaker and less able to alter their own condition. Thus the fantasy of power yet again ensured the acceptance of impotence. Vosughi's screen image was born and reached fruition in an age defined by rebelliousness: the guerrilla movement, the onslaught of terrorism, the assassination of the head of the army. Yet behind the fire and brimstone of his screen anger and rebelliousness, Vosughi actually preserved the status quo.

In March 1971 armed police prevented a group of discontented workers from marching on the capital by shooting into the crowds, killing three people and injuring thirty more in the process. A few days later the military courts handed out death sentences to twelve left-wing guerrillas involved in the 'Siahkal incident' – an attack on a military post in the village of Siahkal on the edge of the Caspian Sea. After a rare television interview with the Deputy General of SAVAK, who announced that guerrillas were plotting against the government, assassins shot and killed Major General Farsiu, head of the army's prosecution services. The government advertised a huge bounty for information leading to the capture of those responsible. Two months later, in an armed conflict, five policemen and three alleged terrorists were killed. A fortnight after this incident, massive numbers of Iranian students in the United States demonstrated against the Shah's visit. During these turbulent times, death and pessimism were slowly permeating Iranian cinema, although newspapers and television were unanimous in presenting an invincible façade. In October the festivities surrounding the 2500th anniversary of the monarchy took place. The festival attracted one of the largest gatherings of heads of state ever assembled in Iran, although it received negative coverage in the Western press. Yet political turmoil continued unabated. In November, Iran took occupation of the Greater and Lesser Tunb islands in the Persian Gulf. Police resisted the invasion, reportedly killing a number of soldiers. In December, Sheikh Saqr, ruler of one of the islands, appealed to the Arab states to force Iran off the islands. Despite reassuring government proclamations, a fresh cycle of violence was set in motion. In October 1973, the government announced the foiling of a plot to kidnap and assassinate the Shah and his family.

Films like those of Kimiai redefined ideas about violence through a radical departure in tone, content, theme and characterisation. Previously, violence had been a convention rather than an ugly reality. Heroes killed for understandable reasons, usually only when severely provoked. Death was often represented as a cleansing force. The new heroes changed all this; violence was depicted as a social condition, feeding on itself in a world almost mad with sadism. For the first time audiences witnessed the actual physical effects of fists and knives. This may have been shocking and distasteful but it was necessary in order to show that violence was not wholesome, but filthy, repulsive and ultimately self-defeating. Yet the escalating body count brought about an exultant feeling of revenge as well as an awareness that violence had become an Iranian way of life, one which was to culminate in the events of the Revolution a few years later.

Thus the vengeance film indicated a change in the relationship between the hero and society, a relationship that steadily deteriorated throughout the course of the narrative. These films revealed the psychic price that the culture paid for repression of the right to disagree with social policy, or even to propose reforms in an inhospitable world: an outpouring of frustration, depression and rage.

The vengeance melodrama was a narrative instrument for managing and resolving social tensions and conflicts. The protagonist's acts were more clearly defined in these films than his politics, absolving the audience of political responsibility in a symbolic and cathartic act of sociopolitical evasion that ignored causes and effects. As long as he operated within certain narrative parameters, and as long as the social order was acknowledged, the avenger could retain the status of hero.

After the commercial success of *Gheisar*, a deluge of embittered anti-heroes swamped Iranian cinema. Vosughi, who had previously specialised in playing gigolos, switched to this new role as the dignified rebel struggling against his inevitable fate, and went on to star in such films as *Tughi* (*The Dove*, Ali Hatami, 1970) and Jalal Moghaddam's *Farar az Taleh* (*The Getaway*, 1971).

The fruitful collaboration between Kimiai and Vosughi yielded five more classic works, *Biker Reza* (1970), *Dash Akol* (1971), *Khak* (*Earth*, 1974), *Baluch* (1972) and *Ghavaznha* (*Deers*,[50] 1975) all of which revolved around the notion of revenge and rebellion. In *Baluch*, Kimiai relocates his familiar themes and obsessions to the province of Baluchistan in the south of Iran – a forgotten, desolate part of the country where time seems to have stood still. Here we see a man unjustly imprisoned, accused of the rape of his wife. On his release from jail, he starts looking for his wife and the two real attackers in the capital. The film becomes a critique of materialism and the urban decadence associated with it. The man's wanderings through a city ornamented with the lavish decorations of the 2500th anniversary celebrations contrasts the wealth of the centre with the poverty at the periphery of society. His acquaintance with a modern 'loose' woman who sets about seducing him is a none-too-subtle assault on urban, bourgeois values.

Arguably the best film of the decade and certainly one of the most politically controversial, *Deers* went on limited release in the winter of 1975, and met with immediate success. Predictably it drew sharp criticism from

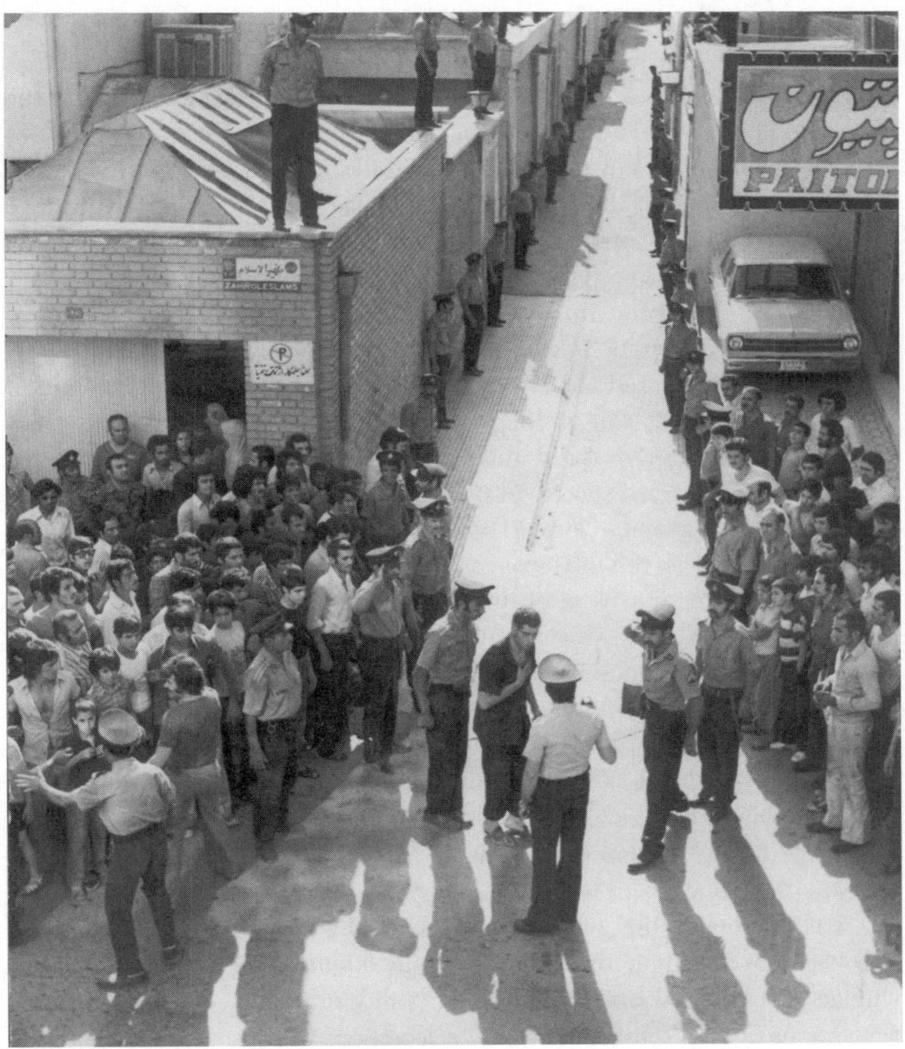

FIG. 17 *Deers* (*Ghavaznha*), Masud Kimiai, 1975.

the Censor's Office. In it, Faramarz Gharibian plays an armed robber who undertakes one last robbery for political purposes, but is shot and wounded. Fleeing with the stolen loot, he takes refuge with an old, estranged friend (Vosughi). In what is possibly the most accomplished performance of his career, Vosughi plays a drug addict who, under the influence of his friend, murders his dealer. Of all Kimiai's heroes, he is the most completely justified in his actions; much of the film's tension derives from his humanity and our consequent concern for his fate. On returning home at the end of the film he finds his house surrounded by police, who have been alerted to his friend's whereabouts. In the original version Vosughi's character is shot alongside his friend and the house is blown up. The censored version has Vosughi lecture Gharibian on the morality of his actions, and the explosion of the house is expunged. Interestingly, even the sanitised version of the script met with a positive audience response.

Deers posits a number of social issues that rested at the heart of 1970s Iran: political conflicts, armed struggle, police brutality, class division and drug addiction. The spatial coding of the film uses populist theatres and crowded poorhouses to portray a society on the verge of explosion. What connects all these fragmented issues is the nostalgic relationship between the two men. *Deers* can be interpreted as an ode to friendship as the one entity that can withstand corruption. This was the first time a central sympathetic character (Gharibian) had played the role of a quasi-guerrilla. For those sensitive to the times they were living through, his call to his friend could be read as an attempt to forge a united front between armed guerrillas and the marginal elements in society. With his humour and sensitivity of expression, Vosughi's character is believable and empathetic throughout. The humour of his character never softens the film's drama nor blunts its political overtones. He dies as a political hero, side by side with his friend.

Children of violence: a new realism

During this period, the filmmaker Amir Naderi was creating his own cult rebels. His first feature, *Kodahafez Rafigh* (*Goodbye Friend*, 1971), was the story of three unemployed friends who, after an ill-advised but impressively executed heist, turn against each other and die one by one. This film created a new 'angry young man' in the shape of Said Rad, and provided directors with an alternative template for future filmmaking. The film brought about a new technical realism in Iranian films; studio lighting did not satisfy Naderi's desire for a more honest, harsh view of Iran. This realist trend succeeded in breaking with the domain of the typical Iranian melodrama by moving the setting into the streets. Zarindast's camera moves through the dirty alleys of lower-class Tehran, capturing the nastiness and desolation of these neighbourhoods. With the black and white, documentary style of its cinematographer Ali-Reza Zarindast, *Goodbye Friend* is a classic example of low-budget, realist filmmaking. The combination of social concern and natural settings inspired many other Iranian films of the period.

While *Goodbye Friend* is based around the fairly standard themes of theft and betrayal, it is stripped down to the very barest narrative bones and opts for an almost clinical minimalism in order to re-imagine the Iranian thriller genre. No scene lasts longer than a few minutes and each is roughly the same length. The effect is of an insistent, almost percussive rhythm, which, as the film progresses, lends it the quality of abstraction. *Goodbye Friend* does not try to elicit excitement, outrage, surprise, or identification. Betrayal is important in the film only for its social and political dimensions, and retribution is no more or less than closure, an ending to the narrative. Naderi is clearly interested in the violence, ethnic diversity and cultural fragmentation that visually define Tehran. The setting invokes the postmodern city as crucible of social history and provides a dizzying premonition of the next decade.

This pessimism reached a peak in *Tangna* (*Deadlock*, Amir Naderi, 1973). A pool hustler, again played by Rad, kills his rival and goes on the run, living in fear in the burnt-out sites of the city. Two of the dead man's brothers hunt him down. He manages to kill one but the other eventually puts him out of his misery. Images shot in the poorest districts of Tehran are calculated to shock the viewer and infuse the film with a sense of gloom. The two women who come across our anti-hero cannot help him. Whilst Kimiai's female characters shifted over the years from passivity towards awareness and activity, women in these films are portrayed as passive, deemed incapable of sharing the young men's sense of rage. They are reduced to the status of helpless witnesses to the man's self-destructive urges. Most of the time, the audience is not even informed about their fate. It is implied though that the dark clouds shadowing the man will sooner or later visit their misfortunes on the women too. The films of this era, until the revolutionary period, were still highly sexist, offering few opportunities for women. But the impossibility of love, of friendship, of self-respect, of life itself, were their crucial themes.

Deadlock is grimmer than any other film of the period. With his usual intensity of purpose Naderi leads us through a whole range of depressing emotions – agony, rage, fear, despair and guilt. An extremely disturbing film whose violence can sometimes hit almost unbearably hard, *Deadlock* captures a rare nastiness that extended the boundaries of Iranian cinematic realism, though in the final scene we are spared the true brutality and ugliness of death. *Deadlock* did much more than make viewers see the brutality hidden within society. It became a powerful political document demonstrating the far-reaching effects of oppression and repression on the psyches of young people whose emotions were in flux, and whose impressionable personalities were still being formed. The film envisions the consequences of an urbanisation that has run amok.

One of the most radical elements of the noir genre was to make heroes out of former villainous types, a switch in point of view that horrified the former purist actors such as Fardin. Lacking the coherence of the traditional hero, Rad has no clearly defined goals. He is both attracted to and repulsed by the city's offer of violence, money and sex. He wants to be a winner, but is redefined as a victim. He is hostile, fearful, and vainly attempts to escape his own fate. Rad is thus an example of the 'new rebel' – totally alienated, totally aware, on the wrong side of the law and with no allegiances to anyone but himself. A man of few words, his actions speak for him; he kills without compunction or remorse. A lifetime of pain and disillusionment is stored up behind his eyes and coiled in the controlled violence of his actions. By making heroes out of the former villains, filmmakers blurred the distinction between good and evil. Since in reality society was populated more by pragmatists than by men of strong moral convictions, this newer, fuzzier moral tone was apposite.

Meanwhile, the newspapers continued to run horror stories.1975 in particular was a year full of extreme events. In March, nine left-wing political

FIG. 18 *Deadlock (Tangna)*, Amir Naderi, 1973.

prisoners were executed. April witnessed an unprecedented incident when the daughter of Professor Adl and her husband, the son of Lieutenant-General Hojjat (two prominent families with links to the highest echelons of the court), were killed by security forces during raids on guerrilla hide-outs. The same month saw the assassination of two more American military attachés by gunmen. There were frequent armed battles in Tabriz and Isfahan. It was also in this hectic year that a group of six guerrillas attacked an OPEC (Organisation of Petroleum-Exporting Countries) meeting in Vienna, taking the Iranian and Saudi Arabian ministers hostage. This last incident was extensively covered by the Iranian media and ended with the Austrian authorities conceding to the demands of the hostage takers. The year ended as it had begun, with the execution of ten more political prisoners. But it was clear that the Shah could not succeed in silencing all dissenting voices.

Official justice and the illusion of enhanced power

Gheisar, which showed four brutal crimes and glorified the anti-hero, remained a landmark film, despite the ruling that stated that the treatment of crime in film should not:

> Teach the methods of crime.
> Inspire potential criminals with a desire for imitation.
> Make criminals seem heroic and justified.

In film after film, family honour was tarnished by an outsider and the hero singlehandedly meted out the justice that the law would take too long to administer. Perhaps this formula reflected the absence of social philosophy, fair legislation, and an attendant lack of concerted social action; it was up to the individual to correct social wrongs, until violent death brought his efforts to an abrupt halt.

The judiciary in Iran had been almost completely absorbed into the ruling executive; its decisions therefore reflected the will of the government. Moreover, its area of responsibility had been gradually eroded by military tribunals and by other special Civil Service tribunals. Under the Shah's reign, the legal system was based on the principle that the state can do no wrong. Military tribunals since the late 1950s had acquired a growing importance. These were staffed by military personnel, held on military premises, and followed military rules. Martial law effectively extended over a large area of national life. Any member of the armed forces automatically went before a military tribunal even if the offence was a civilian one. Any crime that involved the use of a gun came within the jurisdiction of the military. (Significantly, in most Iranian crime films of the 1970s, the hero kills his victims with the traditional knife, while he himself is killed by bullets.) The military courts dealt with all cases affecting 'national security', a blanket term that was loosely interpreted. They arrogated to their own jurisdiction a host of vaguely defined offences and unseen trials.

Where the judiciary had not lost out to the military, its authority was usurped by special tribunals. These were only partially staffed by qualified legal personnel. They had unlimited powers to fine and sentence – powers that could not be challenged by appeal within the normal law courts. In late 1976 the government began to prepare a major overhaul of legal procedures to streamline antiquated practices and cover some of the lacunae in the law. A number of lawyers saw these moves, which included the downgrading of some of the activities of the Supreme Court, as a further shackling of the judiciary.[51]

In June 1977 some amendments were made to the regulations governing military tribunals, including an obligation to hold public trials and the institution of a sort of minimal *habeas corpus* once a detainee had appeared before a military prosecutor. These changes were essentially cosmetic and made no attempt to bring the tribunals under the control of the judiciary. Much also depended upon interpretation; Article 192, for instance, was revised along the following lines: 'Sessions of military courts shall always be public. However, if the prosecutor feels that a public trial is prejudicial to public order and public interest, he may request the court for a secret trial.' Within three weeks of this new provision coming into force, a well-known opposition figure, Ayatollah Taligani, was sentenced to ten years' imprisonment on unspecified charges in a secret trial. Not even the sentence was published.

Since the assassination attempt in 1973, the Shah had regarded SAVAK as a necessary arm of government. The armed forces were the ultimate guarantors of power, but the security services ensured that they would never be used in this role. SAVAK was the Shah's eyes and ears and, where necessary, his iron fist, neutralising all those disloyal to the regime. It acted as both an intelligence service and a political police force, concentrating on Iranian dissidents. The Shah expected his subjects either to follow his political dictates or to remain passive and apolitical. Those who refused to be manipulated or blackmailed into silence suffered the full brunt of SAVAK's repression. The civil courts had no power over SAVAK's investigations since its prosecutions came within the sphere of the military tribunal, though the links between SAVAK and the military establishment were never entirely clear. SAVAK also interfered extensively with the Ministry of Information on matters of censorship and artistic control. The banning of plays and films, or the refusal of permission to publish books, was an integral part of SAVAK's function, and it was particularly concerned with Iran's rapidly expanding and fearless student population.

The number of SAVAK's victims is difficult to establish. In 1975 the Secretary General of Amnesty International described Iran's human rights record as worse than that of any other country in the world. (In 1976 Amnesty International, keeping tracks of 'prisoners of conscience' around the world, estimated that 25,000–100,000 political prisoners were being held in Iran. The Shah's own figure was 3,000–3,500, but he regarded most dissidents as potential or actual Marxist terrorists and thus common criminals rather than political prisoners.) The Shah himself made no secret of the use of torture, though he insisted that it was confined to psychological rather than physical methods.[52]

The effect of the oil price rises throughout 1973 had seen a quantum leap in Iran's annual oil revenue, from $5 billion to $19 billion. Iran, the second largest producer within OPEC and the second biggest exporter of crude oil in the world after Saudi Arabia, took no part in the Arab embargo on selling oil to the West, or in the production cutbacks. This position, coupled with the fact that Iran was not an Arab state, singled the country out for special international attention. The Shah managed to generate a responsible, Olympian image. He cast himself as the man pushing for the correct price for a noble product. Thus his personal standing as a key figure in the Middle East was enhanced. In an interview with Oriana Fallaci in October 1973, the Shah had provided a generally clear and coherent picture of Iranian society. His comments on democracy, however, were in sharp contrast to the prevailing reality:

> I can assure you that in many respects Iran is more democratic than European countries ... It is true that there are only two parties represented in Parliament but these are parties that have signed up to my twelve revolutionary principles. After all, how many parties do you need to represent the revolutionary ethos? ... Also, I do not wish the Communist Party to have legal status... They have no aim other than wanton destruction, and instead of paying allegiance to their country and their king, they do the bidding of foreign powers. They are traitors.[53]

His comments regarding political prisoners also reflected the existing restrictions:

> If you are referring to Communists, I do not consider them political prisoners ... If you are referring to individuals who murder innocent women, children and the elderly, then I do not see them as political ... I feel no sense of compassion for the butchers you call guerrillas, or those who betray their land ... They must be eliminated.[54]

Doomed families and body obsession

Despite the fact that, in Iranian film noir, men and women usually seek happiness within relationships with each other, the lovers or spouses are not permitted the socially acceptable practice of an ordinary marriage. Gheisar, for example, never touches his fiancée, and ignores her wishes to form a family. The wives in *Baluch* and *Sadegh Kordeh* have either been raped or killed. The isolation of the rural couples in *Baluch*, *Sadegh Kordeh* and *Tangsir*, as well as their refusal to conform to certain social norms, was emphasised by the way in which they are presented as being outside of society. Usually the sterility, in conventional terms, of the central male/female relationships in Iranian noir is further emphasised by the childlessness of the couples. In its hierarchical structure, with the father as the head, the mother and children as subservient, the family offered a model or metaphor for hierarchical, authoritarian society. The internal, oppressive, always violent relationships within these films presented a mirror image of violent relationships between classes in the larger society.

In the ideology of what the Shah called the 'Great Civilisation', the royal family was presented as the domestic model. The Shah, as the ideal Iranian man, was powerful, masculine, single-minded, moralistic, protective and the undisputed head of the nation. He believed in the participation of women in society but would not tolerate women who 'tried to imitate men'. He was 'not influenced by any woman' in his life, and 'respected women as long as they were beautiful, feminine, and moderately clever'.[55] Queen Farah Diba represented the ideal stereotype of the emancipated Iranian woman. She left the serious business of the state in the hands of her husband and took up 'feminine' pursuits such as social welfare, education, art and culture. The Shah himself announced with pride that the Queen was the head of more than forty organisations dealing with culture, art, education, health and welfare. Yet even the Women's Organisation of Iran (WOI), established in the 1960s, became in the 1970s an hierarchical, corrupt and non-democratic institution.

The honour of a man was a flexible quantity; depending on his behaviour, his honour could be acquired, augmented, diminished, lost and regained. But women were bound by a specific, inflexible code of honour, which determined their proper conduct and upon which men's honour also depended. A woman was born and grew up with it; she could not augment it, because it was something absolute, but it was her duty to preserve it.

The full dehumanisation of women in commercial Iranian films occurred in the 1970s. Nudity invaded Iranian cinema, and all the tenets of the Production Code on sex were ignored. Most of these films were outlandish, sexually charged cocktails of voyeurism, performance and prostitution. Anything significant in these films' handling of this exploitative material emerged largely, as before, through the differences between traditional and modern women. But these were not mere sentimental melodramas – they were about men exploiting women, pushing them beyond the limits of their traditional boundaries for sex and money. The dramatic failure of these cheap films can be attributed to the fact that they were undiluted examples of poor technique and sheer absence of imagination.

This shift towards the explicit display of the body in commercial Iranian films paralleled many other shifts in Iran. The obsession with the body, sex, good looks, fitness and similar trends reflected a feeling that the only thing one could really change, improve or take control of, in a climate of political impotence, was one's own body. The body and sex therefore became the focus of a new consumerism.

A feast for the male eye, these films offered an explicit extravaganza of acts and body parts previously unseen in Iranian cinema. But the sex itself was the focal point, and in the attempt to make every moment titillating, it would often spill out at bizarre moments. In many films a presumed traditional woman would remove her *chador* to reveal a miniskirt. It seemed these films were homages to the decline of traditional shame. The naked female body was present in such profusion, its nakedness often so incongruously at odds with the tone of the scene played out around it, that its powers of genuine arousal were dispersed into something approaching absurdity.

In the noir genre, the treatment of sex was more ambivalent. Most of the anti-heroes acted as if the women available to them were whores, offering them little affection. The anti-hero's ambition and aggressiveness, including his preoccupation with his knife, seemed to be a result of confused sexuality. Sexual deviancy and jealousy often cropped up in the form of rape, or in the competition of two brothers over the same woman.

The new wave

During the late 1960s, as we have seen, a new wave in Iranian filmmaking had begun, with films such as *The Night of the Hunchback*, *The Brick and the Mirror*, *The Cow* and *Gheisar* dealing intelligently with social themes. In the 1970s, a small group of filmmakers continued to explore social and political issues. Some of their approaches were readily accessible to audiences, since they revised traditional concepts of tragedy and comedy, heroes and villains, good and evil. Others, however, presented crimes that remained unpunished, 'heroes' who seemed to be ordinary men, conflicts that remained unresolved, and stories in which nobody lived happily ever after. The new cinema was sometimes slow and brooding as in *Yek Ettefagh-e Sad-e* (*A Simple Event*, Sohrab Shahid-Sales, 1973), sometimes delicate and lyrical, like *Gharib-e va Meh* (*The Stranger and the Fog*, Bahram Bayzai, 1975), but it always explored the complexities of the social and political context.

The 1970s was a decade full of unanswered questions relating to Iranian identity and native culture. The cinema of the 1970s, more than any other period, tried to identify a true Iranian 'essence'. Ancient parables and traditional characters, locales and architecture predominated in this decade, creating an alternative to mainstream cinema. These works, successful or otherwise, represent the 'golden age' of Iranian cinema before the Revolution, an age belittled by those who equate Iranian cinema simply with its international achievements in the 1990s.

Ali Hatami was a pioneer in the art of adapting Persian folklore for the cinema. He attempted to narrate the history of his land through popular culture. In his pursuit of a new film language, he came to rely on analogies, axioms and recitations from the Koran and other sacred texts. Though Hatami's films always featured a kind of romanticism, it was of a bittersweet nature that was light-years away from the whimsical Iranian film romances.

Adapted from a successful stage play, the musical *Hassan Kachal* (*Egg-Head Hassan*, Ali Hatami, 1971) tells the ancient story of a man who is suffering from a Peter Pan complex and is in love with an imaginary woman called Chehel-gis (literally 'Forty-locks'). The following year Hatami made another musical, *Baba Shamal* (1972), also based on an old tale, about a love triangle involving a woman and two traditional wrestling champions. In this updated version, however, any nostalgia for the innocence of the past is replaced by a particularly Iranian take on shame and self-denial. *Ghalandar* (*The Wandering Dervish*, Ali Hatami, 1972) was a darker, bleaker version of the same theme. Here, a jealous lover becomes incensed on overhearing his beloved whispering sweet nothings to another man in a darkened room. Only after he has murdered them both does he realise that the young man was the woman's son. For Hatami, revenge, which was the bread and butter of 1970s cinema, was synonymous with narrow-mindedness.

The world of money and politics was evoked with great ruthlessness in Hatami's next film. With *Sattar Khan* (1972), he was venturing into the controversial area of national heroes and of the Constitutional Revolution. He followed this with a television series, *Sultan Saheb-Gharan*, set in the final years of the Qajar dynasty, and his dark comedy, *Khastegar* (*The Suitor*, 1972), provided a witty sketch of the follies of the urban middle classes. In *Sooteh-Delan* (*Desiderium*, 1977) the love between a prostitute and a mentally retarded man is portrayed in a tale contrasting simplicity and complexity, honesty and dishonesty.

The quest for a native cinema was often conducted through the device of presenting ordinary people who are forced by circumstance to dwell on their own identities and social context, encouraging viewers to do the same. In 1971 Nosrat Karimi had made both *Doroshkechi* (*Carriage Driver*), at its core an analysis of chastity and women's lack of freedom and self-determination in a predominantly patriarchal society, and *Mohallel*, about divorce and remarriage, which, due to its concern with gender issues, turned into a sex-comedy of sorts. Significantly, it became the first film to be condemned publicly by a cleric – in this case a prominent one: Ayatollah Motahari, who criticised it for its perspective on the religious laws that govern divorce and marriage in Iran. Equally problematic was Naser Taghvai's *Aramesh dar Hozur-e Deegaran* (*Tranquility in the Presence of Others*, 1968), which had finally reached the screens in 1971, after three years of censorship. It narrates the tale of a retired colonel who, accompanied by his new wife, visits his two daughters in Tehran, only to find them enmeshed in a decadent circle of depravity. As the two daughters were nurses, the film ran into opposition from the nurses' union. Moreover, the portrayal of a depressed and authoritarian colonel won no favours with a regime proud of its military credentials. Taqvai's daring depiction of men's alienation and women's sexual freedom had no precedent in Iranian cinema.

Films such as *Cheshmeh* (*Spring*, Arbi Avanesian), *Samad va Foolad Zereh Deev* (*Samad and the Steel-clad Demon*, Jalal Moghaddam) and *Topoli* (*Chubby*, Reza Mir-Lohi), which hit the screens in 1972, were disparate attempts to challenge the clichés of Iranian cinema. Critics attacked the intellectualism and elitism of *Spring*, and the film did poorly on general release, but in truth, Avanesian had made an admirable assault on hackneyed filmmaking. In *Samad and the Steel-clad Demon*, mythical folklore was subverted when the traditional roles assigned in these stories to man and demon were reversed.

Here, the demon was redeemed while the ordinary folk populating the story were demonised. *Chubby* was a reworking of John Steinbeck's story *Of Mice and Men* (1937), which dealt with the universal dimensions of tragedy.

It was against this backdrop that in 1973, fifteen of the country's most respected film practitioners, including Dariush Mehrjui, Behruz Vosughi and Ezatollah Entezami, had formed a syndicate known as the Progressive Filmmakers' Society, in order to oppose the general trend towards sex and vulgarity in cinema. Although this proclamation of autonomy never achieved much practical relevance, it did put under pressure a cinematic apparatus obsessed with commercial imperatives. Yet during the mid-1970s, the Tehran International Film Festival and the Shiraz Art Festival, which could have become occasions for an exchange of views and the encouragement of a film-intelligentsia manifesto, were instead used as forums for the generation of worthless co-productions. Films like *Ten Little Indians* (Peter Collinson, 1975), with Oliver Reed and Richard Attenborough, and *Caravans* (James Fargo, 1978), featuring Anthony Quinn and Joseph Cotton, were the disappointing result.

The year 1973 had seen the release of Parviz Kimiavi's *Mogholha* (*Mongols*), which analysed the changing identity, technology and trajectory of the media within the context of a failing relationship between a filmmaker and his researcher wife (who is completing a dissertation on the Mongol invasion of Iran). Television's invasion of rural areas is compared to the Mongol hordes, and the passive consumer's submission to this full-frontal assault is critiqued. Kimiavi's two subsequent films, *Bagh-e Sangi* (*Stone Garden*, 1977) and *OK, Mister* (1978) were also subtle critiques of the foreign presence in Iran. These latter films were not considered sufficiently commercial, however, to go out on general release.

Sohrab Shahid-Sales's *A Simple Event*, released the same year, captures the slow, everyday rhythms of life in order to describe the melancholic existence of a ten-year-old boy living in a closed village circle, who becomes a metaphor for the Iranian people. His mother is gravely ill and his father drinks the little money he makes. The boy's situation at school is hopeless: he learns nothing in a militaristic system that makes no allowance for the individual. The 'simple event' of the title is the eventual death of his mother.

Shahid-Sales's handling of the story is discreet and restrained; he gets in close to his character, making it easy for the audience to identify with him, although this experience is an uncomfortable one. Each of Shahid-Sales's films hinges on a time of crisis in childhood – the break-up of a relationship, or a death in the family, for example – and in each case the focus is not so much on the crisis itself as on the character's reaction to it.

The prizes won by *A Simple Event* (in Berlin, 1971) and *Mongols* (in France and Italy, 1973) proved that, despite a lack of popular support inside the country, the new wave was capable of sustaining itself abroad. Shahid-Sales was also the first major Iranian filmmaker to make a film outside the country. In 1975 he began working in West Germany, making a name for himself as a creator of quiet, unemphatic but intense observations of the non-events of daily life – films that have attracted comparisons with Anton Chekhov, Robert Bresson and Ermanno Olmi.

Some films of the new wave provided a cynical take on contemporary Iranian events. In 1974, Ebrahim Golestan caricatured the nouveaux riches, intellectuals and artists, as well as the Shah himself, with *Asrar-e Ganj-e Dar-e Jeni (Secrets of the Haunted Treasures)*. His works to date had been testimony to the predicament of a filmmaker who was vociferously anti-establishment yet lacked any well-defined ideological alternative. The sort of freedom his work exalted was essentially primitive, even brutish. *Secrets of the Haunted Treasures* is a viciously satirical film about a country whose leaders do not know what to do with their treasures, a deliberate dig at the oil-obsessed Shah, who is depicted as a cartoonish wastrel. It was Golestan's most ambitious and vociferous film, as well as being the most famous 'anti-Shah' film of the period. Full of funny, anti-bourgeois set pieces, this mind-boggling film stacks analogy upon analogy and allegory upon allegory with hallucinatory fervour. Through the episodic odyssey of a poor rural man, played by Parviz Sayyad, social values regarding sex, consumerism and the family are explored in a variety of surreal ways. The final result is a witty vision of corruption and consumerism in 1970s Iran.

Shazdeh Ehtejab (Prince Ehtejab, Bahman Farman'ara, 1974), based on a novel by Hushang Gulshiri, narrated the dying days of a Qajar royal as an allegory of the problems facing the Shah's regime. Prince Ehtejab, who is suffering from hereditary tuberculosis and will soon die, sits alone in his room recalling a past in which his grandfather killed his own mother and brother, his father machine-gunned a crowd of demonstrators, and he himself ruled through spiritual imprisonment and torture. Such critical trends were reflective of a paradigm shift in people's outlook and sensibilities. As if to underscore the point, *Shir-e Khofteh* (*The Sleeping Lion*, Esmail Kushan, 1976), which employed an adventurous style for the depiction of patriotic opposition to British and Russian military incursions during the Qajar period, failed to impress audiences. History as entertainment had become unacceptable.

Between 1972 and 1977, Bahram Bayzai made three films that engaged with different dimensions of Iranian society during these tumultuous times: *Ragbar* (*Downpour*, 1972), *The Stranger and the Fog* (1975) and *Kalagh* (*The Crow*, 1977). In the last of these the search for a young woman becomes a symbolic yearning for lost youth and an intuitive demonstration that a particular historical phase was coming to an end. It is impossible not to read this parable as a political critique of a regime that had had its day.

Pesar-e Iran az Madarash bi Khabar Ast (*The Iranian Son Does Not Know about His Mother*, Feridun Rahnama) was screened in 1976. Rahnama's abstract, conceptual films were representative of an intellectual trend that was crushed before it could bear fruit. In this film he foregrounds the alienation from their own history experienced by most Iranians, by juxtaposing the notion of faith with cultural diversity. In a similar vein, *Shatranj-e Baad* (*Wind Chess*, Muhammad-Reza Aslani, 1976) sketches the incongruity of a traditional family living in the twentieth century. An abstract cinematic perspective on life became the trademark of this period. Films like Khosrow Hertiash's *Malakut* (*Kingdom of Heaven*, 1976) and Parviz Kimiavi's *Stone Garden*, made near to the end of the Pahlavi regime, talked of birth, dissolution and lack of consciousness in the guise of proverbs and allegories.

The advent of the boom

When in December 1973 the Shah announced a staggering new increase in the price of oil, he had displayed the confidence of a man who knew that his country's financial resources had quadrupled in just over two months. Iran had become one of the world's most prosperous nations, with the chance to play a correspondingly large role in international affairs. A bemused industrialised world, impressed by the Shah, who boasted of Iran entering the ranks of the advanced countries before the turn of the century, was thus forced to come to terms with what appeared to be a major shift in the balance of power, tilted for the first time in the direction of the producers of essential commodities.

The form of the Iranian dictatorship was, however, unique in that it combined the vigorous promotion of capitalist development with a fully constituted monarchist regime, a fundamentally anti-capitalist form of political structure. The gulf between monarchical rule and the Shah's promotion of capitalism would eventually become so wide that an economic crisis resulting from a fall in oil revenue would provoke a revolution. The West, however, seemed totally unaware of this impending crisis and it became an article of faith that within twenty years Iran would become the fifth Great Power.

Dazzled by its new importance, the Iranian response was unashamedly grandiose. The Fifth Plan, less than a year old, was set aside and in its place a new set of objectives was introduced, costing $69 billion: double the original estimate. No developing country had produced such a large investment programme and it was the first to appear in the Middle East. Yet the Shah's calculations were based less on economics than on politics – the politics of his own survival. Within two years Iran witnessed a period of unprecedented boom – in 1974–75 alone the government spent the equivalent of $22 billion. The effect of such an increase in spending was like a car going downhill: comfort and control were sacrificed to speed. The government's policies created a mass of rural migrant workers who found insecure employment on construction sites in urban centres and lived in the shantytowns which rapidly developed on the margins of the cities. The collapse of the construction boom in the late 1970s thus created unemployment, and a high rate of inflation reduced the standard of living sometimes to the point of starvation.

By 1977 the ideology of the Great Civilisation was in full swing, dominating every aspect of Iranian life. The history of Iran had been rewritten and the Iranian calendar itself was changed to convey the sense of a continuous non-Islamic civilisation. The Hezb-e Rastakhiz-e Meli (National Resurgence

Party), set up in 1974 on the ruins of the Iranian Constitution, had finally dispensed with the masquerade of a Western-style political system. It was claimed that class conflict had been eliminated, and thus the Party was to be one of national unity. Used to channel and depoliticise public debate, it became a sort of popular police force and served as another source of information for the Shah regarding rural affairs. The Party's creation also further obstructed the growth of an independent-minded press, which became, in effect, a government public-relations agency.

During the decade, the dramatic increases in oil income led to further capital accumulation by the private sector in at least two areas: the state provided credit to business magnates at favourable rates, and inflation created windfall profits from land speculation and real-estate development. State incentives to substitute domestic products for imports led many importers of industrial goods to establish factories in Iran, which increased the contribution of the private sector to capital acquisition in machinery and construction (from $750 million in 1959 to $6.7 billion in 1977). Huge state growth and increasing urbanisation allowed hundreds of merchants, industrialists, import traders, contractors, consulting engineers, commercial farmers and others to make their fortunes.

The early 1970s had, therefore, formed a prosperous modern bourgeoisie in Iran. This group, however, despite the much closer economic links between the upper middle classes and the state sector, was not allowed to participate in politics, nor to organise autonomously, which meant that they could not voice their concerns through their representatives in Parliament, nor publicise their views through an independent media.

Sociopolitical power was the main theme of *Sazesh* (*Arrangement*, Muhammad Motevaselani, 1974). It starred Vosughi in one of his rare comedies, as a petty thief who suddenly becomes the head of a neighbourhood council, and in the process begins to grasp the bitter realities of society. The heroes played by actors such as Vosughi and Rad rarely had jobs. As the gap between the bourgeoisie and lower classes widened, only by ignoring or denying that earning a living was a critical issue could these films plausibly urge upon men the role of the individualistic, contented hero who, acting alone, can right all wrongs and set an example to the foundering masses. The fear of mass action, however, usually resulted in the depiction of solitary, lower-class heroes who solve their problems for themselves and typically pit the old values against the bourgeoisie more frequently than they toil on the assembly line.

As a Charlie Chaplin-like happy tramp, Reza Beik-Imanverdi, the popular star of 1970s commercial films, had enough leisure time built into his roles to be able to bring the world to rights immediately the call was sounded. His films sought to demonstrate through his characters' charisma the idea that ordinary, jobless men could still flourish as free spirits and defiant individualists; they did not need to band together in groups or organise to make society more hospitable. Beik-Imanverdi used both comedy and his fists as instruments for exposing the contradictions and conflict between the social mechanism and the simplest, most essential human needs. The comedy was in the contradiction between his heroism and his absurdity; it made the audience laugh, while uncovering the harshness of the world around him. As a popular commercial hero, Beik-Imanverdi reflected the tastes of the capitalist bourgeois world during the first half of the decade. For audiences to have picked such an absurd figure as a film hero was profoundly indicative of the period.

An image of prosperity and culture on a par with Western societies was created in Iran during the 1970s. The lifestyle of the royal family was presented as the aspirational example for ordinary people and was imitated by the newly rising, luxury-seeking consumerist upper and middle classes. It became fashionable for well-to-do Iranians to shop extravagantly in Western department stores and to take their holidays in Western ski and beach resorts. Television played a crucial role in this concept, and a good proportion of the material shown by the public broadcasting monopoly NIRT (National Iranian Radio and Television), inaugurated in 1971 with Reza Ghotbi (a close relative of the Queen) as the first Director General, was imported. The main channel's output consisted of classic old films from America, new serials, and musical shows. Much of the cultural programming and advertising served to heighten the gulf in wealth, lifestyle and attitudes between a limited, cosmopolitan upper class and the rest of Iran, leading to mixed sentiments, of envy and outrage, of cultural inferiority and cultural pollution.

One of the major cultural events held in Iran during the 1970s was the Tehran International Film Festival. It tried hard to compete with prestigious international film festivals around the world and many valuable films were screened, yet the typical reaction of foreign guests, invited to confirm that the country had achieved cultural parity with the West, was ambiguous and often ironic, with one British critic noting that:

> the Tehran festival, in its second year, was ostentatiously inviting recognition not just as another stopover on the international circuit but as a four-star attraction. And if a belly dancer at a banquet caused less of a stir than Ann Miller, who danced for old times' sake, that was all part of the circus.[56]

Another took a more political approach:

> The scope of the festival was considerable, reflecting in many ways Iran's mid-way point both geographically and culturally: it is neither Oriental nor Occidental, nor really a part of the Middle East, while its civilisation is caught somewhere between an impressive national cultural heritage and over-paid Westernisation and expansion.[57]

The truth was that class differences had widened due to government policies, with 32.5 per cent of total consumption accounted for by the top 10 per cent of families on the income scale and only 2.5 per cent accounted for by the lowest 10 per cent. An upper class of not more than a thousand households, including royal and aristocratic families and entrepreneurs, owned many of the large commercial firms as well as some 85 per cent of major private firms involved in banking, manufacturing, foreign trade, insurance and urban construction. It was in large part the deterioration of income distribution that led to widespread discontent in the late 1970s.

As a result of investment in health-care facilities, most of it concentrated in cities, by 1976 the population had grown to 33.7 million. Tehran had the largest concentration of economic enterprises as well as the biggest market in Iran. It extracted money and people from all around the country, creating large surpluses of capital and labour, which were increasingly channelled into the built environment. These new developments, supported by the oil boom, ranged from low-rise to high-rise, and from single developments to large new towns, constituting a complex and ever-expanding metropolis.

The city in film therefore came to represent a prison that incarcerated men who had reached breaking point. In *Deadlock* and *Zir-e Pust-e Shab* (*Under the Skin of the Night*, Feridun Goleh, 1974) Tehran becomes a symbol of social injustice

FIG. 19 *Under the Skin of the Night* (*Zir-e Pust-e Shab*), Feridun Goleh, 1974.

and urban squalor. The failure of *Deadlock*'s protagonist to find somewhere safe to hide only serves to underline the city's indifference towards romantic notions such as sanctuary. Similarly, the young protagonist of *Under the Skin of the Night* searches in vain for a safe haven where he can be alone with his foreign sweetheart. At the end, tired and battered, he finds himself in the only place fit for a mid-1970s hero – behind bars. The central character in Goleh's *Kandu* (*Beehive*, 1975) fares little better. His journey from café to café, where he gets through numerous drinks without paying a penny, becomes an excuse to comment on the vast class differences tearing the capital apart. The film presents us with a disquietingly grotesque parody of this dynamic at its most savagely self-destructive.

The struggle of the workers and the rush from Iran

By the late 1970s, the Shah's oil revenues had soared from just over $1 billion per year at the beginning of the decade to $21 billion. This enabled him to buy nuclear reactors from France and Germany, steel mills from the Soviet Union, and telecommunications systems from the USA. In retrospect, it is easy to see that the Shah's oil money was buying trouble as well as power. His army could not protect him from the discontent of his own people, and the boom-town nature of Iran's economic growth nourished that discontent. Glittering apartment houses rose in big cities, but 63,000 of Iran's 66,000 villages still had no piped water. Inflation soared, rising as much as 50 per cent a year, leading many rural residents to seek industrial jobs in the cities. The well-cultivated farmland reverted to desert, and Iran, long self-sufficient in agricultural production, had to import many of its goods.[58]

The peculiar political situation in Iran made its society ripe for radical transformation, and the growing revolution in reaction to this crises had widespread popular support. A range of classes, from urban, traditional groups to the new petty bourgeoisie, the recently proletarianised masses (including the migrant poor) and the richer working class (including the relatively well-paid oil workers) all wanted to get rid of the Shah. The Revolution did not, however, take a classical bourgeois democratic form, primarily because of the lack of strong peasant participation in the demand to overthrow feudal relations. No full account of the role of the working class in the revolutionary process has so far appeared. What has emerged sporadically is limited to praising the determining role of this class in the anti-Pahlavi struggle, rather than offering any critical analysis of its actual involvement and strategies, or strengths and weaknesses.[59]

The initial phase of struggle began in the spring of 1978 with a wave of strikes. Until August, the demands of the workers were largely economic

– but with some political content. By the autumn, there was a progressive increase in the numbers striking; this period also marked a turning point in the nature of the demands that were made, and eventually workers began demanding workers' control. The working class entered the scene of the struggle in the second half of 1978. On 5 September, a religious day, millions took to the streets throughout the country in a peaceful demonstration. Two days later, on what was to become known as Bloody Friday, street battles with the army in Tehran left hundreds dead. When 40,000 oil-workers, 40,000 steel-workers, and 30,000 railway-workers had put down their tools within less than three weeks, the revolutionary process took on a new dynamism. The oil strike was of particular domestic and international significance.

Following a call to strike on 15 October 1978 in the Abadan refinery, troops were called into workplaces, arresting seventy workers and the leader of the union of the Tehran Oil Refinery Workers. Yet the strike committee formulated its demands, including the nationalisation of the oil industry; the unconditional release of all political prisoners; all communication to be in the Persian language; all foreign employees to leave the country; an end to discrimination against women employees, and the punishment of corrupt government officials and ministers. The production and export of oil was brought to a halt; its resumption was dependent on the fulfilment of the demands. Production declined from 5.7 million barrels a day in late October to 1.8 million and then to nil in November.[60] The strike had an international impact, which gave the workers a peculiar social and economic power.

By January 1978, foreign companies, who had once been so keen to invest, were fleeing en masse. There were literally billions at stake. Western banks were owed about $5 billion in outstanding loans for the Shah's schemes, and although there had not yet been any defaults, the huge decline in Iran's oil revenues was a worry for the bankers. About 350 American companies, from small service outfits to giants like General Motors, had invested more than $12 billion, much of which was in jeopardy. The international consortium that was producing oil for the National Iranian Oil Company was already losing millions of dollars a day in profits. For the most part, however, foreign contracts remained in force, and companies were leaving simply because it was impossible to do business under such conditions. Gradually,

United States officials began to criticise themselves for an over-dependence on the Shah's word as a source of reliable information.

In the run-up to the Revolution, Kimiai had made the film *Safar-e Sang* (*Journey of the Stone*, 1977), an accurate echo of the times. The story focused on a group of farmers who decide to stand up to their tyrannical landlord by rolling a gigantic stone from the top of a mountain with the intention of smashing his exploitative mills and production facilities to smithereens. The journey is arduous but the collective will overwhelms all obstacles, finally culminating in the destruction of the mills. This film, however, should not be misinterpreted as simply representing a rural act of defiance against the city. *Journey of the Stone* was a political depiction of a future society and a warning to audiences that passive consumption was no longer an option. The film may seem dated by today's standards but its real value lay in capturing the mood of the times and in expanding on the personal vendettas depicted in earlier films to include collective acts of revolt. By portraying the arousal of a sleepy community, it suggested the larger awakening of society in the struggle for freedom. A prayer scene, a 'chest-beating' ceremony and the unsheathed sword adorning the background of the ritual represented a direct call for the synthesis of religious ardour with armed struggle. The text and subtexts of *Journey of the Stone* thus came to represent in microcosm the wider societal conflict between the people and the regime.

Already by 1977, the bottom had fallen out of the Iranian film market; for all practical purposes it was bankrupt, both financially, and perhaps more ominously, artistically. Many factors were to blame: an increase in the cost of production and promotion; high taxation on filmmaking; disorganised distribution; arbitrary censorship; lack of screening in decent cinemas for native films; lack of support from the Ministry of Art and Culture; the invasion of the market by cheap, vulgar foreign films, and intense competition from national television. The numerous conferences organised to address this issue made little headway, and sectarian politicking overshadowed the process of decision-making.

If the nine-month long strike by dubbing artists in 1975 was a purely economic affair, the strike of cinema owners in 1978 transcended mere professional concerns. On 19 August, the Rex cinema in the southern city of Abadan, which happened to be showing *Deers*, was attacked by arsonists as a symbolic means of hitting out at the regime, with the loss of about 400 lives. Street demonstrations became more widespread and one way to express rage at the regime became the destruction of cinemas. In the capital alone, 31 cinemas (out of a total of 117) were torched. The NIRT was seized on 11 February 1979, when the military forces were ordered back to barracks after a 90-day occupation. That evening some staff returned to the screen, and the two lions of the NIRT logo were shown holding flowers. For the next few days, television broadcast four hours of programmes, with new political graphics, poetry readings from previously banned writers and a good deal of programming that was directly religious in content. A selection of newly composed revolutionary songs providing a background for edited film and photographs of the insurrection, providing an instant historical replay of the Revolution.

7 The 1980s

Spreading to the streets

In 1979, the Revolution became victorious. The new Islamic Republic was declared on 11 February, under the charismatic leadership of Ayatollah Khomeini, and more than 2500 years of monarchy came to an end. Over the next few years it was to weather a series of crises, including the takeover of the US Embassy in November 1979 and the 'American hostage crisis'; a massive bomb blast in Tehran in 1981 that killed many Members of Parliament; a number of military coup attempts; declining oil prices, and eight years of intensive warfare with Iraq, beginning in 1980 with the Iraqi invasions, and at a cost of 140,000 dead, 500,000 injured, and billions of dollars.

By the close of the first year of the Revolution, despite industrial action on the part of many of those without jobs and despite meagre unemployment loans, thousands of unemployed urbanites realised that they must come to terms with their joblessness. Neither the movement of the unemployed nor the efforts of the new government were sufficient to ameliorate the situation. The stagnation of industry and construction, the freezing of recruitment in the state, and an annual release of thousands of urban migrants, all combined to inflate the number of those out of work. In Tehran, unemployment had jumped from 3 per cent in 1976 to some 14 per cent in 1979. A year later it rose to 16.3 per cent. Three main groups made up the unemployed population: laid-off and expelled workers, graduates, and already jobless casual labourers.

So long as the jobless had believed they could gain ground through collective resistance, they refrained from individualistic acts and survival strategies. But these groups had little in common and, whereas a common workplace at least gave laid-off workers a basis for communication, the other two groups lacked even a common space. The struggle of the jobless was therefore somewhat chaotic and by the end of the first year they had begun to resort to individual survival strategies. The black market, largely free from the bureaucratic control of the state, offered the only space in which individuals could exercise their own initiatives to better their lot and, in addition to relying on family, friends and patrons, most found opportunities in casual work.

Street vending was not a novel phenomenon in Iran. Indeed, it was characteristic of pre-modern urban areas, where local traders exhibited their merchandise in public thoroughfares, usually in the vicinity of the established bazaar. Local authorities regulated the use of the streets, which varied according to the local culture. If the state seemed to be far removed from local life, the street vendors were at its centre, performing a highly significant function in the distribution of goods in the local markets and providing services for communities. The collapse of the Shah's regime had brought with it a temporary halt in the bureaucratic control of economic activities and the breakdown of police and municipal control opened the way for thousands of people to undertake their own initiative in economic life. Between 1976 and 1986 this informal economy became the fastest growing sector, second only to the public sector. By 1986 these activities made up some 18 per cent of urban employment.

The post-Revolution period brought changes to the vending sector beyond this sharp increase in its size: a new form of political vending emerged, thus rendering the group more susceptible to control by the state. During the period between February 1979 and mid-1981, many politicised school and college graduates, mainly supporters of the opposition political groups, took advantage of the chaotic freedom and began to set up stalls and kiosks along the sidewalks of the main streets of the capital city. They traded intellectual merchandise such as books, newspapers and cassettes. Political vending, however, represented only a transitory phenomenon. More important were the ordinary vendors, whose main concern was to make a living.

The thousands who joined them following the Revolution were composed of rural migrants, war refugees, young unemployed Tehranis and low-wage state employees seeking a second income. It was Tehran that attracted the largest group of street traders, whose businesses, ranging from the sale of fresh produce or handicrafts to car parts and cigarettes, even stale bread, spread like bushfire. Others offered entertainment, performing as magicians, enacting passion plays or telling fortunes. Or they stood silently next to their handcarts, waiting for someone to buy their muscle power. The more desperate would do anything to ensure survival, including begging, theft, drug-dealing and prostitution.

By the eve of the 1979 Revolution, Tehran, with a population of some five million, exhibited a remarkable and perhaps unique class hierarchy, based on economic, social and cultural elements. Located on a north-to-south sloping landscape, the geophysical pyramid of the city reflected this social structure. To the far north, the highest district was the site of the most affluent populations. The lowest lands of the city were allocated to the poor, new migrants and other strata of the working class. The central areas, from east to west, housed the middle classes. The poor were thus forced to settle in the vast southern plain, encompassing a variety of overcrowded slums and squatter settlements. By 1980, at least one million poor lived in the slums of Tehran, which had provided the setting for Amir Naderi's *Marsieh* (*Elegy*), made in 1978. The film, which contrasted the devastation of poor people's lives with the sterility of the paradise promised by the officials had led, unsurprisingly, to its effective banning by the government.

The new squatters' movement emerged against the background of the Revolution. The central authority had collapsed; there were no secret police, no municipality guards, not even traffic police. Hundreds of factories were taken over by workers and the state offices were run by their employees. The revolutionary youth took charge of the city police stations. A new social order emerged. As we have seen, many business people, frightened by such lawlessness, deserted their companies and factories; the rich abandoned their homes, hurriedly leaving behind million-dollar properties. In the end, some 150,000 housing units – palaces, hotels, villas and unfinished apartment blocks – remained empty. As well as the squatter communities of the southern plain – which included caves, tents, hovels, shacks, shanties and urban villages – it was in these empty properties that, in the days and weeks that followed the insurrection, thousands of homeless families, poor tenants and students took residence.

Stand up cinema

Over 125 cinemas were burnt to the ground during the upheavals of the Revolution. In June 1982, *Etella'at* claimed that out of a total of 524 cinemas in Iran, only 313 remained intact; in April 1983, the newspaper *Kayhan* reported that as few as 400 cinemas remained operational in Iran. In January 1979, speaking at the Behesht-e Zahra cemetery, Ayatollah Khomeini famously remarked that the Revolution was not opposed to cinema *per se*, only obscenity. But this did not help to clarify the direction cinema should now take. Continuing with the old model seemed inappropriate, but there was no agreement as to where the 'new cinema' should be heading.

The provisional government of Mehdi Bazargan, which under instruction from Ayatollah Khomeini had been proclaimed a few days before the overthrow of the Shah, appointed Parviz Varjavand, a university lecturer, to the post of Minister of Culture. The Office for Film Exhibition had been abolished and consequently no department was in overall control of the production and exhibition process. A few weeks before the Revolution, Hamid Ghanbari, President of the Guild of Actors and Film Practitioners, had invited all the branches of the industry to select a representative. These included Hossein Haghighi (representing technical directors), Hossein Gil (actors), Hushang Baharlu (cinematographers) and Reza Allamehzadeh (directors). Three months later, each branch selected five more delegates. The final executive committee was comprised of Masud Kimiai, Muhammad Motevaselani, Kamran Shirdel, Said Motlebi and Reza Allamehzadeh. In a wider move, Varjavand set up the Council for Determining the Political Direction of National Culture, an attempt to create an integral apparatus comprising 20 committees, each responsible for a particular aspect of national culture. Three representatives from cinema were introduced to this council: Shirdel, Baharlu and Allamehzadeh. However, within two months, Varjavand would resign and the council, too, would cease work.

Because of these initial difficulties in the transition from pre-revolutionary cinema to the new Iranian cinema, the period from 1978 to 1982 is considered the vaguest age of Iranian cinema history. Most contemporary critics agree that the films made at this time, whilst attempting to engage with social dilemmas, were empty and superficial. Cinema was after all a twentieth-century art and Muslim theologians had hitherto paid it little attention. The seminal Islamic texts on art such as Ghaemi's *Islam's Artistic Perspectives* (1968) and parts of Ali Shariati's *Art Waiting for Promises* (1970) had, by and large, ignored cinema.[61]

The head of the Islamic Centre for the Study of Art and Filmmaking put it this way: 'In the past, committed Muslims did not tend to take to those arts that the regime promoted … as a result, they are not as well versed in the technical side of things. This is one of our present difficulties.'[62] In reality, there were no criteria by which to judge works and, subsequently, confusion prevailed. The head of the Mostazafin (Foundation for the Deprived), Karim Nuri, was even more upfront: 'At present, our society does not possess a set of aesthetic principles by which to distinguish "good" works from "bad".'[63]

Mohsen Makhmalbaf, later to become one of Iran's most famous film directors, had this to say on the confusion surrounding artistic activity:

> Frankly, our search in the history of Islamic art has not been as productive as we had hoped … [foreign] Orientalist scholars have ascertained various principles of Islamic architecture … but Muslims themselves have not made impressive contributions to this field. In fact, there has been little scholarly work on Islamic art in general. Some of the reasons are clear: the [Islamic] boycott of sculpture and music, as well as antipathy towards painting.[64]

A few months later, he offered the following suggestion: 'I think the best solution is to establish a research institution for the purpose of determining aesthetic criteria by which Islamic art can be assessed.'[65]

Naturally there were conflicting views regarding what Iranian cinema should or should not be in the early years of the Revolution. Initially, realism was offered as the perfect instrument for expressing the struggles of society. This outlook shunned both 'cinema as entertainment' and 'cinema as opium'. In June 1981 the politician Muhammad Ali Rajai stated that: 'People's slogans must be reflected in films. Films should express the people's demands and aspirations and they must also create a sense of hope and a spirit of defiance. The pressing issues of the deprived and the Islamic Revolution must be presented in films.'[66]

The primary criteria, therefore, became the political, ethical and educational aspects of cinema. The Deputy Minister of Culture and Higher Education, Mehdi Kalhor, stated this outlook explicitly: 'Cinema is a school for education and development. It is an activity of which the deprived should make full use.'[67] According to the head of Film Supervision, Hojjatoleslam Sadegh Ardestani, the crucial criterion upon which film might be judged was 'corruptibility', or obscenity.[68]

During this period even managing the extant cinema network proved difficult. From early 1980 the government took over responsibility for importing foreign films, consigning the private sector to the margins. However, the foreign films that were already in the country continued to be screened, and an anti-Hollywood wave in Iran coincided with a rise in screenings of foreign political cinema. The head of the Office for Cinema at the Ministry for the Interior declared: 'It is necessary for every single cinema in the country to be closed down straight away, if only to deny space to the enemies of the Constitution and the Islamic Republic.'[69]

Around this time a seminar entitled 'Analysing the Problems and Shortcomings of Cinema' was held in Tehran, which concluded by denouncing the closure of cinemas. Finally, in June 1980 in an open letter to the President, the Minister of Culture and Higher Education, Hassan Habibi, posed the following testing questions:

> How are we to manage cinema?
>
> Until our film industry has become capable of making products of which society fully approves, by what criteria should we screen foreign and domestic films?
>
> Perhaps more to the point, should we import foreign film at all?[70]

But the political conflicts of the time, which led to the ousting of the Islamic Republic's first President, Abol-Hassan Banisadr in 1981 and his eventual flight from Iran, did not provide the ideal background for dealing with these thorny issues. Later in 1980, another seminar on issues relating to cinema, this time organised by the Mostazafin Foundation with the aid of the Revolutionary Guards, the Reconstruction Corps and the Imam's Office (the office of Ayatollah Khomeini), called for the abolition of the Guild of Cinema Owners. It also suggested that a new committee should be established in order to manage the film industry.[71] This new body, under the supervision of Hojjatoleslam Ardestani, started work in the same year. It consisted of delegates from the politico-ideological department of the army, the Revolutionary Guards, the Reconstruction Corps, the Cultural Department of the Mostazafin Foundation, and the Society of Clerics. However, as the new set of rules and regulations for film exhibition was not decided upon at this stage, the chaos continued unchecked. In 1981 alone, the committee deemed 209 out of a total of 340 films inappropriate for exhibition.

A new political cinema?

At the beginning of the 1980s it was felt by the government that the new cinema needed new freedoms: freedom from the customary conventions of trade; from the influence of commercial partners; from the pressure of vested interests. A concrete notion of the new Iranian cinema was emerging on intellectual, formal and economic levels.

Prior to this period, critical writings on cinema had adopted notions of a national Iranian cinema that had long been informed by the rejection of Hollywood. Certain non-Hollywood-style Iranian films – most commonly art films – were marketed, distributed and reviewed along these lines. They were given a national label promising a cultural difference from American films and from those of other importing countries. Up until the 1980s, national cinema studies had focused almost exclusively on the film texts produced within this territory, sometimes seeing them as expressions of a putative national spirit. This national spirit, and thus the idea of a national cinema, had remained largely in the shadow of the preoccupation with anti-Shah and anti-Western sentiment however, while ideas about the nation-state were conceived primarily in essentialist, albeit anti-imperialist, terms.

A discussion of cultural domination took place. The newspapers, radio and television informed the populace about the various forms of Western exploitation of Third World nations: namely colonialism, neocolonialism and imperialism. Unlike 'classical' colonialism, the public was told, during which the direct political, economic and military control of the colonial power was evident at all times, neocolonialism ensured continued dependence through cultural means. Imperialism was considered a continuation of colonialism in Iran, and was defined as the unequal, oppressive relationship between strong and weak nations.

After the Revolution, filmmakers repeatedly interrogated the question of a national cinema. In the early 1980s, some filmmakers strove to create a militant cinema designed to combat the exploitation of the masses; some moved away from demonstrative cinema towards factual films. The main question was: how could the public be reached? There was a subsequent attempt to make political films, to analyse the struggle of the working classes. Yet there was little attempt to work with the very people whose ambitions and preoccupations these filmmakers were trying to express.

Although the 'political' film could in one sense be said to have had a longer history – an early adventure drama such as Sepanta's *Lor Girl*, with its polarisation of rural and urban, was likely to have been perceived by audiences as establishing the political genre, and many of the early films made during Reza Khan's reign had political aspects – Iranian cinema had never been directly political. How could it therefore adjust itself to these issues? Never had it been so important to fight for creative freedom, so urgent to express the criteria clearly. To create a new wave of political films, a so-called revolutionary cinema that by definition proposed new freedoms of consciousness, would be to renounce the pre-revolutionary filmmakers.

In clichéd terms, revolutionary cinema was a cinema at war with imperialism. This kind of filmmaking excluded profit, the star system and competition. Communication with the people was the objective in film, just as it was the aim of the struggle. To attain that communication, all the frameworks and formulas of an escapist and alienated commercial cinema were rejected. This cinema aimed to tell the truth, to search for another language capable of sending a social message to the spectator. The work of revolutionary cinema, it was claimed, should not limit itself to negative denunciation, nor to appealing for reflection; it must be a summons for action. It must appeal to the people's capacity for tears and anger, enthusiasm and faith; it must attempt to awaken them from the slumber and confusion to which oppression and misery had submitted them. It should be a cinema that would not only rebuild and express history but also actively participate in it.

The new Iranian cinema of the 1980s and 1990s promoted a programme of documentation in the broadest sense, renouncing both individual intrigue and the autonomous, isolated hero. If a single person stepped out from the crowd, he was a type, a social/biological hieroglyphic, an edited image of a real person representing the masses. The asymmetric, irregular, roughly hewn face of this new hero, devoid of stage make-up and symbolising strength, wildness and freedom, was ardently promoted by directors and circulated around the screens of the world. This was an aggressive challenge to the smooth, classical beauty of the past.

The early revolutionary years saw two types of protagonist: those who bring about their own downfall from a position of high social standing by passively maintaining their relationship with the Shah's regime, and ordinary people who become political heroes. Films dealing with this idealised political hero concentrated on his growing social awareness and activism. He must deal a blow to all the forces of the Shah's regime that are attempting to hinder progress, from the security police to the land and factory owners, and must brook the criticism of the passive people around him who disapprove of his revolutionary activism. He invariably loses his job as a labourer/farmer and dies a political hero. Through his death, both his detractors and the audience are brought to an awareness of the just cause of his fight.

Anyone could become a political hero in such films – a theatre actor in *Tareekh-sazan* (*History Makers*, Haadi Saaber, 1980), an artist in *Mojasam-e Saz* (*The Sculptor*, Muhammad Reza Momaged, 1981), a sportsman in *Panjomin Savar-e Sarnevesht* (*Fate's Fifth Horseman*, Said Motlebi, 1981), a technician in *Berenj-e Khunin* (*Bloody Rice*, Amir Ghavidel and Essy Niknejad, 1981), and a journalist in *Efrit* (*Demon*, Farshid Falaknazi, 1983). These emblematic figures would raise anti-Shah slogans, inspiring people to revolt and to die heroically in pursuit of their principles.

In the midst of the political turmoil that was wreaking havoc within the very fabric of society – Prime Minister Mehdi Bazargan's resignation over the hostage crisis, President Banisadr's dismissal by Parliament, and Iraq's invasion of Iran in the summer of 1980 – numerous films with political pretensions were produced. Indeed, every filmmaker became 'political', or at least pretended to be. Films that paid lip service to the armed resistance movement but in reality merely continued the traditions of the action genre flooded the theatres. In pseudo-political works such as *Fariad-e Mojahed* (*Mojahed's Battle Cry*, Mehdi Madanchian, 1979), *Enfejar* (*Explosion*, Samuel Khachikian, 1979) and *Sarbaze Eslam* (*Islamic Warrior*, Aman Manteghi, 1980) the protagonist, usually a devout Muslim, would rebel against tyranny and do battle with the forces of disorder. Some films were wrapped in the thinnest veneer of politics. In *Tolu-ue Enfejar* (*Dawn of Fury*, Parviz Nuri, 1981), a prisoner is released after a thirteen-year sentence, only to find that his son has been murdered. He sets about taking revenge on the four security officers responsible. The template is patently borrowed intact from the revenge genre of the previous decade. Another example is *Dad-Shah* (Habib Kavosh, 1983), whose eponymous protagonist was played by Said Rad, the hero of 1970s Iranian cinema. In the 1980s – and before 1985, when the censorship and control of the film industry was extended and pre-revolutionary actors were banned from the screen – Rad's persona evolved into a kind of political figure. Although *Dad-Shah* was based on the real-life drama of a famous bandit during the Pahlavi reign, it was no more than an action flick aiming to amuse and entertain.

The early political films of the 1980s were often excessively simple-minded and aimed, in terms of audience, at the lowest common denominator. They were badly shot, written and acted, and incoherently edited. The underlying myth of the Iranian political film, though it may not have been acknowledged at the time, had much to do with an increased interest in the significance of urban life, with the protagonist a surrogate for contemporary man, suffering the depersonalising pressures of society. The fight against the Shah was an excuse to express this.

What frequently distinguished these early films about political awakening was a world without humour or comedy. Only a few films mixed serious or dramatic elements with satire, as in Parviz Kimiavi's *OK, Mister* (1979), about the invasion of Western values into a very limited rural area. They also dealt with fewer emotionally sympathetic themes, such as love, since the political hero was more interested in intrigue and activism. He worked first and foremost for the Revolution, and in an almost offhand way courted a farm girl or working woman who was also a revolutionary. Since more often the films of this period were full of fury and rage, the implicit difficulty with the genre was how to make the driven, humourless, political protagonist likeable. Little background information as to his motives for taking the violent political road was provided, and the potential for investigating the social origins of protest was not developed; any true identification with these protagonists was therefore problematic. The explicit message of these films was similar to that of an action film: rebels are born, not made; they are incapable of compromise and can be stopped only by being destroyed by the dominant regime.

Due to the scorn, condescension and frequently violent antagonism of the hero towards the world, viewers were frequently expected to endorse pseudo-fascist doctrines. Indeed, one was often compelled by the political thrust of the film to accept values that one would not brook in a more reasoned environment. The outcry for censorship in the 1980s, then, seems rational enough. Yet it was not a simple matter of manipulation. The films presented political activists as stabilising forces who upheld traditional values, and were seldom concerned with examining the moral structure of their hero's society or the motivating factors in the life of the government agents they pursued. And even though it was accused of distorting values by glamorising violence, the film industry continued to portray the true brutality of criminal life, whose graphic depiction was not obliterated by the presence of charismatic performers.

As morally dubious as the political acts of the main character might be in the abstract, the necessary audience sympathy was usually created – as with all rebels in Iranian films – through his superiority to the corrupt value system or the viciousness of the other characters depicted in the limited world of the fictional narrative. We side with the hero against all opposition, not because we approve of his virtue and ambition but because the opposing characters (usually the Shah's followers) are too passive to attempt any form of protest, or are completely unscrupulous.

Thus the freedom-loving protagonist was – and often still is – portrayed as an admirable figure despite the violence of his activities. This man of the street or village acted as if the world belonged to him, and the audience could not fail to be caught up in the new confidence and strength of the working classes. One of the masses, he trod the path of enlightenment, from a repressed worker or farmer to a politically conscious revolutionary and fighter, from a proletarian victim of society to a leader. Yet this trajectory, we know, will be followed by his precipitate death. The initial contract between the film and its audience agrees on this imposed destiny. Though there is really only one possibility – failure – these films tried to persuade audiences that the final meaning of protest was neither anonymity nor death but to convince others to join the Revolution.

Iranian political films, then, operated in a specially constructed moral universe that resembled the real world but did not attempt to cope with its value systems. These films could not deal precisely with the moral issue of politics without becoming, on the one hand, social documentaries of considerable magnitude or, on the other, mere case studies. It must be remembered that despite the fact that elements of real political events would be used in these films, most gave a highly fictionalised account of history. We might note that there are precedents for this moral relativism in other crucial political periods such as the 1950s and 1960s. This fictionalisation of history applied, for example, to Ali Hatami's films, period pieces about the downfall of the Qajar dynasty or the emergence of Pahlavi power.

Despite the fact that villagers – about half of the country's population on the eve of the Revolution – had remained relatively indifferent to the uprising in comparison to city dwellers (indeed, some peasants took part in counter-revolutionary protests), many filmmakers returned to rural roots, taking flight from urban reality into the arms of nature. They positioned 'pure' peasants against powerful landowners who, naturally enough, stood for the Shah's regime. The farmers' conflict with landowners in *Daneha-ye Gandom* (*Wheat Seeds*, Hassan Rafi'i, 1980), for example, soon turns into a full-blooded rebellion against the state. The youth who picks up a rifle in the final sequence and marches forth with a mixture of courage and dignity is a symbol of the new revolutionary generation. Films like *Esyangaran* (*Rebels*, Jahangir Jahangiri, 1982) and *Dada* (Iraj Ghaderi, 1982) are prime examples of commercially successful adventure stories focused on feudal conflicts.

Films about the struggles of the urban proletariat were less common, since they were associated with leftist ideologies (which were not deemed central to the Revolutionary impetus) and ran the risk of being censored. If the hero was a member of the working class, he was depicted as a loveable *luti* such as Fardin: a man who was devoted to his class values and who never aimed to change the dominant situation. There were a few films, however, that dealt with the working-class struggle. These included *Parvaz be Su-ye Minu* (*Flight to Minu*, Taghi Keyvan Salahshur, 1980), in which a sacked factory worker becomes a guerilla and attempts to assassinate a Member of Parliament, and *Rasul, Pesar-e Abolghasem* (*Rasul, Son of Abolghasem*, Dariush Farhang, 1980), concentrating on brick-burners in the south of Tehran. In *Bazres-e Vizhe* (*The Special Inspector*, Mansur Tehrani, 1984), striking miners are killed by the owner of the mine, while the fishery workers in *Shilat* (*The Fisheries*, Reza Mir-Lohi, 1983) go on strike and kill a government representative. These films asked questions about the roles of and relationships between management and workers. Unfortunately, however, their scripts never delved deep into the issues they raised, opting for pat, simplistic solutions. Today they are largely forgotten.

At times, internal class conflicts were complicated in films by the presence of foreign forces, often culminating in an attempt to martyr their quasi-religious heroes. Three films made in 1983–4 fit this description. *Risheh dar Khun* (*Roots in Blood*, Sirous Alvand) focused on the Law of Capitulation, which had legitimised the Western presence in the 1960s. *Tofangdar* (*Rifleman*, Jamshid Haidari) shows an assault on religious people by the Cossacks of the Qajar; while *Farman* (*Command*, Coopal Meshkat) sketches a struggle between domestic landowners and British military forces. The conflict between the people and SAVAK also became a favourite topic with filmmakers, for example in *Shoja'an Eistade Mimirand* (*The Brave Die on Their Feet*, Abbas Kasai, 1979), which consists of three related stories dealing with different aspects of the struggle against SAVAK. In such films, regardless of whether the archetypal security officer kills or is killed, the people remain the ultimate victors.

The highly controversial commercial production *Doozakhiha* (*Hell-Raisers*, Iraj Ghaderi, 1982) was a defining moment in the cinema of the early 1980s. Its plot focuses on the heyday of the Revolution, during which the masses liberated political prisoners from the jails. In the confusion, a group of non-political criminals also escape and try to leave the country. On their journey, they are joined by a SAVAK agent and a capitalist. However – and this is what caused consternation – when the Iraqis invade Iran they decide to stay and help a village resist the enemy. Throwing themselves bravely into battle, they manage to fight off the invaders, though in the process a number of them are killed. The controversy caused by this sacrilegious distortion of the notion of martyrdom was exacerbated by the fact that its director and main actor (Malak-Motii and Fardin) were associated with the commercial cinema of bygone years. Consequently, *Hell-Raisers*, despite or perhaps because it became a top-grossing film, initiated a backlash against practitioners of the pre-revolutionary era.

As soon as it was screened, the film received a torrent of criticism from cultural policy-makers, with one newspaper writing: 'Those responsible for granting this film a permit are either devoid of a modicum of intelligence or, alternatively, are engaged in a deliberate act of treason against the people.'[72] Another claimed: 'The very least one can do is to ban this film from all Iranian theatres immediately, to apologise heartily to the long-suffering and martyr-breeding *umma* [Islamic community], and perhaps more critically, to bring to justice all those responsible for making this movie.'[73]

This case was seminal for another reason: for the very first time a petition calling the authorities to act against a particular film was delivered to the Hojjatoleslam (the clergy who lead the Friday prayers). The concluding paragraph of the 18-metre-long petition provides a flavour of the grievances it expressed: 'The ever-vigilant umma will not tolerate such insolence aimed at the sacred blood of our beloved martyrs.'[74] Yet the Minister for Guidance, Hojjatoleslam Ma'adi-Khah, who was handed the petition, criticised the media's hysterical campaign against *Hell-Raisers*: 'Sadly I seem to be confronted by people who, under the guise of Hezbollah and religion, ignore the most cherished principles of Islam. After all this ranting and raving, who would dare become a film controller?'[75]

If anything, this statement inflamed the situation. A prominent Member of Parliament, Esmail Fedai stated: 'The treachery, crimes, immorality and vice of pre-revolutionary actors and directors are there for all to see … Not only should their work be denied public exhibition … but they should be arrested and punished as a matter of course.'[76] Following this attack, Haddad-Adel, an influential cultural policy-maker, also criticised the criteria that had allowed the making and distribution of *Hell-Raisers*. Some time later, Ma'adi-Khah resigned; all evidence points to a forceful removal rather than a voluntary departure. After *Hell-Raisers*, almost all pre-revolutionary film practitioners, particularly actors and actresses, were banned from Iranian cinema, and harsher criteria were introduced in order to prevent future anomalies.

For film, this was not so much an era of politicisation as of disengagement occasioned by ideological crisis, and characters were commensurately lacking in emotional depth. A friend was a friend and an enemy was an enemy; villains were still closed and impenetrable – mysterious types from the West. If cinema were to convey a more complex message, these old types would need to be replaced by characters with more psychological depth; the clearness of a single meaning would need to be replaced by a multiplicity of meanings. The 'political' films of this era were more like fairy tales, since although they spoke about justice and political consciousness, they were not really concerned with the actual key events of the period.

Another type of film made after the Revolution, the 'social-study' films, contained direct guidelines as to the desirable qualities of a model citizen living in an ideal society, governed by Muslim laws, and inhabited by people with Islamic ethics, with little mention of non-Muslim Iranians. The society was introduced as one characterised by justice and equality and by a relentless struggle against any form of oppression or moral corruption; free from gambling, drinking, prostitution, seductive music and dance, immoral books and magazines.

The most important characteristics of this ideal person – the New Islamic Citizen – were presented as a belief in God, a love of nature, honesty, thrift, a sense of responsibility and dependability, loyalty and devotion, modesty and a passion for equality and justice. The model individual cleansed him/herself of carnal desires and sins and, as such, differed from Western counterparts whose lives were perceived as being aimed only at pleasure. The audience in such films was frequently reminded that while the imperialist ideologies of the West advocated personal comfort, self-indulgence, and greed above all else, Islam taught co-operation, service to others, defence of the oppressed and downtrodden, charity and self-sacrifice.

On the whole and despite the excitement of the era, the appeal of the majority of Iranian films of the 1980s seemed to originate in the vicarious experience of action, violence, social deviation, corruption and the determined drive for power. Weak action films, they completely missed the golden opportunity presented by the political atmosphere. The prime function of the Iranian cinema in its formative new era – to provide a window through which audiences might see the reality of the Pahlavi era beyond the walls that had blocked their view – remained completely unfulfilled.

Patriarchal attitudes and the politics of recuperation

Clearly, what was needed for culture was a period of calm, of recuperation and affirmation, even in the face of events (post-Revolutionary tensions and the bloody war with Iraq) that would appear to render these impossible. In this respect, Ayatollah Khomeini was an extraordinary phenomenon. He did not merely articulate the language of Iranians; he was the centre of Iran, polarising politics with a personality that spoke deliberately, assertively, and with complete conviction, and focusing the various ideological elements of the post-Revolutionary spirit. Moreover, he became an ideology in himself. Ayatollah Khomeini represented everything that religious people wanted to see and hear. His aggressive, anti-Western, anti-Communist discourses, his promise of a free utopian country in which every Muslim (of the appropriate gender, politics and colour) might thrive without interference, his offer to act as paternal guide, made him both an ideological magnet and a hegemonic force for religious people.

Gradually, the character of a brave paternal mentor, whose role it was to guide the hero towards wisdom, became a familiar narrative figure in Iranian film, appearing in a variety of guises. In many films the hero emerges from a de-classed mass and is raised up to religious and political consciousness by the wise man. In order to do so, he must accept everything the wise man says to him; a typical device of the genre that not only established the notion of compliance but also suggested that political activists had a superior impetus for their intense dedication to the movement, an ideological plan of action rather than an individual emotional response. The morality of the activist is in his readiness to think and operate politically from the moment he is confronted by the old man.

The wise-man persona not only teaches and legitimises the hero but, perhaps even more importantly, provides a sense of security for the audience. While the hero may go beyond his mentor's guidance in his deeds, the old man remains present as a control or safety limit. He looks out for the hero and reassures the audience that he will not get hurt, or overstep established bonds. The audience is therefore given a comforting, sustaining – even maternal – image of patriarchal power.

Certain veteran pre-revolutionary actors with theatrical backgrounds, rather than careers in films of a violent or sexual nature, were permitted to carry on working in cinema. Davud Rashidi in *Sheitan* (*Devil*, Akbar Sadeghi, 1980), *Marz* (*Border*, Jamshid Heidari, 1981), and *Tatooreh* (Kiumars Pour-Ahmad, 1984), and Jamshid Mashayekhi in *Peerak* (Koopal Meshkat, 1984), established this patriarchal mentor figure. Replacing the biological father, this mentor, wiser and more protective than the hero's own relatives, gives the young protagonist direction and control. The new maternal–patriarchal mentor supplied the ideological demand of the nation.

Spiritual themes

In 1983, the Farabi Cinematic Foundation, established as part of the Ministry of Islamic Culture and Guidance, announced its programme, proclaiming its role in setting the parameters for cinematic activities. The Foundation made a film entitled *Ansu-ye Meh* (*Beyond the Mist*, Manuchehr Asgari-Nasab) in 1985 as the ideal archetype for Iranian cinema. Part political, part religious, part mystical, *Beyond the Mist* was considered a model film, not just as a new genre, but also as a narrative pattern for religious analysis. Muhammad Beheshti, the head of the Foundation, wrote the screenplay, and the leading actor was Ali-Reza Shoja-nuri, the Foundation's Head of Foreign Affairs.

The film is about a man who travels to a northern city as the new Governor. Three terrorists try to assassinate him en route, but they mistake an identical car for his vehicle and are eventually killed by falling rocks. The spiritual theme of *Beyond the Mist* breaks through during the action sequences, in the course of which the Governor and his colleague are trapped in a wild river. They are miraculously rescued, and their surprising journey brings them to a new understanding of destiny, faith, life and death. At the end of the film the Governor is a changed man: merciful, self-sacrificing and heroic, and spectators are offered participation in this conversion by virtue of our identification with him. The river signifies his new spiritual and social freedom.

This genre offered a form of divine or sacramental experience to the audience through identification and assent. The most successful of the numerous and diverse films in this mode was *Nar-o-nay* (*Fire and Reed*), made by Said Ebrahimifar in 1989, in which a photographer embarks on a search to discover the identity of a man who has suffered a heart attack, a search that becomes a spiritual journey triggering nostalgic memories of a lost past.

At the centre of these films is a disruption of the primary narrative in which the central character undergoes a transcendent experience and finds a renewed faith in God. But the specifics of the spiritual dimension were secondary to their symbolic function. Religious films of this type had a decidedly Islamic tenor, inviting the audience to participate in the celebration of faith, and exhibiting a yearning for a personal relationship with God. But the audience did not welcome this highbrow genre, heavy with uninspired symbolism. By the end of the decade, the trend was over.

Anti-Americanism

One of the primary goals of the post-Revolutionary cinema was to establish an anti-Western attitude. Such an attitude saw the West as an oppressive, criminal force driven by an inhuman quest for profit, whose primary aims were to conquer the Muslim world, steal its natural wealth, exploit the cheap labour of the oppressed people, create a safe and expanded market for its manufactured goods, and crush its spirit. During the revolutionary period, Ayatollah Khomeini's inflammatory rhetoric played a major part in the wave of Muslim fanaticism and anti-American violence that swept far beyond Iran. In Saudi Arabia, a band of extreme religious zealots seized the Sacred Mosque in Mecca, the holiest shrine in all Islam. In Pakistan, a group, enraged by radio reports claiming that the USA had inspired the attack on the Mecca mosque, stormed and set fire to the US Embassy. Two Americans were killed, and 90 were rescued after seven hours. Angry crowds also threw rocks through the windows of the US Consulate in Izmir, Turkey; another crowd chanted outside the American Embassy in Dhaka, Bangladesh, and demonstrators in Calcutta stoned the US Consulate.[77]

Perhaps the most notorious attack, that on the US Embassy in Tehran, had occurred immediately after the Revolution, on Sunday 4 November 1979. A group of Iranian students had laid siege to the US Embassy in Tehran, seizing 44 American hostages. US President Jimmy Carter responded with a warning but to no avail. He then ordered a specially trained team of American military commandos to try to pluck the hostages from the heavily guarded Embassy. The secret operation failed dismally, ending on the powdery sands of Dasht-e Kavir – Iran's Great Salt Desert – in the shape of the burnt-out hulk of a US aircraft lying next to the scorched skeleton of a helicopter. In the wreckage were the burned bodies of eight American military aircrew. Iranian cinema never referred to the hostage crisis, but in 1988, Barbara Trent, an American producer/director, made a controversial documentary called *Cover-up: Behind the Iran–Contra Affair*, in which former presidential campaign aide Barbara Honegger testified that Reagan and his staff had tried to contact the Iranians prior to the presidential elections of 1980, to delay the release of the hostages as a campaign ploy.

Since 1979, despite the newfound political impetus, the staple of Iranian cinemas had consisted of the latest releases from the West, which included a generous dollop of soft-core porn. The sell-outs were films with revolutionary, and preferably anti-American, themes such as *State of Siege*, Costa Gavras's 1973 indictment of CIA activities in Latin America. Audiences could also see occasional features produced by their own film industry, which until recently had been concentrating largely on erotica but which was now in the business of dramatising the Revolution.

On 3 July 1988, US–Iranian relations reached an all-time low when the American warship *Vincennes* shot down a civilian Iranian airliner over the Persian Gulf, killing all 290 people on board. The American pilot claimed he had mistaken the airbus for a fighter warplane. Less than a week later, it was announced that the US officer who ordered the shooting of the airbus was to receive a 'mild reprimand'.

Unseen films

Between 1979 and 1983, a plethora of films were made that never saw the light of day, due to tightened censorship rules and internal quarrels at a time when a purely political perspective overshadowed all considerations. These films were rejected for their ideological confusion, irreligious themes, communistic influence, darkening of reality and threatening revisionism. Other reasons put forward for confiscating them, owing to the prevailing confusion in the laws governing distribution, were cited as follows:

> The employment of actors or directors belonging to the pre-revolutionary era.
> Lack of proper *hejab* for female performers.
> Plot lines about leftist groups and other illegal organisations.

During this period, the processes of controlling filmmaking and screening also became more and more complicated, and included four stages: 'Script Approval', 'Production Approval', 'Final-Cut Check', and 'Rating' into groups A, B, C and D. Classification was made on the basis of three criteria: technical sophistication, aesthetic qualities and content. Those films that were given 'A' classification were shown at peak times in the best cinemas, with higher ticket prices and longer runs; those classified 'D' were briefly shown in minor venues with the lowest ticket prices.

In *Mofsedin* (*Corrupters*, Aman Manteghi, 1980), a group of the Shah's supporters try to escape the country by boat. During their journey they encounter many obstacles and adventures, tensions come to the surface, fights ensue, and they set about killing each other. By the end, only two remain alive: the daughter of a general and a worker, who find themselves back in Iranian waters. The official reasons for confiscating the film were cited as: the misrepresentation of the Islamic resistance; misinformation; the promotion of violence, and the legitimisation of corrupt and sinful activities under the guise of humanitarian concerns. On top of the official justification, it should be noted that the film's director, Aman Manteghi, was a famed and successful commercial practitioner associated with the pre-revolutionary era, which, due to the lack of genuine cinematic criteria, is likely to have been the major reason behind the censors' decision.

Gholam-Ali Erfan's *Mr Hieroglyph* (1980), about the politics of a leftist young woman who is killed at the end of the film, was denied a permit on the grounds that it clashed with Islamic principles; promoted left-wing and atheistic ideas; encouraged terrorism and based itself on the dictum 'the end justifies the means'. The producers of Erfan's other film of the same year, *Goft Har Se Nafareshan* (*He Said, All Three*), who anticipated problems with the authorities, did not even bother to apply for an exhibition permit. *Mr Hieroglyph* was sent to the Cannes Film Festival. As luck would have it however, an Iraqi film entitled *Ghadesieh* was also sent to the festival in the same year. The festival organisers deemed the latter to be tinged with marked anti-Iranian sentiment, and it was rejected. In order to maintain a semblance of impartiality, they decided to reject *Mr Hieroglyph* as well, depriving the film of its one chance of finding an audience.

With *Panjomin Savar-e Sarnevesht* (*Fate's Fifth Horseman*, Said Motalebi, 1981), a fictive account of the developed world's export of addictive drugs to Iran, the censors' judgment was particularly severe. The central character is an addict who, due to his religious beliefs, resists the Pahlavi regime. The film was accused of superficiality in dealing with the root causes of social problems; opportunistic usage of religion to trick the masses; the promotion of corruption and indecency; the distribution of an ambiguous message; and the involvement of 'corrupt' film practitioners such as Iraj Ghaderi, whose films had been popular in the pre-Revolutionary period. The producers employed a two-pronged strategy for gaining a certificate: they altered substantial parts of the film whilst seeking the personal consent of key political and religious figures, but the censors remained unimpressed.

Kimiai's *The Red Line* (*Khat-e Sorkh*) was banned in the same year. It narrates the story of a high-ranking SAVAK agent, played by Said Rad, who gets married during the insurrectionary phase of the Revolution. At the beginning of the film he is a kind bridegroom but when he learns that his bride's brother is a political prisoner, he is unable to come to terms with the discovery. He subsequently becomes the victim of the changing system. Kimiai made some major alterations to the film including re-shooting many of the scenes and changing the dialogue so that the brother-in-law was transformed from a leftist into an Islamist. Despite all these efforts, the film, after an initial screening at the Fajr Film Festival, was denied a general-release certificate.

A film that ran into severe difficulties with the censors was *Whirlpool* (Hossein Davani, 1982). Centring on a dirt-poor family in the south of Tehran, it fell foul of the authorities because it dealt with touchy subjects like drug addiction and prostitution. In addition, the film was accused of promoting indecency; putting forward a non-Islamic economic manifesto; insulting the poor; depicting family members in a cold, irreligious and heartless relationship; and, more generally, of portraying theft, prostitution and addiction from a non-Islamic perspective. So scandalised were the censors that not only was the film banned, its negatives and soundtrack were also impounded.

Bahram Bayzai's career during this period reflected the tribulations involved in trying to make films within a cinema controlled by changing rules. His first two films of the 1980s, *Cherike-ye Tara* (*The Ballad of Tara*, 1981) and *Marg-e Yazdgerd* (*Death of Yazdgerd*, 1982), commented on contemporary Iran through reference to the past. *The Ballad of Tara* was banned because its actresses performed without scarves or veils. *The Death of Yazdgerd* was also banned and denied a certificate indefinitely for the same reason. It was based on a successful play about the death of the last Persian king before the Arab conquest, and boasted strong performances from a female cast that included Soosan Taslimi. Illegal videos of both were later issued, and were passed around interested circles, becoming cult films. Amongst numerous other films by various directors, two by Amir Naderi, *Josteju-ye Yek* (*The Search 1*, 1979) about the days of Revolution, and *Josteju-ye Dow* (*The Search 2*, 1981), about soldiers missing in action in the Iran–Iraq war, were also banned during this time.[78]

New hymns for the new decade

When the old social structure was overthrown, cinema was for a time virtually extinguished. When it gradually returned to life, it was peopled with new faces. Most of the pre-revolutionary Iranian film stars simply vanished from the posters, and many of them emigrated to the West. The representation of women continued to be one of the most problematic issues in the new era, when Iranian women went back under the veil, sometimes by force, hiding their hair and bodies. The main strategies adopted to deal with this situation in cinema were either to avoid stories involving women altogether, or adherence to a rigid code requiring that Muslim women be shown as chaste and maternal, never sexualised. Parliament occasionally debated the dilemma of television images of women, as in 1988 when the neck of an Iranian actress protruded from under her headscarf in the popular serial *Paiz Sahra* (*The Plains in Autumn*).

The most important thing about the emerging new heroine was her immutable clarity, her wholehearted nature and optimism. She talked in revolutionary hymns, her gestures expansive, her stride resolute, her voice loud and clear (essential for addressing meetings). In these films there was no hint of intimacy or of sensuality. The heroine never received declarations of love, since her affections could not be directed towards a single person but must be shared between everyone. If she did feel love for one person, it was of the platonic kind.

The heroines of the 1980s gradually descended from the heights of glamour and stylisation to the level of everyday life – they were forced to settle in the same neighbourhood as the audience. After the Revolution, society demanded from art a visual demonstration of an ideal life, a pledge to the audience that happiness lay neither too far in the future nor too distant from home. The simple boy and girl next door – familiar and ordinary – were elevated into this ideal.

After the Revolution the traditionally beautiful actresses did not immediately disappear, but the films in which they appeared went through a distinct change and their role within them shifted so that they took on a more negative image. Melodramas underwent their own revolution; the former regime now took the blame for destroying the happiness of the heroes. The film temptresses of the 1960s and 1970s such as Fakhri Khorwash and Farzaneh Taiedi were presented in films like *Dada* and *Miras-e Man Jonun* (*Madness My Heritage*, Mehdi Fakhimzadeh, 1981) as relics of the past, or as counter-revolutionaries. They represented the exotic remnants of a bygone age, playing tormented heroines in stories about life in a former decadent era. The camera, which had previously looked down on them from above, underlining their oppression, now began to look upwards from below, as if they were monuments.

Gradually, the beautiful, delicate Iranian heroine with her perfect face, narrow eyebrows and curled hair – the suffering victim of her circumstances – was replaced by the lower-class worker or peasant, the woman of the Revolution. This sharp change in the social status of the film heroine resulted in liberation from the prevailing 'star' conception of female beauty. Both the male and female 'anti-stars' of the 1980s were distinguished above all by their unattractiveness. In the case of the female protagonist, this apparently gave freer rein to the social role and behaviour permitted her.

This unattractiveness was unique in the history of Iranian cinema. The heroines of the 1980s were not complex, restless characters but were open and direct. Sensuality (in a highly veiled form) was now permissible only in women of the petty bourgeoisie – the idle 'boudoir' wives and daughters of the 'big bosses'. These women were now portrayed in an entirely negative way. Although they emulated the former queens of the screen, they became comic caricatures. Instead of learning how to operate industrial machinery, they struggled against weight gain, fussed about their big noses, constantly gazing at themselves in the mirror and changing their outfits. The former heroines could no longer appear even on postcards or advertisements, or in fashion magazines. And it was unthinkable that the new heroine would appear in this context; for her, only the political poster was appropriate. The 1980s struck a complete blow to the artificial model of womanhood; the new actresses were supposed to represent the masses.

A powerful indictment of the repression of villagers, *Madian* (*The Mare*, Ali Jeckan, 1985) is the most memorable film of the 1980s about women. The characters immediately breathe life onto the screen, remaining interesting despite simply pursuing their fate and without clever plot twists or surprises. When a farm belonging to a widowed mother of four is destroyed by heavy rains, her brother persuades the woman to alleviate her family's problems by giving her teenage daughter in marriage to an old man. Soosan Taslimi, a theatre performer who became an exceptional screen heroine of the day, is astonishing as the tough mother and Jeckan goes for the jugular in depicting her challenges. Taslimi expresses various degrees of rage at a system that she is powerless to change. In a scene in which she fights with her brother over a horse, such a tangible sense of reality is achieved that the audience can almost feel the grim clamminess of the rain.

This film presents the typical characteristics of the early 1980s protagonists – simple, of the people, and unburdened by a surplus of knowledge – but unlike the films of previous decades, Taslimi's character is less idealised than poeticised. She is granted a banal personal life: working on the farm, doing the laundry and so forth. She is allowed to be ordinary. The audience's ability to identify with such a heroine as mother, friend or sister was total.

The following year she was cast in the role of an energetic, cheerful mother in *Bashu, Gharib-e Kuchak* (*Bashu, the Little Stranger*, Bahram Bayzai, 1983), to which I shall return. Taslimi never reached the unattainable brilliance of a film star but she remained simple and accessible, and was embraced by the audience on the basis of her social optimism and her contagious conviviality. Her towering, dignified performance in *Bashu, the Little Stranger* was to play a significant role in the transformation of the Iranian heroine.

In *Shayad Vagti Digar* (*Maybe Some Other Time*, Bahram Bayzai, 1988), Taslimi delivered a particularly intense performance, acting out three different roles. The film was an exploration of the dilemma of women in the 1980s and became a rhetorical sounding board for the issue of identity. A TV commentator happens to spot his wife in a documentary about air pollution, seemingly engaged in conversation with another man, and becomes suspicious of her behaviour. With his usual intensity of purpose, Bayzai leads us through a range of emotions – agony, fear, jealousy, despair and guilt. But this is not an epic about repressed jealousy and family secrets. It illustrates the process of recovering one's identity through recollection of past experiences. Via flashbacks, we learn that the woman has undergone a strange childhood and is questioning her identity. There are several elements (such as the reference to air pollution), which are self-conscious in their social commentary. It is a dark, claustrophobic work, depicting an angst characteristic of the country at the time: suspicion, untrustworthiness, loss of identity. Sadly, this was to be Taslimi's farewell; she later emigrated to Sweden, never to return.

Ethnic minorities: distrust and anxiety

The Revolution constituted the most popular political struggle in modern Iranian history. It had drawn the majority of the population, especially in urban areas, into political activism aimed at the overthrow of the monarchical dictatorship. However, its participants did not have a common goal. Visions of a future Iran were diverse, ranging from an Islamic regime to a democratic socialist state. Activists among the non-Persian peoples, especially in Kurdistan, Turkman Sahra, Baluchistan and Khuzistan, sought a federal state, allowing extensive autonomy in administration, language, culture and economics.

The population of Iran is diverse in terms of national, ethnic, linguistic and religious formation. At the time of the Revolution roughly half were Persians who inhabited the central regions of Iran, especially the provinces of Tehran, Isfahan, Fars and most parts of Khorasan. The rest were Azerbaijani Turks or Azeris (making up 24 per cent), Kurds (9 per cent), Baluchis (3 per cent), Arabs (2.5 per cent) and Turkmans (1.5 per cent), who lived in their ancestral territories in the western, southeastern and northeastern regions. Other ethnic peoples include Armenians and Jews, dispersed throughout the country. They are distinguished from other non-Persian peoples by their lack of ancestral territories.

An important feature of the nationalities system is that each race is part of a larger nation, separated by international borders. Thus, the Turkmans are part of the Turkman nation, most of whom live in the neighbouring republic of Turkmanistan. The same is true of the Arabs, Baluchis, Kurds and Azerbaijanis. While there are independent Azerbaijan and Arab states, the Kurds and Baluchis do not have a state of their own. Thus the social, cultural, linguistic and political life of each nationality is shaped, to varying degrees, by developments in neighbouring countries. Another feature that complicates the question of nationality is the further division of ethnic groups along religious lines. The Persians and the Azeris are Shi'a, whilst Baluchis, Turkmans and the majority of Kurds are Sunni. Most Zoroastrians (a small minority religion) are Persians, whilst some Arabs are Shi'a and some Sunni. The Armenians, as an Assyrian people, are Christians. Socioeconomic and cultural differences are also significant. Persians and Azeris are more urbanised, while Turkmans and Baluchis are more rural and, to some extent, have retained tribal relations. Under these conditions, the question of nationalities during the early years of the 1980s was an enduring dilemma of the state.

When the monarchy was overthrown, the Islamic government gained full control of the country. Tehran was unable to exercise power over the ethnic groups, the privately owned mass media, or the universities, where a situation of dual power prevailed. Moreover, a considerable number of political parties, old and new, religious and secular, liberal and leftist, had come out into the open to seek a role in the post-monarchist state. Under these circumstances, the Islamic Republic tried to extend its control over these autonomous entities while striving to Islamise the vast state machinery inherited from the Pahlavi monarchy. On 8 April 1981, Iran's state radio had announced a ten-point programme granting legal recognition to groups that had waged an armed struggle against the Islamic Republic, provided they laid down their weapons and changed their attitudes. The offer appeared to be aimed mainly at the Kurdish Democratic Party (KDP), which had been fighting the government in Kurdistan.

Several films of this period reflected such ethnic diversity and conflict. The events depicted in *Moj-e Tufan* (*Wave of Storm*, Manuchehr Ahmadi, 1981), for example, took place on the shorelines of the Persian Gulf. *Tofangdar* (Jamshid Heidari, 1983) was about the people's clash with the Cossacks in the Gilan province. The fishermen in the northern part of Iran rebelled against the government in *The Fisheries*, while the people of *Sirus Alvand* (*Rooted in Blood*, Risheh dar Khun, 1984) protested against the Capitulation Law during the 1960s. *Otoboos* (*The Bus*, Yadolah Samadi, 1985) was about a cynical competition between two dynasties in an Azerbaijan village. Even *Samandar* (Mahmud Kushan, 1985), ostensibly a film about horseracing in Turkmanistan, demonstrated ethnic barriers.

Blood and battle: war comes to Iran

The eight-year Iran–Iraq war had begun on 22 September 1980, when Iraq invaded Iran at eight different points, bombing ten Iranian airfields. Iraq's

President, Saddam Hossein, had announced his country's unilateral abrogation of the 1975 Algiers agreement, which had arbitrated on the various boundaries and borders between the two countries. His goals seemed to have been to defeat the Islamic Revolution, to win the territorial concession from Iran and to establish himself as the Arab world's leading figure. Iraq turned out to have more allies than Iran during this period. Only Syria and Libya, whose leaders were rivals of Saddam, sided with Iran. Saudi Arabia and Jordan, fearing the spread of Islamic Revolution, backed Iraq, as did the Soviet Union, as well as France, which depended on Iraqi oil. For years the war remained at a stalemate, with Iraq bombing Iranian cities, refineries and in some cases oil tankers and then deploying more firepower and poison gas, despite a long-standing international ban. Moreover, the United States increasingly sided with Iraq. From 1983, America supplied Saddam with grain credits and satellite intelligence.

Years later, Abolfazl Jalili, a young Iranian filmmaker, wrote in the catalogue of the 1999 Fukuoka Film Festival in Japan:

> We experienced a long war. It was a war that hurt our spirits much more than our bodies. Every day, radio, television and newspapers sent messages of 'blood' and 'battles' ... There were bombardments while people were working away from their families. No one could tell which part of the city was attacked and whether their loved ones were alive or not.

The role of the Revolutionary Guard in the war became the subject of a number of films. A military body, this was one of the strongest institutions to be produced by the Islamic Revolution, and was a primary instrument in promoting its goals. It became a complex and cohesive body without losing its ideological zeal. Although it was instrumental in perpetuating ideology, the interests of the organisation ultimately took precedence over ideological purity whenever there was conflict between the two. The durability of the Revolution lay, in part, in its ability to create revolutionary institutions to absorb the many social forces that had contributed to the overthrow of the Shah. Despite Ayatollah Khomeini's personal authority, the regime would have been unable to handle the many challenges it faced had it not established this institutional base. The Guard proved itself adept at parrying the many political challenges it faced during its existence, especially in its early years. It was flexible enough to survive beyond the Revolution, emerging as a separate institution despite many calls for its complete dismantling. It also survived rebellion by several ethnic groups, as well as bombing in Tehran that resulted in the death of several major leaders in 1981, and the Iraqi invasion. It was then able to modify its strategy and tactics for prosecuting the war against Iraq during the US occupation of the Persian Gulf in 1987.

Films such as *Jan-bazan* (*Bravados*, Naser Muhammadi, 1983) demonstrated the co-operation between the Army and the Revolutionary Guard during the war through the relationship of two old friends on either side. In *Parchamdar* (*The Standard Bearer*, Shahriar Bahrani, 1985) the Guard fights the enemy both at the front and in the cities. It is also active in the war-stricken cities of *Balami be Suye Sahel* (*A Boat towards the Shore*, Rasul Molagholipur, 1984) and in the battlegrounds of *Ofogh* (*Horizon*, Rasul Molagholipur, 1988) and *Ensan va Aslaheh* (*Man and Weapon*, Mojtaba Ra'i, 1988).

The great impact of the war on Iranian society was reflected in every aspect of life, and steered Iranian cinema in a new direction, with the depiction of ground, air and sea battles, as well as the bombing of cities and Iraq's use of chemical weapons. These war films flooded into the theatres. Most of the early Iranian war films were commercial ventures, aimed at entertainment, and the characters were one-dimensional – stereotypical 'good guys' versus 'bad guys'. The Iraqis were depicted as barely human, cruelly evil, sinister and deceitful, spitting out harshly accented commands. But even in this time of war, screen depictions of Westernised Iranians were more negative and stereotyped than those of the Iraqis. The ideal Iranian soldiers, proclaimed these simple exercises in propaganda, were honourable sons and good husbands.

Of all the major Iranian genres, only the war film has been a consistent outlet for propaganda – that is, for the delivery of a social message with a predetermined point of view rather than a message evolving from the dramatic conflicts portrayed on-screen. In order to get this message across, the characters frankly expressed what they stood for and what they opposed. War films were considered by the authorities to be a necessary aspect of national life, since stories of individual tragedies were seen as having an ennobling effect on those going to the front. The majority of war films focused on battle situations, and described the pressures on soldiers, their relationships, fears, hopes and values amid the continual violence and imminent perils of their environment. The very act of delineating a group under battle conditions created sympathy for their hardships and respect for their survival strategies. Numerous virtues were propagated through these films, including courage against great odds and strength through unity, described in terms of a small group of soldiers who are able to prevail when attacked by a much larger group of Iraqi soldiers.

Yet the main aspect of the glorification of war was the depiction of the successful strategy of the country as a whole. The detailed and intricate problems involved in taking a well-defended enemy referred in a larger sense to the Revolution itself. The propaganda value of most Iranian war films was in their justification of the way in which society went about the business of conducting a war that could lead either to victory or to terrible defeat – a defeat that would mean conditions far worse than those endured during combat, since it would be considered the defeat of the Revolution. Films used the war to rally support for the ideology of Islam and to issue a warning about the dangers of complacency. The repeated message in the media was: 'We are not fighting with Iraq, we are fighting with the enemies of the Revolution.'

The war film was an important genre in terms of quantity, if not in terms of quality. In early films, emotional factors tended to determine the portrayal of conflict, and the majority were poorly made or highly forgettable minor films glorifying war. The best only partially portrayed the aspect of battle, putting emphasis instead on the gallantry and self-sacrifice of individual soldiers. However, Iranian cinema gradually grew up during the war. The gravity of the situation – the proximity of the enemy, the bombardments, the sacrificing of the pleasures of civilian life to the rigours of military service – meant that audiences demanded either better escapism or more reflective content in their films and, after it had adjusted to the new situation, the industry began to answer their needs.

In the meantime, a large proportion of Iranian war films not only relegated the actual conflict to the background, but focused either on a personal relationship unravelling during wartime or on a theme that required the atmosphere of war without the turmoil of actual fighting. Sometimes the subtlety of their references to the war makes these films only borderline members of the genre. Love stories set against the backdrop of war take on new dimensions, with the lovers placed in a precarious position and facing an uncertain future, finding love at a time when life itself may have little meaning.

One of the most significant aspects of the war films of the 1980s lay in their equation of patriotism with friendship between men. The metaphoric equation of war with religion, gender, country and family was inevitable. All could be understood through the window of war.

Within the genre of the war film are two sub-categories: the prisoner-of-war film and the special-mission film. The first category deals with the problems of maintaining a decent standard of daily life in captivity. As the plot develops in the Iranian prisoner-of-war film, the prisoners effect their escape both through their religious faith and through the subversive harassment of their Iraqi guards. Their continual attempts to escape preoccupy the prison administration and undermine the self-confidence of the Iraqis. Their escape attempts, in other words, might be seen as an extension of the military campaign, and considered successful regardless of the outcome. Almost as consistently structured as the prisoner-of-war category, the special-mission film adheres to a certain narrative pattern in a variety of situations. The special mission is usually devised in answer to some urgent, unexpected problem or opportunity: a small group of fighting men volunteer for a dangerous assignment. In Iranian special-mission films these men exhibit two obvious characteristics: physical toughness (sometimes represented through a crude attitude towards the reality of their surroundings) and, almost paradoxically, religious sensibility and a near-philosophical approach to what they are doing and why. Their heroism aims to demonstrate the inseparability of war and religion.

A further group were the action combat films that were especially popular among young audiences. Akbar Sadeghi's *Payegah-e Jahanami* (*A Military Base in Hell*, 1982), Samuel Khachikian's *Oghabha* (*Eagles*, 1984), and Shahriar Bahrani's *Gozargah* (*Passage*, 1986) were particularly successful. These films about special combat forces became the model for the war films to come: action as an entertaining morale-booster.

At the peak of the war, many films were made in which ordinary, simple men go to the front voluntarily, encouraging the younger generation to join

FIG. 20 *The Scout* (*Dideban*), Ebrahim Hatamikia, 1988.

the battle. *Rahai* (*Deliverance*, Rasul Sadr-Ameli, 1983) and *Hesar* (*Fence*, Hojjatollah Seif), *Do Cheshm-e Bisu* (*Two Semi-Blind Eyes*, Mohsen Makhmalbaf), *Zang-e Aval* (*The First Bell*, Nezam Fatemi), *Ma Istade'im* (*We Are Standing*, Akbar Hor) and *Sarbaz-e Kuchak* (*The Little Soldier*, Said Bakhshalian), all made in 1984, showed the anger, the religious and patriotic stirrings and other 'gut feelings' of the ordinary citizen.

As the war developed, Iranian cinema had to deal with new themes and stories. One of the first films to take a new approach was *Dyar-e Ashegan* (*Lover's Place*), directed by Hassan Karbakhsh and made in 1983. It told the story of a young man of no particular convictions or beliefs, who at the end of the film volunteers for military duty, believing that the war will purify his soul. Other films treated the subject of war not as an over-sensationalised action-packed adventure but rather as a bleak reality with serious consequences. These films inevitably placed human motives under a microscope, representing a journey of self-discovery. Most were based on the actual experiences of their young makers, who had served in the military or the Revolutionary Guard and endured war at first hand. Ebrahim Hatamikia, Rasul Molagholipur, Hossein Ghasemi-Jami, Kamal Tabrizi, Jamal Shurjeh and Javad Shamaghdari are notable among this group of filmmakers. Hojjatollah Seif's *Kilometer Five (The Fifth Kilometre)*, made in 1980, also offers a more realistic portrayal of war, avoiding the usual sensationalisation of action films, and aimed to shift public opinion against the war.

Ebrahim Hatamikia is the best known of the war filmmakers. His three films, which also explore Islamic culture, *Hoviyyat (Identity*, 1986), *Dideban (The Scout*, 1988) and *Mohajer* (1990), were highly praised by critics in Iran. *Identity* is about a young, irresponsible man who is mistakenly identified as a wounded soldier. Having witnessed the bravery and sacrifices of others, he undergoes a moral and personal transformation. Hatamikia is concerned here with the religious identity that was forged during the war. In *The Scout* and *Mohajer*, he effectively portrays human beings in the heat of battle against the background of personal adventure.

The central theme of most of the films by this group of directors was martyrdom in the service of faith, formulated into a slogan by which the protagonists live. In most of the films a lonely man denounces all material possession and earthly desires to find salvation in martyrdom. Kamal Tabrizi's *Obur (Crossing*, 1988) and Hossein Ghasemi-Jami's *Cheshm-e Shishei (The Glass Eye*, 1991) were exemplary of such films, in which the hero transforms concepts such as loyalty, sacrifice and nationalism into a spiritual journey. Audiences witnessed his loneliness and pain in separation from his family and loved ones, but victory for him did not necessarily mean returning home alive.

These films were particularly vulnerable to conflicting ideological pressures, since filmmakers often depended on the armed forces for expensive props: planes, ships, tanks, and so on. The army's aid to Iranian cinema in the form of these materials came with strings attached. It required that each film adhered to its guidelines for a true interpretation of military life, and complied with accepted standards of dignity and propriety. Support was forthcoming only for scripts that satisfied the army's interpretation of these requirements.

One of the most significant results of this phenomenon was the production of numerous war documentaries by institutions such as the Art Department of the Islamic Relations Organisation and the Islamic Republic of Iranian Television. In the early 1990s the Cinematic Institute of Holy Defence was founded for the sole purpose of making war films. As part of this movement, specially designed towns were built, and the army was used for shooting war scenes, with the government providing special assistance. These documentaries included Rahim Rahimi-Poor's *Doleto* (1984), about a famous prison in Kurdistan, and his *Otagh-e Yek* (*Room One*, 1986) focusing on the Hezb-e Kumeleh (Kurdistan Kumoleh Party), which fought against the government during the war. *Hamaseh Darreh-ye Sheeler* (*The Myth of Sheeler Valley*, Ahmad Hasani-Moghaddam, 1986) was based on the leftist Hezb-e Democrat-e Kurdistan (Kurdistan Democratic Party).

Ownership and the commercial bourgeoisie

At the heart of the economic debate in the Islamic Republic of Iran was the question of ownership. Should state ownership be consolidated and even extended further, in accordance with the provisions of the Constitution, or should clear and legal frameworks be introduced that would give the private sector confidence and an important and legitimate role in the economy, in order to offset the Constitution?

Even though much economic activity had by now come under central government control, the debate about how to construct an 'Islamic' economy raged on. The commercial bourgeoisie became the most active faction of the ruling class. The importation of intermediate industrial products, capital goods and consumer goods continued unabated. The economy as a whole was increasingly crisis-ridden throughout the Mir Hossein Mussavi premiership (1982–89). Rising food imports testified to the continuing deficiencies in agriculture, and stagnation was evident in the manufacturing and industrial sectors. Many of the state-owned establishments were operating at a loss.

The government's problems were magnified in the second half of the 1980s with the substantial drop in oil prices and the subsequent decline in Iran's revenues.

At the peak of the war, *Ejareneshin-ha* (*The Lodgers*, 1987), a comedy of extremes written and directed by Dariush Mehrjui, became a controversial commercial success. *The Lodgers* brimmed with satirical allegories concerning ownership, class differences, and the general life of the middle classes in the 1980s. When a landlord in the Tehran suburbs dies without an heir, leaving the ownership of his building up for grabs, a confrontation between the lodgers is inevitable. The outstanding cast, including Akbar Abdi, unravel the personal repressions of each family member. But it is Ezatollah Entezami who is most captivating. He plays the landlord, a charismatic conman, whose every act has a hidden agenda, despite his surface affability. Mehrjui is adept at weaving multiple subplots and characters into the main story, imposing order, good humour and a rattling momentum on a naturally chaotic subject. The sequence in which the lodgers decide to compromise, getting together to pacify a group of labourers at a supper ceremony, is particularly memorable.

During the 1980s the transition from the strong, masculine hero to screen comedians such as Ali-Reza Khamse and Akbar Abdi – and occasionally Mehdi Hashemi – hinted at a social order in danger of collapse. In an era of deteriorating cities, unemployment and escalating violence, the underdog again became the Iranian hero. Though idealised images of soldiers at the front existed side by side with these comic figures, audiences preferred the humorous antics of the latter. It was with lackadaisical and cowardly relatives or with the lurking counterculture of corrupt black marketeers that these men did battle. Comic heroes, little men beset by their circumstances, appealed to an audience composed not of the elite but of ordinary people, for whom life was a struggle. Khamse and Hashemi often starred in films that forced the audience to choose between the attractions of being a good person or of being successful. The comic heroes were often outsiders, unsuccessful, lacking in physical prowess but battling against hostile forces and callous social institutions. Khamse, who became a highly successful comic actor, often directed his wit against himself. Though acquiescent to authority, his enthusiasms and mannerisms frequently estranged him from

FIG. 21 *The Lodgers (Ejareneshin-ha)*, Dariush Mehrjui, 1987.

the other characters. This coalesced with the counterculture's continuing estrangement from the family.

The politics of paranoia and the films of Mohsen Makhmalbaf

The mid-1980s was characterised by paranoia and this was reflected on the screens. Secret or 'parallel' police forces were so ubiquitous that innocent individuals often fell into their clutches. Justice was political and was rarely done. The rich and influential could get away with anything; the media cared nothing for the truth. Within this established order only an occasional examining magistrate or investigative journalist stepped out of line, and he was likely to end up dead. Anyone could fall victim to manipulation, and the state locked up those who stumbled upon uncomfortable truths, or created scapegoats for particular crimes and disorders.

Zang-ha (*Rings*, 1985), made by the young religious members of the Hozeh-ye Honari-Eslami (Islamic Centre of Art), is the best example of the new political films that sprang up in response to this climate. This allegorical film presented an unnamed, deeply disturbed society embroiled in a futile search for an unknown killer, who seems to pick his victims indiscriminately. The murderer is 'death' itself. The police, whose tentacles reach everywhere, are under the total control of political power and are licensed to use any method against those who step out of line.

Among the figures who had risen to prominence over the first years of the Revolution as the creators of the New Iranian Cinema, Mohsen Makhmalbaf remained the most persistently unclassifiable maverick. The religious aspects of his early films; the handling of history in *Naser al-Din Shah, Actor-e Cinema* (*Once upon a Time, Cinema*, 1981); his ironic treatment of leftist groups in *Boycott* (1985); the philosophical points in *The Pedlar* (1986); the anarchy of *Marriage of the Blessed* (1989); the humanism of *Bicycle-Run* (*The Cyclist*, 1989); the controversial sexual subject matter of *Time of Love* (1990); and the lush, colourful wilderness of *Gabbeh* (1996) together constitute a lucid exploration of the most bizarre and inexplicable manifestations of life in post-revolutionary Iran.

A dedicated Muslim, Makhmalbaf was born in Tehran in 1957, and lived with his grandparents following the separation of his parents. He left school at the age of 11 to help support his family, joined a militant anti-Shah group and, at the age of 17, was seriously wounded after attempting to steal a policeman's gun in order to rob a bank for the cause. After four years in prison, he was released along with many other political prisoners a few months before the Revolution. Following his release, Makhmalbaf engaged in political activities for a short time, then began a period of extensive artistic experimentation, during which he wrote plays, short stories and screenplays. At the same time, he set up the Islamic Propagation Organisation in collaboration with other artists devoted to Islamic ideology. Among its proclaimed objectives was: 'Presenting Islamic ideology through artistic media, and challenging artists whose ideas and modes of expression are not harmonious with those of the Organisation.'

Makhmalbaf began working in radio, published his first novel in 1981, and made his debut film, *Tobeh Nassouh* (*Nassouh's Repentance*) in 1982. All three of his first films reflected his strict adherence to Islam in his approach to religious themes, and did not arouse much interest. Their simplicity contrasts with the questioning sense of anarchy in his later work. His fourth film, *Bykot* (*Boycott*, 1985), confirmed his status as a talented and controversial political filmmaker.

Boycott deals with the themes of man, faith and death. It focuses on a leftist guerrilla in prison during the 1970s. (Makhmalbaf's preoccupation with the roles of leftist groups is also reflected in some of his plays and stories.) The volatile young protagonist, played by Majid Majidi, has been arrested by SAVAK and sentenced to death. Initially, he cannot understand what is happening to him, but is finally forced to come to terms both with himself and his ideology. His nemesis comes when he discovers that the other leftist prisoners do not consider him a reliable ally. Thinking about his past relationships with them, he begins to doubt the validity of the ideas on which he has based his life. He decides to face himself and break the leftist codes. Redeemed in time for his execution, when he eventually faces death it is for a different, more spiritual cause.

Boycott is a melodrama set against a stormy political background. In the course of combative conversations and action sequences, the political duplicities and personal secrets of its characters are finally brought out into the light. In this stagnant enclave, the atmosphere, almost tangible to the audience, is more gloomy, dank and tense than had been risked by an Iranian picture for years. In its pessimism *Boycott* is reminiscent of the films of the 1970s but added to this is Makhmalbaf's great energy and psychological accuracy. It is the central human relationships – emotionally caustic, damaged, perverse and nihilistic – that make this one of the most original Iranian prison dramas. In the end, however, the unimaginative solution of redemption is insufficiently bold.

Dastfroosh (*The Pedlar*, 1986) constituted a turning point in Makhmalbaf's career. The film is set amongst the poor city folk of modern Iran, and its main theme is humanity itself. The first of three episodes tells of a couple driven by poverty to seek adoptive parents for their newborn daughter. The next concerns an unstable man, laughed at by his neighbours, and with only his aged mother for company. The last tells of a youth (the pedlar), who is suspected of betraying his colleagues. The stories portray those at the bottom of the pile, yet the light of the human spirit flickers on. Each character embodied an extreme stereotype of what Iranian society had become.

These films were symbolic without being poetic. Underneath the continuous stream of political agenda slumber allegories of man, God and life. *The Pedlar* is full of cynicism: its references are to a doomed life and its characters are sometimes grotesque and bizarre. This exotic treatment was a pretext for subjectifying Makhmalbaf's political fantasies. The subject was 'us' – the viewers, our deepest fears, and the ease with which we can be made to lose ground, delude and hate ourselves, to surrender our spirit.

Arusi-ye Khuban (*Marriage of the Blessed*, 1989) protests against the dominant economic situation, governed by the rich, during the war. A young fundamentalist Muslim, who is suffering from shell shock, leaves hospital having only partially recovered. He is advised by his doctors to get married in order to help him recuperate. His fiancée's father, however, is a businessman who plans to marry off his daughter to a rich man. While trying to resolve this problem, the protagonist gains a new understanding of social issues, and decides to go back to the battlefront – the only place where he believes he belongs. This disturbing film constitutes a rare display of political and moral surgery that goes far further, for once, than merely laying out the instruments.

In a key scene, during his marriage ceremony, the man indulges in a political outburst against the materialistic way of life in the city, which was most evident during the war. We see the anxiety of battle through the eyes of this tormented veteran, who is not a typical war hero or anti-capitalist youth. He is a protestor, haunted by the desire to revenge the dominant system. He resents the hypocrisy of those who make the rules, which seem to his sense of social justice crooked and full of traps. He is an anarchist in the true philosophical sense, a man who sees all social life as a cunning force and rebels against every possible system, protecting his spiritual freedom whatever the cost, either to others (including his fiancée), or to himself. Yet his honesty redeems his moral cynicism. Another way to see

FIG. 22 *Time of Love (Nobat-e Asheghi)*, 1990.

him is as an idealist at heart, so disgusted by the hypocrisy of society that he reacts with apparent nihilism.

In 1990, Makhmalbaf released two particularly controversial films: *Nobat-e Asheghi* (*Time of Love*) and *Shabha-ye Zayandeh Rud* (*Nights of Zayandeh Rud*). After their screening at the Fajr Film Festival in Tehran, the fundamentalist papers attacked Makhmalbaf for making films, especially *Time of Love*, about illicit affairs. Islamic protestors focused on the theme of adultery in the film, claiming it a profanity against Islamic rules and Iranian culture. They accused Makhmalbaf of lack of dedication to the Muslim faith. Adultery remains a controversial subject in the Islamic world and cannot be filmed in Iran; *Time of Love* is still seen as problematic despite the fact that Makhmalbaf shot the film in Istanbul in 1989 and cast Turkish actors in order to distance the story from Iran. Puzzle-like in structure, *Time of Love* narrates three versions of a woman's extramarital affair, each with a different ending. In the various versions of the story Makhmalbaf plays with the dynamics of the three-way relationship and the changing roles of the characters, causing the meaning of the adulterous act to shift on the slippery slope of conventional morality. *Nights of Zayandeh Rud* focuses on the obsessions of a retired colonel and his young unmarried daughter. The colonel, who is anti-Shah, has lost both his wife and the use of his legs in a car accident.

Neither film was ever released in Iran; *Time of Love* was screened at a few film festivals years later. When it was shown in Israel in the 1990s, it provoked yet another debate, to which I shall return. To view Makhmalbaf's development as either a progression or regression would be to assign a system to one of the most unsystematic careers in Iranian cinema. Even to regard his work as a totality is difficult because it is so varied. How, for instance, does one link *Marriage of the Blessed*, a protest against defiant capitalists who ignore their war veterans, with *Gabbeh*, a panoramic fairy tale shot in the heart of the countryside?

Several years later Makhmalbaf expressed his dismay at the popularisation in the West of the notion that restrictions placed on filmmaking somehow contributed to the quality of cinema: 'This is nonsense. You can't create in such a restrictive, controlled environment.' He argued that the best Iranian films came out in 1985–90, when censorship was at a low ebb, adding, 'Every time there is a bureaucratic shake-up, a whole new set of technocrats comes in. At the beginning they cause a lot of problems. But after a few years, things get better. They come to love cinema. Because good cinema makes people more human.'[79]

Makhmalbaf's attitude towards cinema, and his rigorous cinematic dialectic, offers an inexhaustible source of energy. Even when not overtly political, most of his films seem to have drunk from political and religious springs. Gradually, Makhmalbaf's work began to move away from political dilemmas. In these later films he asked his audience: 'Do politics mean more than everything else to us?' By the 1990s, he was clearly answering this question in the negative.

Little Stranger

Bahram Bayzai's *Bashu, the Little Stranger* (1983) was a landmark of 1980s Iranian cinema. It tells the tale of a boy who loses his family in war-torn southern Iran and escapes to the peaceful north. There, the dark-skinned, foreign-speaking boy is homeless and alone. Controversially, he is taken under the wing of a stern farming woman and mother of two, played by Soosan Taslimi, whose husband has gone to war. Bayzai was known for his positive images of strong women, and was consistently interested in observing the struggle of a central character who is neither morally despicable nor particularly heroic, yet is forced to criticise the political authoritarianism overshadowing life. Dealing with recent history, the film takes political aim both at racism and at those in power, using the forgotten children of war as ballast for its drama. It deals not with the waging of war, but with its effects, concentrating on civilian victims.

Remarkably, despite its loaded premise and its unavoidably dark themes, the picture was praised on its initial release, though it was banned from 1986 to 1989 and, re-released just before the end of the war (which ended in 1988), was only screened for the public a year later. Tender, intelligent and affecting, it was successful partly because its appearance in Iran in the 1980s was so unexpected, and partly because its anti-war message was hungered for so universally. It also laid emphasis on overcoming the physical and psychological problems of rehabilitation, a theme that is explored more generally when, at the end of the film, the woman's husband returns home as a casualty of war.

Bashu, the Little Stranger remains a sincere, sometimes shattering and often courageous attempt to depict the scars of war through human relationships. Not just a beautiful piece of work, this is a film that grasps the political nettle and hangs on for dear life. The splendid performance of Adnan Afravian, an ordinary young boy from the war-stricken regions of southern Iran, as the trapped, intelligent refugee torn between racism, war and love, epitomises all that was best in Iranian cinema in this decade.

It was the humanist, anti-war and anti-racist sentiments of the film that kept it from the screen for three years. Years later Bayzai commented:

FIG. 23 *Bashu, the Little Stranger (Bashu, Garib-e Kuchak)*, Bahram Bayzai, 1986.

> At first, the censors saw no problem; then, they kept looking at the movie and found many problems. The film was set during the Iran–Iraq conflict. A boy from the south witnesses the massacre of his family and flees north where a peasant woman whose husband is at the front takes him in. He becomes head of the family although he is black, they are white, and they do not speak the same language. One of the objections was that a good Muslim boy would have stayed to fight; he would not have deserted.[80]

Bashu, the Little Stranger not only brought Bayzai immense success at home but also introduced him to a wide international audience. Into an otherwise conventional narrative structure, Bayzai inserted values that had been both scorned by avant-garde theoreticians and ignored by a commercial cinema thriving on a diet of sentimental fantasy. His techniques included unobtrusive camerawork, quality acting and visual clarity without fussiness. He treated the audience with neither contempt nor obsequiousness, and was comfortable with both melodramatic sequences and intimately subtle emotional scenes.

The film also posed interesting questions concerning the relationship of politics, cinema and audience, without laboriously dwelling on secondary issues. In the context of a degenerating political system that encouraged nepotism rather than merit, *Bashu, the Little Stranger* was seen by Iranian film critics as a bastion of hope, honesty and integrity. For those depressed by a seemingly endless trail of films dependent on visceral pleasures aimed at the titillation of jaded emotions, his example was a positive relief.

Bashu, the Little Stranger did nothing, of course, to stop the war, but its anti-war theme remained almost unique in the films of the 1980s. It captivated Iranian audiences through its ability to summarise and encapsulate the complex effects of the war, and through its vivid visual statement of social malaise. Increasingly, films became vehicles for the dramatic analysis of the collapse of social morality, destroying the lives of private, impotent individuals.

1988: the turning point

With the end of the Iran–Iraq war in 1988, Iran's regional and international policies were concentrated on an attempt to restore and improve relations with its neighbours and the West. This was seen as a precondition for the end of Iran's diplomatic isolation, and the return of stability to the Persian Gulf region.

The hunger for information and coverage of events during the war had created a new, informative role for the media. With the end of the war there were signs that the decade's strict rules were giving way to a marginally more relaxed cultural atmosphere, and a debate about social reconstruction began. In September 1988 Ayatollah Khomeini gave his official blessing to the use of musical instruments and approved the playing of chess, which had been banned after the Revolution. Beyond the eclectic internationalism of film and television, a new atmosphere of public criticism and a concern with national culture would be ushered in.

The 1990s 8

Western challenge

By the beginning of the 1990s, a change of theme had become necessary in Iranian cinema. To the policy-makers, the next step was obvious: the problems of contemporary life must be dealt with. Due to the initial difficulties in the shift from the war period to the post-war era, and the vested interest of those who still wished to glorify the war, the early 1990s constituted a period of transition. Yet, looking back, strong claims could be made that this period witnessed a renaissance, since it saw the production of a far wider variety of films – albeit of fluctuating quality and ranging from the simplistic to the polemical – than in any other period.

The more extreme religious figures of the Revolution had relied on a mixture of national chauvinism and xenophobia to rally the people against the monarchy for absorbing foreign influences. This nationalism was also an undercurrent in some urban guerrilla and revolutionary ideology, especially amongst those recruited from religious families. At the end of the 1980s, the impact of this xenophobic attitude, and of Iran's decreased contact with the Western world throughout the 1980s, came to light in the cinema.

At the same time, American and Israeli films began to portray Iranians in a negative light, with Iranians taking the place of Orientals as the alien 'other'. The American coup of 1953 had rendered Iran a 'good' Muslim country, as opposed to those 'bad' Muslim countries favourable to the Soviets. But when Iran deposed the Shah to establish a Muslim state and subsequently took the American hostages, it became evil, radical and terrorist in the eyes of the USA, while other Arab countries became 'good' by virtue of their war with Iran. Iranians in major Western films of this period were often depicted as rich and stupid, or as barbarous, irrational terrorists. *Down and Out in Beverly Hills* (Paul Mazursky, 1986), in which one of the families in the neighbourhood is an unhappy Iranian household ostracised by the community (in one scene, a lonely Iranian boy looks sadly at the Americans in their big house and sighs) provides a positive representation in comparison with that of *Into the Night* (John Landis), made a year before. This comedy revolves around an American nerd (Jeff Goldblum) helping a beautiful woman (Michelle Pfeiffer), who is being pursued by a band of zany Iranian killers. These figures of fun destroy everything in their path, even a chatty parrot. Interestingly, Landis casts himself as one of the unshaven Iranian bad guys. David Zucker's *Naked Gun 2 ½* (1991), a slapstick comedy starring Leslie Nielson, also alluded unfavourably to Iranians. The film was censored in Turkey due to the Turkish government's concern about damaging relations with Iran.

Walt Disney's animated film *Aladdin* (John Musker, 1992) was one of a series of clichéd, often self-contradictory narratives underlining popular American assumptions about the Muslim Middle East. In the mythical 'Arabia' of this film, Iran and Iraq are represented at one remove. The CIA substitutes for the British regiment of the original story, and the representation of the East is normalised through a Western-style romance.[81] *Aladdin* posits the immense destructive potential of an armed Muslim Middle East by connecting, in the film's Westernised notion of Iran and Iraq, the dishonesty and disloyalty of the Eastern Other with the dangers of its lust for power. The East is reconfigured through a pastiche of its own myths and codes as forms of exotic performance within the spectacle of Western entertainment, defining the Muslim identity through shifting sands, minarets, confused identity, unstable power and nomadic allegiances.

Perhaps the best example of a Western film of this time featuring a negative portrayal of Iranians is *Not without My Daughter* (1990), directed by Brian Gilbert for MGM and Pathé Entertainment, and filmed in Israel. It starred Sally Field, whom some Iranians remembered as the likeable but ridiculous nun in the American series *The Flying Nun*, which ran on Iranian television in the late 1960s. Field played the real-life American woman Betty Mahmoody, on whose book the film was based. Betty accompanies her Iranian-born husband, Moody, a doctor who has lived in the USA for twenty years, on a visit to his homeland in 1984. Once there, he decides to stay, and she learns to her horror that in Iran she no longer has any rights. Not only is she restricted to her home, but she is not allowed to use the phone, has her passport taken away, and is told that her daughter will be raised as a Muslim. She decides to find a way to flee the country with her daughter. As related in William Hoffer's simplistic screenplay, Iran turns Moody from a civilised, sophisticated man into an intolerant monster within a fortnight. The basic issue is in this transition from sympathetic husband to violent oppressor; there was little the actor Alfred Molina could do to clarify the psychological issues ignored by the script. Sally Field, on the other hand, is given enough screen time to engage the audience's sympathy, which she does with an earnest, emotional performance as a stereotypical middle-class American. When Iranians viewed the film on pirate videos, they saw not just a propaganda film against the Iranian government, but a story with the mythical 'Beauty (American) and the Beast (Iranian)' theme at its core.

The film was not much admired by the critics, however. An American video guide wrote: 'Cartoonish Iranians and heavy-handed melodrama make this true story hard to take.'[82] Even years later, debate about the film was still hot. When *Not without My Daughter* was shown on a French television channel just a few days before the highly publicised Iran–USA World Cup football match in 1998, Iranian officials protested harshly, claiming it was 'a conspiracy, an intrigue against Iran'.[83]

Yet Iranian filmmakers were also making anti-American films. The most notable anti-Western Iranian film of the 1980s had been *Tigh va Abrisham* (*Blade and Silk*, Masud Kimiai, 1986), in which the Western block plots to send tons of heroin to Iran in order to weaken its war effort by turning young men into addicts. But in the 1990s the enemy was more directly targeted. In Ahmad-Reza Darvish's *Eblis* (*Lucifer*, 1990) the wife and children of the depressed hero die in the commericial Airbus that was notoriously – and supposedly accidentally – shot down by the Americans in 1988. In *Dadsetan* (*Prosecutor*, Bozorgmehr Rafia, 1991), an inspector investigates a medical scandal in pre-Revolutionary Iran, and traces it back to an American company. When two Americans are arrested in Tehran and sent to prison, a US colonel comes to free them. His agents massacre an Iranian family, and at the end of the film he escapes with the Americans. In a scene in

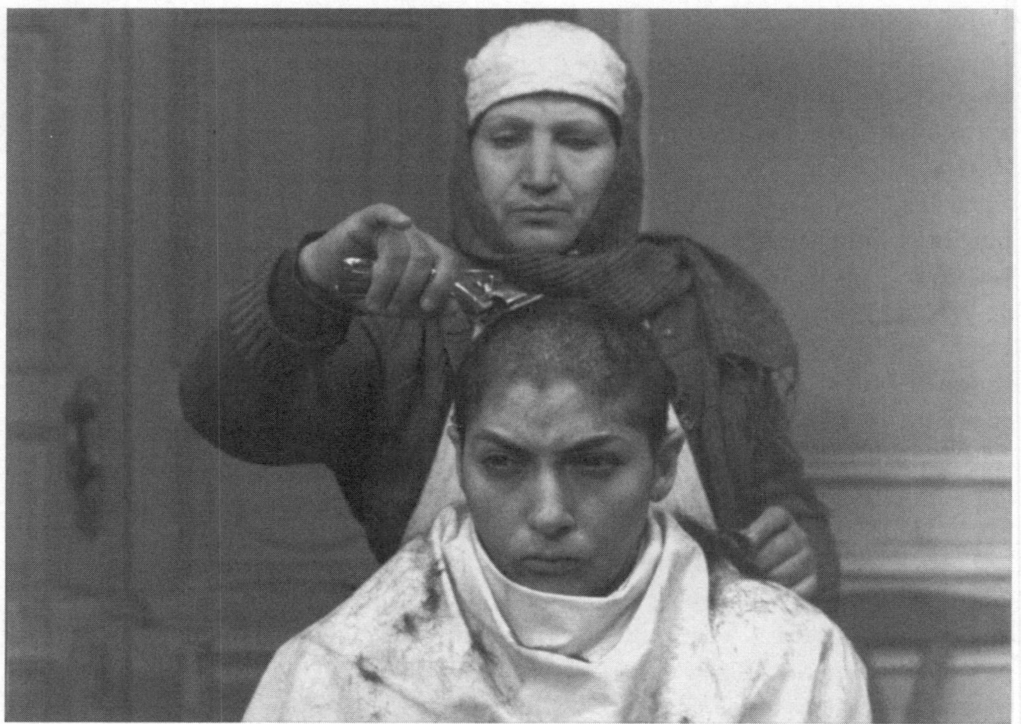

FIG. 24 *Lead (Sorb)*, **Masud Kimiai, 1987.**

which an Iranian man shouts 'American idiots!' the colonel kills him in cold blood.

In a number of films, foreign enemies plotted to overthrow the Iranian government. In Ali Shah-Hatami's *Taghib-e Sayeha* (*Chasing the Shadows*, 1991), a well-shot action film, the explosion of a bomb in the heart of Tehran is the first step in a major plan to attack the state. A royalist group in *Ruz-e Sheitan* (*The Devil's Day*, Behruz Afkhami, 1994) transport parts of an atomic bomb to Iran a week before an inspection of the Iranian nuclear installation by representatives from the International Agency for Atomic Energy. The sabotage theme is repeated in *Hadeseh dar Kandovan* (*Accident in Kandovan*, Jahangir Jahangiri, 1995), in which anti-government groups send millions of false messages to Iran, and the young Iranian official in *Diplomat* (Dariush Farhang, 1995) finds himself up against hostile opponents in Turkey. Occasionally major projects were sponsored by large organisations. *Jang-e Naftkeshha* (*Battle of Tankers*, Muhammad Reza Bozorgnia, 1994), for example, based on attacks on Iranian oil tankers during the war, was made with the direct support of the National Oil Tanker Company.

The history of anti-Zionist Iranian film goes back to the mid-1980s. Farshid Falaknazi's *Efrit* (*Demon*), about the activities of Zionists in Iran, was made in 1984 but was never screened. Masud Kimiai's exceptional film *Sorb* (*Lead*, 1987), set in 1948, featured a young Iranian Jewish couple who wish to move to the newly founded state of Israel in Palestine; they come of age when they experience the violent scene of immigration to the Promised Land. Between 1990 and 1997, numerous Iranian films about the threat of Israel and Zionism were made. The events of Habib Kavosh's *Atash-e Penhan* (*Hidden Flame*, 1990) take place in Lebanon, where the members of a Jewish Lebanese family are massacred by Israeli agents and a young couple tries to fight injustice and discrimination. *Bazmandeh* (*Survivor*, Seifollah Dad, 1994), based on a novel by Ghasan Kanani, is about a Lebanese doctor and his family, who are forced by Israelis to leave their homeland in Haifa. Abolghasem Talebi's *Virangar* (*Destroyer*, 1995) tells of an Israeli plan to send seven special agents to Tehran for the purposes of sabotage and the overthrowing of the Islamic Republic of Iran. These themes reached their peak in 1997 with *Zan-e Royai* (*An Ideal Woman*, Hassan Karbakhsh) in which a Lebanese woman journalist writes an article against Israel, loses her job in London, and is then kidnapped by the Israelis.

In the summer of the same year the screening of four films by Mohsen Makhmalbaf at the Jerusalem Film Festival caused a huge controversy in Iran. These were *Time of Love* (which had not yet been released in Iran due to its adultery theme), *Salam Cinema* (1994), *Non va Goldun* (*A Moment of Innocence*, 1996), and *Gabbeh*. All the films received warm reactions at the festival but when the news of their screening spread to Iran, the authorities described the situation as another conspiracy on the part of the Israelis, condemning the showing of Iranian films in Israel.

Meanwhile, the West was still considered to be guilty of *tahajom-e farhangi* (cultural invasion). Cited amongst its major offences was the distribution of immoral films, music and literature; encouraging higher levels of consumption and the use of luxury items manufactured in the West such as cosmetics and fashionable clothes; and attacking the cultural heritage of once-proud nations by taking away their national identity and replacing it with pale carbon-copies of the Western personality. Young Iranians were encouraged to battle against such tyranny and oppression.

Yet cultural contradictions were rife and debates continued to rage in the newspapers and journals. The government ban on satellite dishes, for example, was often ignored, so that viewers were able to see female actresses unveiled. Thus a gulf developed between Iran's Islamic public culture and a private, illicit subculture. Moreover, some 14 years after the Revolution, Iranian television channels still consisted of English, American, Japanese, French or Russian films and cartoons.

In July 1993, the Ministry of Guidance and Islamic Culture assigned a team to develop video clubs, to buy film and video rights selectively from international television production companies and to develop cable television in order to prevent the expansion of black-market video piracy and the spread of illegal satellite dishes. The young urban generation, especially in Tehran, began to focus on video and computer games, Western music and fashionable clothes and trainers. The main debate therefore revolved around the idea that Iran was caught between two conflicting cultural pulls. The question being asked was: should Iran go towards the indigenous and the religious or towards global popular culture stemming mainly from the West? If anything, the demand for the latter was stronger than ever.

In 1990 the United States census reported that 226,123 Iranian immigrants were living in the USA, a growth of around 100,000 since 1980. These were individuals who had either been born in Iran, or were of Iranian ancestry but born neither in Iran nor in the United States. The rapid growth of this population, combined with the variety of the group's socioeconomic conditions, created some of the most diverse ethnic geographies in the United States. The themes of immigration and the influence of Western values, which had been present in Iranian cinema from the second half of the 1980s, were carried through into the next decade in films including Bahram Reypur's *Visa* (1987) and Manuchehr Askarinasab's *Hey Joe* (1989), in which a young man who is desperate to emigrate to the USA meets a cowboy called Joe, and makes a dream-like voyage to America. *Adam Barfi* (*Snowman*, Davud Mirbagheri, 1994), in which an Iranian man dresses as a woman to secure his visa to America, was the quintessential film on this theme. It was banned for three years and only came to the screen during the presidency of Muhammad Khatami, who was elected in 1998.

Political loyalty to the home country was axiomatic to most of these films, often symbolised at an allegorical level. Whether they worked with fact or fiction, their main theme was the struggle against Western values. With the exception of *Snowman*, they were seldom courageously controversial or free from romantic tendencies but they had undeniable political implications. They were films made in a socially aware but still isolationist Iran.

Yet despite these hostilities, it was a time of reconciliation with the West in terms of cinema exhibition and distribution. Iranian films travelled around the world, and Abbas Kiarostami's *Zir-e Derakhtan-e Zeitoon* (*Under the Olive Trees*) was nominated for an 1994 Academy Award. This was the first Iranian film to receive major distribution in the United States by Miramax. Iranian cinema was beginning to act as a political envoy.

Questions regarding the past

After the Iran–Iraq war, men came home to pick up the pieces of their lives. Audiences were exhausted by the tragedies of clichéd melodrama and a gradual reappraisal of values produced a new protagonist for the screen. At last, here were films that did not celebrate the historically pompous or heroically solemn but concentrated with a newfound sophistication on ordinary, prosaic existence. In place of the flamboyant, monumentalising war films with their abstract ideals, the camera began to look at daily life as if through the eyes of the veteran. Cinema rediscovered the value of unobtrusive details, the pleasures of family life, or of simple friendship. For the first time, heroes had to tackle difficulties – including the questioning of their faith – that came from within their own lives.

As at other points in Iran's recent history, economic collapse led to a redefinition of appropriate male behaviour in film. If the post-war era questioned the viability of free enterprise in Iran, its cinema produced

FIG. 25 *The Sergeant* (*Goruhban*), Masud Kimiai, 1991.

types who could make any business work; who could overcome adversity through individual perseverance. In this way, the economic system was not subjected to critique. The message of these films was that if a man were aggressive and competitive enough, all would be his – as if such dreams had not been shattered.

Cynicism stemming from the aftermath of war was evident in Kianush Ayari's *Abadaniha* (*Abadanians*, 1993), based on Vittorio de Sica's classic 1948 film *Bicycle Thieves*. This simple but emotionally powerful story is seen through the eyes of a young boy from a war-refugee family living in Tehran and focuses on his father's struggle to provide for his family during the war. The father works as a driver, using his own car, of which he is very proud. Disaster strikes when the car is stolen. Father and son set out on a desperate quest to find it, a quest that not only leads them into the bowels of

Tehran but also forces them to question their priorities and values. Ayari's deceptively simple black-and-white camerawork keeps us rooting for them every step of the way. The man is pitted against an entire city of nameless and insensitive faces, his plight even more tragic when seen through the tear-filled eyes of his son. The boy brilliantly symbolises the innocence that can be endangered during hard times.

As the decade progressed Iranian films became markedly more sardonic. The acquiescence of the Iranian public in the late 1990s to an all-pervasive corruption further encouraged filmmakers in their insistence that evil stems from ordinary people's devotion to individual success and material gain. This trend was directly demonstrated in many films in which a serviceman returns from the war to find that his wife has become a stranger, or that his business partner is cheating on him, and consequently begins to question whether society has been worth fighting for.

Although many Iranians had seen all the war films they wanted to see, they continued to be produced in the 1990s, although they now tended to suggest a pragmatic stoicism on the part of the soldiers. If these films were not unduly troubled with a well-drawn enemy it was because the new enemy was within, just as the real drama lay not on the battlefield but in a cynical struggle between the individual and society which began to overshadow all other concerns.

As these films began to accord a less important role to the Iraqis, they started to depict more candidly the adverse effects of war. Masud Kimiai in *Dandan-e Mar* (*Snake Fang*, 1989) illustrated the harsh way of life experienced by young immigrants who had come to Tehran during the war. If this film is about the lives and loves of the socially excluded, it is also about Tehran, whose poor areas are portrayed as a dilapidated wasteland of stagnant water and tiny dwellings. Kimiai's achievement is to make visible the gritty lives of refugees, the unemployed and orphaned children. The attentive, indefatigable camera lingers over their faces, moving doggedly back and forth through the space of the film. Films such as Kimiai's slightly later *Goruhban* (*The Sergeant*, 1991) and Ebrahim Hatamikia's *Vasl-e Nikan* (*Union of the Good*, 1992) looked sensitively at the veteran's agonising experience of the military/civilian culture clash. Gradually, war films became even grimmer and less hopeful, revealing the savage excess of casualties and martyrdom.

Towards the end of the decade, in 1998, the jury at the Fajr Film Festival in Tehran chose *Ajans-e Shishei* (*Glass Agency*, Ebrahim Hatamikia) as the best film. An Iranian version of Sidney Lumet's *Dog Day Afternoon* (1975), in which a man in need of money for his friend's operation tries to rob a bank and becomes a media sensation, Hatamikia's version centres on the attempts of a panic-stricken *Basiji* (a member of the volunteer forces) to save the life of his comrade, who has a piece of mortar shell embedded in his neck. He needs to be dispatched immediately to London for surgery but does not have a plane ticket. By taking hostage the people in a travel agency and threatening to shoot them unless he and his friend are delivered to the airport, the *Basiji* ultimately reaches his objective. Parviz Pasrastooie, as this most unlikely hostage-taker, is both amusing and tragic. The taut script and Hatamikia's disciplined and insightful direction highlight both the suspense and the absurdity of the situation.

Glass Agency, produced late in the decade, was nevertheless the first film of the 1990s to critique Iran's social tensions through the eyes of political fundamentalists and extremists. As such, it worked as a useful model for the production of other films that cast a critical eye on Iran's social and political circumstances. Although it operated primarily as a satire on extremism, it managed to popularise a contemporary type of drama that, while still concentrated on the war, was aimed at those who did not remember it, focusing on the undiagnosed tensions of the past that lurked behind a surface normality. The hero of the post-war era was forced to confront social problems that had long been ignored or wished away in facile invocations of reformism. Thus *Glass Agency* became one of the most controversial and political films of the period.

Notwithstanding romantic illusions about valour, liberty and righteousness, the ultimate reality of the war was the desolation of its heroes. It was no wonder then that the tone of Iranian films in the 1990s should make the drastic reactive shift into the personal universe of the lonely and alienated ex-soldier. They took as their task the refurbishment of post-war life, and their protagonists were confused and bewildered.

Rasul Molagholipur's *Majnun* (*Possessed*, 1991) differs from its predecessors in its acknowledgement not only of the pressures of poverty after the Revolution but also of the presence of anti-government groups. In it a young man agrees to collaborate with these groups in the planting of a bomb in Tehran in order to raise money to marry the girl he loves. The difficulties of post-war Iran, still torn by internal dissension, are brought to life in *Possessed* in all their ambiguity, and the social antidote to economic hardship is seen as ever greater ruthlessness. The film's excessive violence and rapid-fire editing had special relevance to a society in which the jobless had no idea which way to turn, and whose younger generation was fixated on violence. Its depiction of the vulnerability of youth was unique for its time. With its compelling action and depiction of a repressive, dark city, *Possessed* created an atmosphere of intense claustrophobia. The frank treatment of the drive to protest was a recurring motif in Molagholipur's films. The fight against the inevitability of social forces was central to his works, intensified by its combination with the theme of anarchy, which became the protagonist's only possible expression of defiance.

Molagholipur's was a cinema built on tension and paradox. Though he was a sensitive filmmaker, his films are notable for their violence. His work should be seen in its political and social context, where desperation in the face of a rapidly changing society was never far below the surface. His strategies could generally be explained in two ways: as motivated by the desire to make the spectator aware of social values, and as the expression of his own uncertainties regarding the war. In his *Safar be Chazabeh* (*Journey to Chazabeh*, 1996), two friends travel back in time to the 1980s, where they meet their old war companions. In this rapid-edit time-travel drama with virtually no plot, the war scenes are presented with a new sense of understanding. The infliction of horrible, excessive damage by troops on the civilian population is depicted for the first time. Molagholipur seeks to immerse the audience totally in the nightmare of the two men on this misguided adventure, and manages to do so in a number of highly effective war scenes. He avoids glamorisation through gritty sets and authentic clothes and mannerisms, while the camera is not squeamish in its increasingly lurid depiction of dead bodies. A surplus of lingering long-take scenes concentrating on the corpses almost brings the narrative to a halt. The invisible enemy is everywhere, swiftly dispatching the young soldiers.

Journey to Chazabeh asked questions that had never before been asked by Iranian films. Had the military action been dictated by good organisation or bad bureaucracy? Who had held the authority to command the troops? Had he put the mission before his men? Was there an army doctor, and if so, was he truly available to tend to the wounded soldiers? Who died and who survived?

It is still a harrowing and very effective political war film. The battle scenes showing the suicide attacks in which scores of soldiers rush to certain death are devastating and brutally authentic; the barrage through which a commander leads his men – the camera moving inexorably through the carnage – is a hurricane of death. Molagholipur profiles in this film naked power and its effects with a graphic explicitness seldom seen in Iranian cinema. A particularly striking and effective strategy is the use of mesmerising, inhuman tracking shots for the trenches and battlegrounds while employing circling camera movements to convey the discomfort of civilians. What is particularly valuable about this unique film is that it treats its characters as human beings; it reminds us of the reality behind what we are seeing.

Molagholipur consistently expressed the struggle between spontaneous impulse and conscious control. Much of the quality of his work stems from the interaction between these opposed drives. He implicitly acknowledges the validity of each, and the dislocation (*Journey to Chazabeh*) or delusion (*Possessed*) inherent in the human condition. *Hiva* (2000) is a grim drama about a woman who accepts a marriage proposal a decade after the disappearance of her husband during the war. In her search into the past of her lost husband, she reads his letters and remembers the war years. The war scenes are well shot and throughout the film various attitudes to war and faith are explored, compared and juxtaposed. Reliving the man's life, the woman realises that she has led an empty existence without the values her husband believed in and fought for. Nightmares, dreams and reminiscences blend together as space and time are dislocated. It is a brutal work that uses flashback to show how much Iranian society has changed since the war.

Hiva lays emphasis on the character of a woman at the heart of the war, and conveys a message familiar in Iranian cinema: that while a man is defined by what he is capable of doing to or for others, a woman is defined by what can or cannot be done to her. This dynamic had operated in a particularly interesting way in Iranian war films of the 1980s. The image of women in that decade became the ideological matrix from which Iranian cinema constructed its image of the audience – an audience that the state wished to create as passive, inactive, fearful and submissive – in other words, 'feminine'. The aim of this 'feminisation' was to defuse social and political dissent. Cinematic narrative often seeks to resolve contradictions and to provide models for action in the present, though it may use the past to achieve this. *Hiva*, on the other hand, was directed at those who wished to enact social change through violent or radical confrontation – women, veterans, and others who were pressing society for recognition of their political position. It made use of images of women and the feminine to prepare audiences for a different view of the significance of female roles during the war.

Children: utopia or reality?

That the cinema of the 1980s had tended to favour older actors and actresses revealed a suspicion in society regarding the younger generation. Those who attacked Westernisation saw the youth of the Shah's era as the enemy within, while the older generation represented social order. This was also, as we have seen, the time of the anti-star, when non-commercial filmmakers were insisting that cinema should move closer to life and further away from fantasy and mystification. The generation of actors and actresses who came of age in the late 1940s and early 1950s were thus well suited to the main roles, and those who had seldom appeared in commercial films before the Revolution were preferred – notably Ezatollah Entezami, Ali Nasirian, Muhammad-Ali Keshavarz, and Soraya Ghasemi.

Gradually, however, children began to constitute a significant presence in Iranian cinema, defying the domination of these older actors. Through their use of children, a handful of directors not only changed Iranian cinema but also altered the vision of Iran from the outside. These films were identified at international film festivals as belonging to a 'new wave' in Iranian cinema. They were praised as non-commercial artworks with a new form and vision. The children in these films could be monumentalised into a universal alter ego, and provided a contradiction of the view of an uncivilised Iran promoted by the foreign media over the previous two decades.

In the immediate post-war years, poetic realist films, notably by Abbas Kiarostami, provided an immediate response to the desire to wipe out the material and ideological legacies of violence. The use of children in these films denounced the horrors of the war and/or dealt with themes central to reconstruction such as poverty, unemployment, the shortage of housing and social strife. Moreover, in their social and geographical inclusiveness they represented a bid to redefine the coordinates of national and cultural identity. This realism suited Iran's post-war mood: a public desire for a more honest view of Iran. It succeeded in taking cinema away from the domain of melodrama, placing it where it more properly belonged: in the streets with everyday people. Iranian realist films registered ambivalence toward technology and progress based on Western attitudes, and realism as elaborated here gave shape to the Iranian social/national imaginary at that time. It can thus be seen as a historical and political phenomenon, not new in the late 1980s and early 1990s, but privileged in that period as a nation-building tool.

Reality is a slippery concept at the best of times, however, and our understanding of it is more or less a subjective matter. Realism in the context of these films suggests morality and sincerity of purpose rather than a strict adherence to the principle of impartial observation of social phenomena, and in the case of Abbas Kiarostami's films, which employ personal subjectivity, subverts the notion of objective empiricism. The filmmakers whose work was shown outside Iran during this period (from veterans such as Amir Naderi to Kiarostami and the younger directors including Mohsen Makhmalbaf and his daughter Samira) were theoretically pledged to realism, yet the reality they served up was far from raw. This is partly because it was filtered through the new filmmaking regulations, sometimes as a tool of education, and in a few cases reflected an interest in developing cinema as an art form. In addition, the use of contemporary characters and themes, the focus on the lower classes and the casting of unknown, non-professional actors as authentic characters distinguished these films from local commercial productions of the period. Yet they presented a curious contradiction. On the one hand their stylised artistry and fictional narratives constituted a divergence from real life, and on the other they could be seen as a true reflection of the bizarre reality that characterised Iran. *Sib* (*The Apple*, 1998) by Samira Makhmalbaf, and *Zendegi va Digar Hich* (*And Life Goes On…*, 1990) by Kiarostami, for example, were personal artistic statements and at the same time films about contemporary Iran.

The major impediments to the creation of a self-image that Iran could embrace were excessive social problems including the plight of refugees from war-stricken cities, poverty and unemployment. But there were dangers in endorsing too strongly its opposite: namely, material affluence. Affluence had negative connotations in the popular imagination: the eager pursuit of money could unleash the undesirable social traits of cupidity, violence and criminality. Since implicit in the creation of a new society is a vision of utopia, an idea of what kind of society is desirable and what sort of citizens should inhabit it, forms of mass culture can become instrumental in embodying the tension that results between the utopian ideal and the bedrock of practical considerations to which it must be linked.

Much of the realist cinema of post-revolutionary Iran can be seen in this 'utopian' vein. Broadly speaking, the utopian sensibility was linked to a strong moral stance vis-à-vis fetishistic images of material objects such as money and cars. Filmmakers could provide what seemed a naturalistic portrayal of social reality – the world of business, money, corruption and greed – while at the same time implying through point-of-views shots and sympathetic, morally upright characters the availability of a utopian solution. This ethical code suggested that honest hard work was a desirable social virtue. At its simplest level, this was conveyed through the poor, steadfast villager, the honest labourer, and hardworking children who were touched but not corrupted by their social environment. In other films the utopian sensibility was replaced by an exploration of anxiety, pessimism, fear and resignation. Such films took as their raw materials the contemporary experience of the lower and labouring urban classes, and presented the city as the microcosm of the people.

Simple stories such as the search of a child for a lost friend or stolen money now became common. The Revolution, the occupation of the US Embassy, and the war with Iraq had made a profound impact on the way in which cinema developed in Iran, and on the kinds of films produced in the country, with respect to Islamic rules, anti-Western attitudes and propaganda. These events had brought about the isolation of the majority of Iranians from direct contact with the outside world. The political struggle between the Iranian government and Western powers led to an external perception of ordinary Iranian people as rough, ruthless and inhumane. Cinema was the only medium to attempt to show a different image of Iranians. The representation of children obviously had a long and complex history in Iranian cinema, shaped by a concentration on the family order and the rules of melodrama, but the conception and importance of childhood on screen in the 'golden age' of Iranian cinema, from 1984 to 1994, represented something quite different.

If one considers some of the most important features of cinema after the Revolution, it is easy to see why children came to the forefront. These features include the abandonment of the majority of familiar actors and actresses from the industry, and the exclusion of sex, song and dance. It was harder to get scripts passed by the censorship board and many of the codes and symbols used in the Shah's era had been disposed of.

The appearance of children in the films of the 1980s was not unique to Iran and other countries such as Brazil, France, Sweden and Yugoslavia were experimenting with similar subject matter. But in Iran the tradition had roots as far back as the late 1960s, when a government agency known as the Centre for the Intellectual Development of Children and Young Adults (CIDCYA), which Iranians refer to as Kanun, was founded in order to make films and publish books for children and young adults. Starting out as a producer of short films and animation, CIDCYA employed few directors and animators in the beginning but its early results were very different from the commercial films of the period.

In 1969, *Nan va Kucheh (Bread and Alley)* by Abbas Kiarostami was one of seven films produced by CIDCYA. This 11-minute experimental film was about a small boy confronting a menacing dog in an alley. It marked the beginning of Kiarostami's journey with children and drew both on his documentary and experimental strands. Bahram Bayzai also made the short film *Amu Sibilu (Uncle Moustache)*, for CIDCYA in the same year. During the 1970s, CIDCYA grew rapidly, releasing about ten productions per year. Its films and animations received around sixty awards in international film festivals

FIG. 26 *Where is the Friend's House? (Khaneh-ye Dust Kojast?)*, Abbas Kiarostami, 1986.

but it never seriously attempted to screen its films to ordinary audiences and was criticised for its elitism and intellectualism. Accordingly, CIDCYA films might be seen to depart radically from the conventions and production values of the studio system of the 1960s and 1970s. Location shooting and the use of available light resulted in more naturalistic photography, closer to documentary than the studio-made fiction film.

After the Revolution, CIDCYA continued its activities on a smaller scale due to financial problems, although a few of its films were screened in theatres. Between 1980 and 1990, a handful of realist feature films on the subject of social problems was produced by CIDCYA, including Kiarostami's *Khaneh-ye Dust Kojast? (Where is the Friend's House?*, 1987) and *Mashgh-e Shab* (*Homework*, 1989), and Bayzai's *Bashu, the Little Stranger.* These films, revolving around the problems of children, are among the classics of contemporary Iranian cinema. This type of filmmaking, based on the CIDCYA model using non-professional actors in studies of everyday life, was reinforced by the huge success of Kiarostami's films outside Iran.

Homework was based on interviews with schoolchildren. Ostensibly it focused on their problems with their homework but its themes extended to deeper issues regarding the family and society, and aspects of war and militarism in Iranian society. Ebrahim Foruzesh's *Kelid* (*The Key*, 1986), also made for CIDCYA, was highly successful in international festivals. It told a simple story about a four-year-old boy who takes responsibility for his infant brother while their mother is out. All the action, during which the camera scarcely leaves the cramped little rooms of the house, revolves around the boy's efforts to find the key to the main door. Each event and situation can be seen as a part of a puzzle, a reflection of Iranian life. The boy, for example, represents the young generation, while the series of adults with whom he communicates from the window represent different layers of society. Foruzesh's *Mardan-e Kuchak* (*The Little Man*, 1994) is about the 12-year-old son of a farming family who decides to help his mother by using some abandoned land for horticultural plantation. The title is indicative of the responsibility he takes on.

These films sketched the historical changes taking place in Iran during the 1980s and 1990s, with the children representing the Iranian people. The symbolic device of the pretty, idealised, innocent and hardworking child was used to convey certain abstract ideas, such as lost innocence in a politicised world, while never straying far from the field of realism. One of the first Iranian films to be welcomed by international festivals in the early 1980s was *Davandeh* (*The Runner*, Amir Naderi, 1981). The lack of political dogma and the dominance of the man-versus-nature theme in this film gave it universal appeal.

Naderi traces a boy's growth from a chaotic existence into manhood and spiritual maturity under harsh conditions. Lonely Amiro dreams of journeying to an unknown destination. He lives in a rusty, abandoned tanker hulk beached in a shantytown, earning a meagre living through rubbish-picking and peddling water. After bigger boys steal his water bottles and ice he learns to fight back, beating them in a race. The cinematography is aptly simple and conventional, with a taut composition that conveys the cramped living conditions and winding beaches. The constant promise of escape and eternity is represented by the Persian Gulf sky and the welcoming sea, a device which tells us more about the social and economic context of the story than the somewhat superficial attempts at political analysis conveyed by the main character.

In Naderi's slightly later film *Ab, Bad, Khak* (*Water, Wind, Dust*, 1983), the young hero, a boy searching for his missing parents in a vast, parched desert, is once again pitted against cruel nature in an exploration of the liberating power of youthful energy in an oppressive situation, while the last inhabitants of the city flee from the region amid rising sandstorms. The opening shot, which cuts from a dreamy portrait of the young boy in ragged clothes to an establishing shot of the deserted city, perfectly embodies the conflict in the film. The speechless young boy is part of his environment, whether the sandy wastelands of Southern Iran, or the exquisitely organic architecture of the deserted clay houses. He has no history, but is himself a state of being.

Majid Majidi's debut, *Baduk* (1992), depicted a brother and sister who are sold to Arab drug smugglers. A black and bitter film set on the border of Iran and Pakistan, it was successful at the box office and at film festivals; his second film, *Pedar* (*The Father*, 1995) was about a boy who rebels against his mother and stepfather. In this rash of films about children, triggered by the international success of films like *The Runner*, it is hardly surprising that the title of the first Iranian picture (also by Majidi) to be nominated for an Oscar (Best Foreign Film) was *Bacheha-ye Aseman* (*Children of Heaven*, 1998). A brother and sister, the children of a poor family, share the same pair of shoes for going to school. The sister, for whom they are far too big, puts them on in the morning, then runs back home to give them to her brother in the afternoon. Majidi's intense study of a family living in the grip of poverty is exaggerated in mood, but this is a work characterised by visual quality and emotional generosity, which impressed the Academy members. It offered an opportunity for international audiences to observe characters whose lives might be very different from their own but whose concerns are ultimately universal.

The irresistible, serious little seven-year-old in *Badkonak-e Sefid* (*White Balloon*, 1995) by Jafar Panahi is the quintessential heroine of the Iranian child film. When she loses the money she has been given to buy a goldfish, she sets out on a determined quest to recover it. Like other characters in this genre, she moves from an overly naive and passive position to a condition of extreme action. In this sense the film carries implicit political content. This is sentimentalised socialism, however, suggesting that poverty is not an obstacle in a world in which people are all kind and generous. But that is its least important feature and hardly crucial to its success; its sentimentality feeds into a universal humanism, and its ideological nostalgia and naivety only add to the old-fashioned charm of this well-told story. *White Balloon* won a prize at the Cannes Film Festival and became one of the most profitable foreign films in the United States and in Europe.

Children liberated films from the domination of plot, introducing inessential actions and occupations, such as loafing around on a street or biding one's time in a rural area. They also avoided the many restrictions on showing the real emotions of adults. The child genre does not display any kind of stylistic coherency that would allow for easy categorisation but we usually see the world through the child's eyes. Sometimes the action realises itself in terms of resistance to the adult characters, creating a situation of challenge. The family, of course, receives much attention in this genre but it is not proclaimed the basic cell of society or the ultimate source of love, support or morality. It is depicted as a mass of tension and conflict. The adult characters come off badly in comparison with these children, who acquire a tone of elevated romanticism denied to their indifferent parents. Represented from the point of view of the child, the parents do not seem to speak the same language as their offspring.

In the 1980s a few women directors had made successful sentimental melodramas, including Puran Darakhshandeh's *Parandeh-ye Shirin Khoshbakhti* (*Sweet Bird of Fortune*, 1986) and *Parandeh-ye Kuchak-e Khoshbakhti* (*The Little Bird of Happiness*, 1988), and *Bachehha-ye Talagh* (*Children of Divorce*, 1988) by Tahmineh Milani, which depicted children as victims and relied on their vulnerability to impress all types of audiences. Images of the family had also often been used in the past to purchase emotion at the expense of analytical alternatives. In so many Iranian films, from box-office hits to art-house films, the family had served a crucial function in inserting within the film narrative the established values of competitive, repressive and hierarchical relationships in order to legitimate and naturalise them. The viewer of these more recent films, however, was not given any assurance that what they saw would affirm the status quo. This time round, narrative images of home and safety, of protecting fathers and comforting families were not a part of the discourse. Paternal sacrifice was exchanged for child sacrifice. The prevalence of the theme of hardworking children, together with the increasing elevation of childhood to the margins of adulthood, suggest the importance of young adults to Iranian society over the last two decades. The absence of family – which as we have seen functions as an ideological cornerstone embodying a range of intertwined traditional values, including love of country – suggests a sense of uncertainty about the smooth functioning of society and provides a dark commentary on the dominant social values.

In Kambozia Partovi's *Bazi-ye Bozorgan* (*The Adult Game*, 1993), set shortly after the outbreak of the war, the Iraqi army occupies a small Iranian border village. Most of the inhabitants take refuge in the mountains. Among the survivors are a small girl and boy, who find a baby still alive among the corpses. The film's *verité* ambience teeters at times on the verge of documentary-style realism, and then shifts off down more overtly stylised avenues. The young couple, forced to act almost as mother and father, are non-idealised, sour-tempered children who must fight with hostile enemies.

A similar role-reversal can be seen in other films, though the genre was becoming more and more varied. Slapstick comedies like Muhammad-Reza Honarmand's *Dozd-e Arusakha* (*Doll's Thief*, 1989) about a brother and sister fighting a witch, or Abolhasan Davoudi's *Patal va Arezouha-ye Kuchak* (*Patal and the Little Wishes*, 1991), about siblings who play-act the role of their parents, were box-office hits. The child 'couples' in these films are freer and more autonomous than any of the adults in the stories and the little girls, without veil or scarf, are able to accompany their brothers in every scene.

While the first Iranian film musical after the Revolution, Muhammad-Ali Talebi's *Shahr-e Mushha* (*The City of Mice*, 1984), based on a successful TV cartoon for children, had been animated, Kambozia Partovi's *Golnar* (1986) was the first post-revolutionary live-action musical. Its teenage heroine, who gets lost in the jungle and sings and dances with animals, was a new type of female star

– cool, indifferent and contemporary. Children thus provided an excuse to include song and dance once again. *Golnar* was a box-office hit and became a model for a whole series of entertaining films. The traditional order of gender relations was eliminated, since children were perceived as sexless. Such films displayed love from the point of view of children, rather than focusing on the sexual love prevalent in Western films. The children's complete absence of sexual knowledge became an outer display of freedom.

The history of Iranian cinema is dominated by the critical centrality of the group of films made between the mid-1980s and the mid-1990s, commonly described as 'Iranian poetic realism'. This genre, however, cannot be traced back to a consciously thought-out and publicly circulated manifesto or movement. The term is a descriptive category that has evolved through critical discourse. The continuing interest in poetic realism lies in the fact that it is not a straightforwardly homogenous or unitary phenomenon but successfully crosses the boundaries between highbrow and lowbrow, tradition and modernity, serious engagement and pleasure. The films are relatively few in number, constituting no more than 40 or 50 over a period in which domestic film production figures were high. Yet discussion of them has been substantial and has encompassed a complex range of theoretical, methodological and historiographical debates.

The use of children and amateur actors as central characters is a means of representing ordinary people, but it also allows the projection of ideas about what people should ideally be like. With their extraordinary dignity (as seen in the hero of *Bashu, the Little Stranger* or the characters in *Where is the Friend's House?*), unlike film stars, these children are easily seen as real people, so that the values they embody are all the more persuasively and authentically disseminated. Perhaps the most compelling factor offered by the use of children in these films is that it eased the problem of political judgement by throwing it into the realm of personal experience and feeling. Children could depoliticise the audience's reactions. They promoted the private and personal, as well as a kind of mass consciousness, since their characters' personal troubles were also universal. They reconstituted social difference into a new collective experience.

The plain, untrained style of acting employed by these children heralded a new generation of non-professional actors, who gave the best performances in Iranian cinema since the beginning of the 1980s. The subtle and genuine acting style and the authenticity of everyday life combined to present the unremarkable presence of real people, who nevertheless exhibited strong individuality. The performances of Babak Ahmadpoor, for example, in *Where is the Friend's House?*, or Adnan Afravian in *Bashu, the Little Stranger*, were compelling evocations of an intense inner life. The only remarkable thing about these simple, sweet boys and girls was their absolute mediocrity. A close-up shot in the cinema was like a blow-up of a passport photo taken at random – one person, no different from any other. They also represented a conscious break with the past.

Abolfazl Jalili had directed several 16 mm shorts and documentaries for television related to the Iran–Iraq war. His themes centred mostly on the victims of war, natural disasters and the hardships of children. His first two feature films, *Milad* (1983) and *Bahar* (*The Spring*, 1984) were also made at the peak of the war. Soon, he turned to the dramas of daily life using a more experimental style. In his films, the moral crisis created by the grip of urbanisation, the anticipation of a dark future, and issues of illiteracy, addiction and the inadequacy of the social system became highly colourful.

His *Gal* (*Scabies*, 1987), which deals with teenage delinquency, was followed in 1990 with *Dan*, a docudrama about a real nine-year-old boy who was never issued with a birth certificate, which meant that he could neither go to school nor find a job. Like the other children in this genre, he sets out on a quest for his own identity. It is a portrait of a small, vulnerable human being, doing his best to cope with unfathomable rules. Complementary to this story is that of a girl who yields to a marriage of convenience to help sustain her family. As a wrenching portrait of a nightmarish existence in a crime-ridden world, *Dan* was one of the most disturbing Iranian films, though it was never screened for the Iranian public since it was deemed suitable only for foreign markets.

Raghs-e Khak (*Dance of Dust*, 1992) is Jalili's most poetic film. It contains very little dialogue, being made up instead of a combination of abstract sounds and images, metaphors and symbols. This highlights the silent intensity of emotion between two young children who speak different dialects. Having come under heavy criticism for alleged impersonation of intellectual European films, it was not released until 1998.

In Jalili's films, space is alien and threatening, allowing the central characters no escape but providing a testing ground for their moral sense. The big city is a closed urban milieu that is claustrophobic, evil, corrupt. Moral victory can only result in withdrawal to a 'nowhere' beyond the scope of the information provided in the films, and no reassuring sense of a secure future is provided.

Life goes on…

The phenomenon of Abbas Kiarostami came about partly through his great endurance. Kiarostami was one of the few Iranian filmmakers from the old generation of the Iranian new wave that emerged at the end of the 1960s to work continuously after the Revolution. He pioneered new forms and a boundary-breaking language in docudrama filmmaking. The new rules forbidding sex and violence did not affect his films, since they had never contained either. He remained in his own territory, untouched. The great fantasist of Iranian recuperation, assuring people through his films that they could survive, he was seen as the quintessential modern narrator of fulfilled aspiration.

Kiarostami came to the notice of the West with a trilogy of films: *Where is the Friend's House?* (1986), *And Life Goes On…* (1992) and *Under the Olive Trees* (1994). For Westerners, it seemed magical that in a country such as Iran, which had undergone such profound historical changes, political tension and social upheaval, a filmmaker could continually focus on the small but valuable pleasures of the most simple and innocent kind. His success, starting with *Where is the Friend's House?* and climaxing with the 1997 Cannes Film Festival winner, *Tam-e Geelas* (*Taste of Cherry*), had a profound influence on non-commercial Iranian cinema. In *Where is the Friend's House?* he took his camera to the northern Iranian village of Kokar, to tell the story of a boy who, having inadvertently taken his friend's homework book, tries to return it to prevent him from being punished.

Kiarostami's 1988 film *Close-Up* was based on the true story of a man who fooled a family into believing that he was the famous filmmaker Mohsen Makhmalbaf; he is revealed at the end only to be a harmless film fan. Makhmalbaf makes a cameo appearance in the film as himself. This is a moral enquiry into the possible benefits and benevolent motives of imposture and deceit, and works overall as a redemptive film with reference to the younger generation's desire for success at any cost. The fusion of fiction and reality fascinates Kiarostami, not simply in aesthetic terms but as a strategy with which to deal with censorship, and is a tactic he would use again in his next two films.

And Life Goes On... investigates the aftermath of a devastating earthquake that claimed the lives of 50,000 people in 1990 in the area north of Iran in which he shot *Where is the Friend's House?* The director (played by an actor), accompanied by his son, travels to Kokar to see if his cast members are still alive. This is a tale of life and death, destruction and reconstruction, pain and loss. Filmed largely in silence, it is a masterly demonstration of how death and devastation can become a dramatic source of life. Kiarostami examines the impact of the disaster on the human population by showing it through the eyes of a man – himself – who is used to supplying an organising structure for his portraits of the human condition. His profound and fragmented examination of this shattered population attempting to restore the structures of normal life mirrors Iran's attempts to rebuild itself after the war.

Under the Olive Trees is the final segment in the Kokar trilogy. It takes the structure of a film-within-a-film – a fictionalised account of the making of *And Life Goes On...* The two amateur actors who play a newly married couple in this film are, in fact, embroiled in a real-life romance. Hossein, a local handyman, who plays the groom, is desperately in love with Tahereh, but she is reluctant to play opposite him as the bride. This simple tale of two young lovers shrugging off their grief in the face of the earthquake attempts to transcend the unsettling dichotomy between their desires and the reality of their lives. While taken by itself, *Under the Olive Trees* functions as an offbeat, whimsical love story that is barely resolved; seen as part of the trilogy about this disaster-torn, mountainous part of rural Iran, it develops and intensifies the ongoing themes of image and reality, social inequity and the determination to survive tragedy. In the last sequence of the film, Hossein follows the girl he loves across the fields, pleading his case all the way. Finally, in the far distance, we see her turn to him, and he runs back towards the camera, seemingly elated. This hint is enough to suggest a parallel with Iran's tentative new relationship with other countries. The film seemed apolitical to foreigners, but had a strong message for Iranians.

The innocence and unpretentious values associated with the rustic hero of *Under the Olive Trees* tended to give way in other films of the 1990s to more worldly, sophisticated and cynical characters. Yet the traditionalist populist hero still spoke for contemporary Iran. Hossein's simple but very real aspiration is to get married and have children who will not be poor and illiterate like him. His role is innately political, since *Under the Olive Trees* is an investigation of social issues. The values of the world around him are changing in response to the social turmoil of the time but his convictions remain constant; he adheres to the straightforward maxims of his class. His naive optimism and honesty hark back to the utopian Iran envisioned by populist ideology, recalling the films of Majid Mohseni in the 1950s and 1960s. Kiarostami captures the widening of the gap in society and uses humour as his instrument for exposing it.

Perhaps the most immediately recognisable formal element in Kiarostami's films, his stylistic signature, is his use of the long shot. Breaking with cinematographic tradition, he uses extreme long shots in combination with closer shots to convey the polarities of threat and protection, fear and security. The long shots play on both, violating the viewer's safe distance from the narrative by demanding attention, forcing the gaze, hiding objects and then revealing them, surrounding them with a protective glow. Such self-conscious gestures are never distancing; they propel the viewer into the real world. The space created between the audience and the characters heightens the seductive pull of the images. Kiarostami manipulates the gap separating his texts and reality itself, generating a tension between desired security and narrative uncertainty.

Gradually, Kiarostami became an unusual ambassador for a politicised Iranian cinema abroad. In an interview with the British magazine *Sight & Sound* he asserted:

> Any work of art is a political work, but it's not party political. It doesn't approve one party and attack another, and doesn't support one system over

another. Our understanding of 'political cinema' is that it should always support one specific political ideology. I think if you look at my films from this point of view, they are definitely not political … I think that those films which appear non-political, are more political than films known specifically as 'political' films.[84]

The success of Kiarostami's films outside Iran was a motivating factor for other Iranian filmmakers. Their production greatly differed from other films since they required no sets, props or special effects, and were made on a modest budget. This new approach to cinematic form and content, the film within a film, or the docudrama, was highly successful, finding great support at foreign festivals, whilst the commercial release of his films in Europe and the United States brought Kiarostami financial rewards. This was the first time in the history of Iranian cinema that it had found an audience abroad.

One American film critic wrote:

What is uncommon, and particular to Iran, is how [the CYDCYA] aesthetic was preserved virtually intact for future decades via the curious cultural processes that surrounded the Iranian Revolution and the early years of the Islamic Republic. While the rest of the world was swept up in an increasingly globalised and video-dominated media climate, Iran shut off almost everything coming from the outside, and then, circa 1983, encouraged its filmmakers to resume their former preoccupations (albeit with new restrictions on content). Thus did the modernist-cinematic '60s/'70s survive to enjoy a vital afterlife, two decades later, in a particularly unlikely corner of the globe. Obviously, this touches on the appeal of Iranian films to Festival World: in some lights, they uncannily reincarnate the auteurist spirit, the politique that brought many festivals into being in the first place.[85]

New President, new era

The year 1997 was a landmark in the post-Revolution era, both politically and in terms of film. On 10 April a German court ruled that Iranian officials had in 1992 ordered the murder of four Iranian Kurdish leaders. On 30 April *Taste of Cherry* shared the Palme d'Or at Cannes. On winning his award, Kiarostami took the stage and exchanged a polite kiss with its presenter, Catherine Deneuve. This two-second transgression of Islamic propriety instantly set off a polemical firestorm in Iran. On Kiarostami's return from France a welcoming reception at the airport was derailed by angry fundamentalists; Kiarostami was spirited through customs and out through a side door.

On 23 May Muhammad Khatami was elected president of Iran in a landslide victory on a platform of cultural and social change. He introduced Ayatollah Mohajerani as his Minister of Guidance and Islamic Culture. On 29 November, Iran's national football team qualified for the World Cup finals. On 9–11 December, Tehran hosted the Organisation of the Islamic Conference after years of tensions with its Arab Muslim neighbours. Also in December, Iranians flocked to see *Snowman*, the bitter comedy whose protagonist dresses as a woman in order to secure a visa to America. The film had been banned for three years.

During the presidential elections, some notable Iranian filmmakers involved themselves directly by making short propaganda films for the candidates. Seifollah Dad and Behruz Afkhami made one for Khatami, Rasul Sadr-Ameli made a film on Seyyed-Reza Zavarei, and Behzad Behzadpur (an actor) made one for Ali-Akbar Nategh-Nuri, Khatami's main rival. Khatami was still a few weeks away from assuming office when Khaneh-ye Cinema (House of Cinema), the umbrella organisation for Iran's filmmaking guilds, held its annual ceremony. The evening included special awards for the outgoing President, Hojjatoleslam Hashemi Rafsanjani, and to Abbas Kiarostami.

President Khatami, in an exclusive interview for CNN in January 1998, called for greater cultural 'dialogue between civilisations' (Iran and the West). His strategy was no secret: he wanted to use cinema, sport and other cultural avenues to improve the country's standing. Filmmaking, nurtured by Khatami when he was Minister for Guidance and Islamic Culture from 1982 to 1992, had won the country acclaim at international film festivals. There were many rumours that Kiarostami's Palme d'Or at Cannes was a positive response from the West to President Khatami's offer. When *Time* magazine selected *Taste of Cherry* as its first choice for the 'Ten Best Movies of the Year' it commented: 'Kiarostami will find a quiet place and listen to a man's heart, right up until it stops beating'. In the same issue, readers were told: 'President Muhammad Khatami, considered a moderate force in Iranian politics, called for a dialogue with the "great" people of the United States – a statement considered the most conciliatory toward the USA by an Iranian head of state since the 1979 Islamic Revolution.'[86]

In July 1998, Abbas Abdi, one of the student leaders who had planned and directed the storming of the US Embassy in 1979, met in Paris with Barry Rosen, who had been amongst the Americans taken hostage. In November of the same year a documentary film by Leslie Woodhead, *444 Days: The US Hostage Crisis in Iran*, an eyewitness account from both Iranians and Americans, was shown in the United States and Britain. In February 1999, two groups of Iranian and American film practitioners in Tehran and New York talked together on an Internet website about dialogue between their cinemas. The Iranians included the directors Dariush Mehrjui, Behruz Afkhami and Ali-Reza Davudnezhad, and the actress Niki Karimi; the Americans included directors Jim Jarmusch and Nancy Sawkaw, the producer Warington Hodlin, the critic Andrew Sarris and Richard Penia, Director of the New York Film Festival. The detail of this dialogue, however, never appeared in the Iranian media.

The arts in general, and particularly film, had long been targeted by Iran's self-appointed moralists. Before Khatami took office, zealots who attacked cinemas often enjoyed tacit government backing. Many theatres had been forced to close. After the new president took office, the situation was reversed, with cinemas showing films that spoke directly to popular sentiment. The bureaucratic running of the film industry and total bans on films considered objectionable became a thing of the past. Before 1998, Iranian cinema had occupied two utterly divorced worlds: the officially sanctioned and the officially semi-tolerated. Some of the films most widely respected outside the country, like those by Abolfazl Jalili, had received the scantest domestic distribution. Khatami's election signified the beginning of a new era.

Films by Jalili, Kiarostami, Makhmalbaf, Panahi, Bani-Etemad and Mehrjui were not only successful abroad but also touched the hearts and minds of Iranian audiences. To differing degrees, they were all based on a quality of calculated allusion, making their critique of contemporary Iranian society through a variety of metaphoric techniques. Sometimes these films seemed enigmatic to Western audiences, but their disguised references to internal problems had a tremendous impact on Iranian viewers. Their achievements were not merely cinematic but political, using a cunning art of inventive criticism that occasionally managed to sneak past the rather dim censors. Their interest for the most part lies at the junction between the expression of cultural dilemmas and experimentation with genre.

If film had moved into the shadows of conservatism a decade before, by the mid-1990s it was heading in new directions. With more freedom to show images of women, along with the virtual dismantling of censorship and above all the fast-growing analysis of the effects of war, a new climate emerged that was increasingly conducive to the production of films critical of Iranian institutions, which would have been unimaginable a few years before. The basic settling of accounts with the past began with the screening of banned films made in Iran over the previous two decades, such as *Snowman* and *Banu* (*Lady*, 1992, Dariush Mehrjui), a black comedy on post-revolutionary debates about the values of rich and poor, which offered a droll portrait of an Iranian lower-working-class family. Due to its criticism of consumerism and of the oblivion to elementary moral norms, it had been banned for three years.

Filmmakers were now able to play with taboos. They often referred to subjects associated with Islamic codes and rules pertaining to women after the Revolution. In an allegorical scene in Mohsen Makhmalbaf's *Sokut* (*The Silence*, 1999) made in Tajikistan, a teenage girl dances unveiled to rhythmic music. Though this scene was still considered controversial, Makhmalbaf succeeded in his challenge to the authorities to release his film uncensored.

Maryam Shahriar, a young woman who had studied cinema in California, made another polemical film in Iran, *Dokhtaran-e Khorshid* (*Daughters of the Sun*, 1999). In a rural area a poor young girl lives with her father. To help her find a well-paid job, while protecting her virtue, the father shaves her head and disguises her as a man. The girl changes her name and finds employment in a carpet factory, where most of the workers are women. She encounters no problems in moving from her native village, passing as a boy, or with her work in the factory, where her status as a man allows her to get a better job than her female colleagues. But her false identity causes other problems.

At last, viewers could see a female character in an Iranian film without a veil. In 1987, Farima Farjami had appeared in the film *Lead* with a shaved head and without a scarf as a Jewish immigrant, but she appeared in only one very brief scene. *Daughters of the Sun* results in tragi-comedy when a brash, attractive female worker befriends and progressively falls in love with the disguised girl. This theme was too much for the moralistic authorities, and *Daughters of the Sun* only received a few screenings, none of which was in a public theatre. However, it won first prize at the Montreal Film Festival in the same year.

The semiotic system that maintains Iran as a gender-divided society was repeatedly violated in this way. A play on visual signifiers kept gender constructions shifting, producing an image of sex and gender that was often funny and surreal. The theme of cross-dressing was repeated in *Tondar* (Hamid-Reza Ashtianipur, 2000), a fairy tale in which a young girl puts on a wig, disguising herself as a man, and beats all the men of her village in battle. For women characters, cross-dressing often meant a taste of male privilege, the relinquishing of which they commonly resisted. In the end, however, the female character usually sacrifices her temporary mobility for permanent heterosexual love. But the necessity of giving up the disguise is, just like the prior necessity to adopt it, the product of a governing limitation.

The cross-dressing films of this period shared a large number of elements: the narrative necessity for the adoption of a gender-coded costume belonging to the opposite sex; the way in which this disguise is credible to the characters in the film but completely lacking in credibility to the audience; visual, behavioural and narrative clues as to the character's real sex; references to the difference between the sexes and to their cultural/religious separation and, finally, heterosexual desire, which was still a taboo, thwarted by the character's disguise. The simultaneous diegetic adequacy and extradiegetic inadequacy of the disguise provided a field in which established visual codes, conventions and regulations could be ignored.

Ghete-ye Natamam (*Unfinished Sonata*, 2000) by Maziar Miri was another intriguing and controversial film. In it a young researcher goes to the Khorasan province to record the songs of native local women. He is trying to find the famous but elusive local singer, Heiran (literally 'bewildered'). At last, the man finds her in prison, where she sings a melancholy song directly to camera. Seeing – even hearing – a woman singing is still banned by Islamic rule and this was the first time since the Revolution that an Iranian woman's singing voice had been used in a film.

The film was banned because of the short song, performed by Sima Bina, one of the singers of the pre-revolutionary period. Muhammad-Reza Darvishi, the composer, sent an open letter to the Minister of Guidance and Islamic Culture, Ayatollah Mohajerani, and the banning of the film was publicised in the newspapers. After Mohajerani's resignation following pressure from fundamentalists on a number of issues, the ban on the film was maintained. At last Davud Rashidi, the producer, visited President Khatami and suggested a compromise. When the film was screened at the Fajr Film Festival, the last song was deleted, but in some scenes a hymn-like song, which was performed by a woman, could be heard on the soundtrack. Although the ending was thus unfulfilling, and the film lacked its original richness and depth of character, it was carried by its insistent single theme about the taboos surrounding Iranian women.

When the young man in *Unfinished Sonata* visits the female singer in prison, and the woman suddenly closes her sad eyes and sings her heartfelt song, it is a moving experience. Whether or not one liked the film, it was clear that Iranian cinema was acknowledging its power, and was struggling to create a niche for itself in the political arena.

Fear of youth

Since the 1980s, young people had become increasingly visible in Iranian society. But it was only after the election of Muhammad Khatami that their presence was fully acknowledged. Before the election the media had reported that in a demographic shift, the vast majority of Iran's people was young – 54 per cent were under 18, and 65 per cent were under 25 – and that they were waiting for change. This propelled the moderate reformer to his surprise win and put political and social change on the agenda. A cultural tidal wave was hitting Iran. The Minister of Guidance and Islamic Culture, Ayatollah Mohajerani stated: 'We believe that if [the young generation] understand our beliefs, they will accept them'.[87] President Khatami benefited from the promise of change. His pledge to modernise Iran by replacing zealotry with the rule of law won him more than 70 per cent of the vote in the election.

Youth was driving the change. Iran's young people today are more numerous, more literate, and thanks to radio and television, more widely aware of the outside world, than any generation of Iranians before them. Some conservatives would have banned sports if they could but the fever that built up around football among young people as the Iranian team fought its way through the qualifying matches of the World Cup in 1998 won the nation over.

With the radical political changes brought about by the election of a reformist president based on the votes of young adults, a new era began. Fresh themes and stories in Iranian cinema began to develop, along with the hope that hidden obsessions, the secrets of inner life invisible from the outside, would be presented on screen.

What had started out as a rhetoric of concern in the child genre, however, progressively evolved into one of moral panic, a fear of youth. Discourses surrounding youth concerned both internal and external manifestations of power. Youth was visualised in Iranian films as a menace, a spectacle of otherness. Young people were not presented as part of an ordinary way of life, but were seen to occupy a social site on the periphery, a site of contradictions that often challenged the safe borders of the dominant order.

Part of the 'problem' of youth is that it contains within its own representation of itself a passion for new codes that outsiders cannot read. This illegibility brought about a fetishisation or a spectacularisation of youth-as-violence that said more about the fear of changing boundaries than it did about youth itself as a fundamental threat to the social order. Why else would it be seen as a single social category, as a unity, when this group was as diverse as any other category or age group? A profound ambivalence towards youth therefore prevailed: films revealed both paranoia about and fascination with its transgression. A mistrust similar to that which had permeated earlier representations of women in Iranian cinema was manifested, so that young people, like women, were fetishised and made into the object of speculation, but were nevertheless punished as offenders or violators by the end of the films.

One film of the early 1990s which dwelt on these themes was *Dow Hamsafar* (*Two Companions*, Asghar Hashemi, 1993). Never released in its original version, it is about a female obstetrician and a truck driver – two characters from opposite poles – who are forced together for a short time following the arrest of their sons. Their 'relationship' becomes a poignant parody of the familiar dilemmas inherent in each of their worlds. The film is a deadpan, ironic satire about urban angst, circling around the themes of the invasion of a young new breed, its conflict with the law, and the inevitable parental or patriarchal compromise that it brings about.

The most fascinating example of a film about the youth invasion during the Khatami era is by Samira Makhmalbaf, Mohsen Makhmalbaf's daughter. In 1998, just after the election, this 18-year-old screened her film *Sib* (*The Apple*) around the globe. It was highly acclaimed, winning seven international awards. In the same year she went to the Cannes Film Festival as the youngest director in the world, ironically from a country that had always been described by the Western media as torn between the isolationism of religious fundamentalists and its efforts to open itself up to the world. Referring to the new atmosphere in Iran, she said to a Western magazine: 'After the election of President Khatami the censorship is less than before … and when Iran's national football team went to the World Cup, I saw for the first time the joy of the Iranians in the streets.'[88]

Her film, based on a true story, is a reflection of the prevailing attitude to the younger generation. An old man and his blind wife keep their 12-year-old twin daughters locked up from birth. *The Apple* begins with concerned neighbours reporting the case to the welfare services. A social worker comes to the house to investigate and promptly sends the children out to play in the street, before locking up the father. The film traces the girls' first wide-eyed encounters with the outside world.

The Apple uses symbolism to create broader social comment. The central symbol of the apple, which features in several scenes, is intended to signify freedom, a new beginning for the young generation, rather than the biblical fall of Adam and Eve, since in Iranian poetry it is a symbol of life and knowledge. Some Western magazines and newspapers summed up the film's

FIG. 27 *A Time for Drunken Horses* (*Zamani Barayeh Masti Asbha*), Bahman Ghobadi, 1999.

liberating political tone through their headlines: 'The teenager who turned politics into art'; 'An Iranian Dynasty, a young director claims her own spotlight'; 'Forbidden Fruit: Freedom and Happiness'; 'Born Again'.[89]

On her long journey around the international festivals, Samira Makhmalbaf challenged the public image of young Iranian women. With *The Apple*, she not only drew these children out of their locked room, but also extracted herself from her country so that she could see the world. Most Western people have a mental picture of Iranian woman wearing full-length black dresses and veils. But with her teenage acne, jeans and T-shirt (albeit with the addition of a headscarf), the young Samira belied this image. She commented, 'People ask me, is Iran the kind of place where two twelve-year-old girls can't come out and see the world? Or is it a place where a girl who is eighteen can make a film about them?'[90] This question encapsulated the irony of Iranian life during this period.

It was the documentarists who first addressed themselves in the new political climate to a series of formerly closed contemporary problems, and Iranian documentary became more successful than ever before. Two films on the hardships of the Kurdish people, Samira Makhmalbaf's semi-documentary *Takht-e Siah* (*Blackboard*, 1999), and Bahman Ghobadi's *Zamani Barayeh Masti Asbha* (*A Time for Drunken Horses*, 1999), which provoked considerable discussion, were extremely successful abroad. *A Time for Drunken Horses* was a poignant story depicting the courage of orphaned Kurdish children, forced to support themselves under the harshest of conditions. Portraying the hardships faced by the Kurds was previously taboo, though they had been documented before in an earlier short film by Ghobadi. Ghobadi's unflinching and rigorously minimal approach, mostly delivered in a hand-held documentary style, was tempered by the deep emotional bond shared by the three siblings it portrayed and the appeal of their naturalistic performances. These films offered a broad social portrait of the young generation, and showed the complex and problematic nature of the choices they face in Iran.

Meanwhile, some films dealt with the rebellion of the new Iranian teenagers. These include *Dokhtari ba Kafshha-ye Katani* (*The Girl in the Sneakers*, Rasul Sadr-Ameli, 1998) and *Masaeb-e Shirin* (*Sweet Agony*, Ali-Reza Davudnezhad, 1999). *The Girl in the Sneakers* focuses on the psychological preoccupations of a number of young people. The central character is a middle-class girl who is treading the narrow path between childhood and maturity. Having run away from home in pursuit of forbidden love, she gains a limited freedom, meeting a boy of her own age with whom she sits on a park bench on a long night, discussing personal myths and her favourite book, *Don Juan*. But above all she confronts the horrifying reality of society, witnessing the struggles of the poor and narrowly escaping a rape. The film is an uncompromising portrayal of an urban teenager struggling with her shattered dreams, and hangs on the knockout performance of Pegah Ahangarani as the lonely heroine. She brings an instinctive intensity to her role as the social outcast, seen constantly on the move, trying to find a place to sleep for the night. This is underscored by the visual style of the film, as the camera follows her movements through the bleak, cold landscape she inhabits. The hallmark of her personality is a combination of aggressiveness and passivity, which reveals itself not only in her relationship with the people around her, but also in her concern for society itself. The film indicates that society is not yet ready for unlimited freedom, asserting the need to create a balance between total liberation and excessive restriction. It asks us to question our response to her needs, and whether, either directly or indirectly, we are responsible for her plight.

Sweet Agony is the story of a boy and girl in their late teens who have been engaged since childhood, played by Reza and Mona Davudnezhad, the director's children. They want to marry as soon as possible, but their parents are against the idea since they are still too young. The drama unfolds around their discussions about their families, life, freedom and love. Due to the fact that the cast of the film is largely made up of the director's family and therefore permitted to embrace, the story has great authenticity. It is a critique of both generations: the older one for living in the past, unable to deal with the present except in the most conformist way, and the younger one for being overly demanding.

The irony embodied in much of the treatment of young people in films at this time is that they are punished for their transgressiveness at the same time as being fetishised as objects that can neither be read nor understood. In the final analysis, the youth was seen as an outsider who must become an insider by upholding the social order. While this youth was the nation's necessary future, and the group on which it pinned its hopes, these hopes were deeply ambivalent. There was a tension between the desire to control youth and despair regarding an (imagined and imaged) inability to do so. Many of the youth films of the 1980s and 1990s did not really represent the point of view of young people, although they sometimes pretended to in order to caution adults about youth. Rather, they systematically co-opted the narrative into the fully socialised adult gaze. The politics of youth were constructed as a kind of spectacle of waste. The common discourse on youth suggested that they chose to be outside of society by rejecting its norms, rather than that they were excluded by society. But this was to provide an easy excuse for so-called youth violence and served to justify the culture of surveillance in which they were made to live.

The energetic filmmaker Mohsen Makhmalbaf also tapped into the youth obsession, but for him the gap between yesterday and tomorrow was much narrower. *A Moment of Innocence* of 1996 recreated his encounter with a policeman whom he had wounded before the Revolution. The film's style shows the influence both of Kiarostami and CIDCYA. Reality meets fantasy in a work that shows that life and art can triumph over theory and politics. The bread and vessel – symbols of life and friendship – presented in the last shot, significantly replace gun and knife. The result is both a perceptive personal historical document and a typical Iranian love story of the period.

Quantitatively, certainly, the greater part of Makhmalbaf's theoretical work dates from the early 1980s, but his later films reflect the ultimately insoluble conflict between the filmmaker's own questions and the constraints imposed by religious propriety. It was this conflict that led Makhmalbaf, previously a political filmmaker, further away from politics and even from contemporary problems. It caused him to seek refuge in eschatological considerations, which were often extremely illuminating, but shed light mainly on paintings, literature and at best on a fictive type of cinema conceived as art form.

Gabbeh, for example, is a great panorama of traditional life in the far plateaux that demonstrates Makhmalbaf's visionary gifts and love of national ethnography and folklore. An astonishing example of Iranian cinematography, it makes use of carefully rendered colour schemes to heighten the emotional impact of Makhmalbaf's message regarding the alienating effect of religion on his people. At the heart of this exquisitely told tale about the frustrated love of a young woman in a nomadic world, an ancient form of rug-weaving results in the precious *gabbeh* – a carpet into which is woven images of timeless tales and legends.

In this era, with its youth explosion and unemployment, popular Iranian films turned with unprecedented openness and intensity to the exploration of the rebel: rebels with or without a cause, standing between childhood and adult life. Films of this period acknowledged the prevalence in the tame 1990s of antisocial behaviour in young people who had been deprived of any form of rebellion other than the irrationally destructive. To young men who were unaffected by the war, yet felt anxious about their masculinity, the rebel hero suggested that the traditional superiority of the strong, silent male could be recovered. Men could live vicariously through these images revealing the hidden potential of male capacity. Quick, decisive action unhampered by introspection became especially popular with the young generation, who felt powerless in the face of threatened lay-offs and unstable employment. Actors Fariborz Arabnia and Abolfazl Purarab provided a reflection of the real dilemma of young male Iranians, and their characters were typically given beliefs that put them in opposition to the demands made upon them by others. The typical heroes of the 1990s were simple, strong, somewhat rough, and not burdened by an excess of intellect. In the 1980s, young men had been absent from mainstream films; in the 1990s, they directly addressed the specific difficulties of the post-revolution years.

The hero's external appearance and his fate did not necessarily go together: he might not be particularly handsome, but he was still noble. Conversely, he might have a fine face, but turn out to be an arrogant dogmatist, while the heroine might be beautiful but could be vain or egotistical. These were the first timid steps towards a more complex characterisation in mainstream cinema. At this point, however, it was still a simplistic formula, since the old one had simply been reversed: a beautiful appearance normally went with a negative character, while a plain appearance had spelt a positive character. More recently, this urge for greater divergence and complexity between the type the actor portrays and the function he or she serves has become more marked.

The stabilisation of cinema had made possible the appearance of such young heroes, with their freedom from the burdens of the past – the era before 1998. Now their range was greatly extended. No longer limited to the abstraction of ideas, they became individual, concrete people. The focus shifted away from the heroic past to the prosaic present. On-screen male personalities crackled with undirected energy, sexually alive and refusing to conform. But although Purarab and Arabnia seemed to be pure rebels in these 1990s films, at the end of many of them, traditional values were reasserted. By the late 1990s the job of the strong screen male was the overt protection of a social order in danger of economic collapse. In an era of unemployment and escalating violence, the hero is not the underdog but the smuggler, finding his own solution to poverty and unemployment. Eventually, he is brought around and forced to conform, but these *pro forma* endings fooled no one – the audience responded largely to his independence and irrepressible energy. Proletarian characters such as those played by Purarab and Arabnia were applauded for their daring and brashness and, like the revenge films, such films showed that survival was a matter of individual effort, even if it was outside the bounds of official morality.

Despite the limitations imposed by a repressive society, film recovered for men an image of the individual self with a distinctive identity and a flourishing ego. Audiences were encouraged to experience a vicarious thrill through the sight of violent individuals lusting for – and obtaining – money and power in films like *Arus* (*The Bride*, Behruz Afkhami, 1990), a big box-office hit starring Purarab. Those who identified with these male stars could imagine themselves to be free, autonomous and self-determining. But, as has so often been the case with Iranian heroes, Purarab and Arabnia offered through their personal magnetism and inward exploration an inventive obeisance to those frightened by political debate and to the frantic orthodoxy engendered by the economic situation. One could see *The Bride* as a story about class and economic conflict focused through the lens of sexual obsession. From another viewpoint, however, it was a story about the futility of reliance on conscious planning in human affairs without making allowance for the unconscious.

The intense sexuality of these young rebels also acted to emasculate the audience. If being tough was the hallmark of virility, then social cooperation and the common struggle for a more humane society were implicitly sentimental and effete. Manliness was defined in terms of rebellion and defiance of all moral ties to others. It was the struggle of a drowning man who claws at those going down with him. To the beleaguered, young post-war viewer the mood was seductive, even if it was also intended to encourage the debased panic of 'every man for himself'.

The heroic image proposed in such films derived from the same values demanded by official Iranian culture at the height of economic prosperity in the early 1970s. Only in his lawlessness did the rebel violate the norms conducive to competition within the free-enterprise system, and this was shown as admirable in spirit if misdirected in practice. Thus personal initiative and drive, and the demand that men define themselves through their superiority to others, were the qualities required of ordinary men both in times of economic prosperity and of economic collapse. If the opportunity for success was being denied in reality, the values had long since been internalised and the system absolved itself of failure.

In these films, violence was intuitively celebrated as an inevitable outcome of the hero's ideals; it seemed to be the appropriate expression of young Iranian aspirations. The drive for 'success' was by nature immoral and violent. Iran exalted the rugged young individualist, the self-made man who won a place in the sun of his own ambition, regardless of the means he used in his struggle to the top. The cool, young, handsome liar who used his fists was rewarded in these films. On the way to the top he acquired elegant clothes in imitation of the rich men whom he admired. In one witty scene in *The Bride*, for example, the groom shows off his money to his beloved as if he were demonstrating his desires. His motto is one to which most young Iranians would have responded: 'Always look after number one.'

Yet film males began to be granted a new and greater psychological space. As well as assertiveness and flair, they came to display sensitivity and concern, articulating attitudes on sex, politics and life. Muhammad-Reza Forutan in *Showkaran* (*Hemlock*, Behruz Afkhami, 1999) and *Zir-e Pust-e Shahr* (*Under the Skin of the City*, Rakhshan Bani-Etemad, 1999) brought to the cinema of the late 1990s the image of a more sensitive male through his portrayal in both films of men in their twenties, not yet hardened by life or alienated from their feelings. Forutan's personality appealed to young people, who immediately welcomed him as an important figure in Iranian cinema because he evoked their own submerged pain, the sense of being stifled and smothered by values not their own. In both films, Forutan's character refused to conform to someone else's idea of right and wrong, and he managed as a sincere and caring young man to make his immediate world respond in some measure to his outcry. In *Under the Skin of the City* his younger brother is a political agitator (the film begins with a speech by Khatami, and the street protests of the brother), and his mother, the main character, who displays humanity in an otherwise emotionally barren environment, talks frankly about her political beliefs (the film ends with her voting during the presidential election). The naturalistic style, and editing that is unobtrusive to the point of being elliptical, are perfectly suited to Bani-Etemad's demonstration of the fact that social and political crises, far from being exceptional, are the norm.

Films like *The Bride* and *Under the Skin of the City* presented the sense of immorality and disorder that were subtly manifest in Iran's economic situation. Everything is for sale; families are betrayed, mothers abandoned, honour smothered through unlawful acts, and the hero is eventually at the mercy of the success for which he has sold himself. This ambivalence regarding the fiercely pursued dream of success and its ultimate reality is manifested through intense feelings of guilt and regret on the part of the hero. The success story is often told as one of destruction and remorse. Thus these films celebrating youth slip again and again into dark, vivid melodrama. The harsh struggle for economic survival, coupled with the culture's insistence that a real man must achieve financial success, continued to influence the image of men in films. Yet there were, and still are, enough Iranian films linking success and violence to suggest that the theme is an important one for Iranian writers and directors.

Also revealing of the mood of society was the unpopularity of *Eshgh-e Bedun-e Marz* (*Love without Borders*, 1999), a film by the female director Puran Darakhshande. It was intended as a riposte to *Not without My Daughter*, the anti-Iranian American film of the early part of the decade. Yet audiences now wanted to see their own lives on screen, and were more interested in their own social and political internal affairs than in the anti-Western sentiment of *Love without Borders*.

The alienation of intellectuals

There is a long history of anti-intellectualism in Iran, particularly evident in its cinema. This is linked to a kind of xenophobia, since the intellectual is seen as a Westernised presence. Each generation has habitually made fun of those with intellectual pretensions, creating an absolute and value-laden division between ordinary people and the intellectual, who is the negative against which traditions are measured. While ordinary men are equated with masculinity, outdoor life, activity, adventure, emotional restraint and public power, intellectuals represent passivity, softness, introspection and femininity. According to cinematic depictions, they are incapable of forceful action, incompetent, and often commit villainous acts; they are willing to express emotion, and are idealistic and sentimental. In the symbolic universe of Iranian cinema, the intellectual is represented as a threat to society, inevitably divided between two cultures, and therefore subject to contradictory behaviour and accorded a highly circumscribed place in the plot structure.

The intellectual has often been a figure of fun, as illustrated by the whimsically absurd debate amongst the intellectuals in the famous café scene of *The Brick and the Mirror*. A notable early exception to the rule was Parviz Fanizadeh's character in *Ragbar (Rainfall*, Bahram Bayzai, 1972), an intellectual who was far from ridiculous. He played a new teacher in a traditional neighbourhood, and his rivalry with the local butcher over the heart of a woman was more than a battle of wills: it was the symbolic clash of two opposing elements of society.

A host of iconographic elements have come to distinguish Westernised intellectuals from ordinary people. The significance of clothes, veils and hats during Reza Khan's era has already been noted. Westernised modernity also relates to a wider economic and cultural shift that has led contemporary marketing to encourage people to conceive of themselves and their bodies as sites for consumer attention and cultural invasion. This legacy of modern, Westernised habits versus national traditions has become encoded in the garments of the intellectual, who is also distinguished by a fastidious neatness, a carefully manicured and pressed appearance that signals effeminacy and potential dishonesty. This code of cleanliness has played a significant role in the history of intellectualism on screen.

The character of the intellectual can be defined in terms of four major traits: deep insecurity, political cynicism, personal mistrust and self-destruction. As we have seen, no other psychological theme has featured so prominently in the discussion of Iranian cinema as that of insecurity. This theme and its relationship to several other character traits and attitudes in the context of contemporary politics was most fully developed in the insightful *Hamun* (Dariush Mehrjui, 1989). Mehrjui was the representative of intellectuals in this period, and *Hamun*, a landmark of Iranian cinema, captured their sense of malaise. Though non-commercial, this psychodrama was highly popular in Iran, especially with young audiences. It may have continued to ridicule the intellectual, but it took this figure beyond cliché towards a more interesting and rounded protrayal of a character who talked frankly about sex, employment and money, and was in a sense a new kind of rebel, questioning the values and limitations of those around him.

Hamun centred on a man on the verge of losing his job, his wife and his mind, and launched the career of Khosrow Shakibai as one of the most successful actors of the 1990s. The film benefits greatly from his performance, and from that of Bita Farahi, who plays his wife, as the two battle out their jealousies and neuroses, revealing their deepest feelings. Hamun is a frustrated writer/translator who takes on job after job, not because he is in search of wealth, but in order to protest against social wrongs. Torn between dreams and reality, passive against both society and his wife (who is having an affair and has been driven by his obsessiveness to ask him for a divorce), he is experiencing an existential crisis. Anguish and tortured self-examination had long been part of the heroic experience, but they were brought to the surface in this obsessive, misguided intellectual. Shakibai was to define this type of personality in the early 1990s.

Externally, Hamun is a man of great physical vitality and charm; internally, he is weak. He brings a raw, even brutal, masculinity to the screen, slapping his wife's face in one scene, an act which masks his own vulnerability. (Ironically, this slap was the first time since the Revolution that a man had touched a woman on screen.) But the association of sexuality with violence is challenged here. However much the audience thrilled to Shakibai as a physical male, his image is modified by the perception that he is often no more than a scared little boy who cries for his forgotten past and for his mother. When he understands that his wife is having an affair, he bursts into tears. Without her, he is helpless. Far from the domineering, educated handsome man he had seemed earlier in the film, he is revealed as a needy person, whose anger with his wife stems from his own weakness. Mehrjui takes pains to show the emptiness of his world – his barren apartment and his scattered papers symbolising his state of mind. For all his loud pretence, he has no real control over the circumstances of his life. He is a confused, uncertain, threatened, ordinary man.

Gradually, as the brash optimism and confidence of the post-war era began to dwindle throughout the 1990s, before the election of Khatami, more new protagonists were introduced into films who were characterised by a lack of self-confidence. The world in which they had to make their way was perceived as shaky and unknown. The optimistic films of the post-war years, when one could assume that sooner or later a happy outcome would prevail, were thus replaced by those exhibiting a contradictory mixture of romanticism and despair, sometimes dwelling on the theme of death.

An early example of this is Bayzai's *Mosaferan* (*Travellers*, 1992), an engrossing, thickly textured film about the nature of faith. The film recounts the allegorical story of a young couple preparing for their wedding. With the death of the bride's elder sister, along with her husband and children in a tragic car accident, the ceremony turns into a wake, at which the couple are somehow forgotten. This duality of wedding and funeral is expressed through the symbolic device of mirrors. These act like eyes, continually observing the characters' movements, creating a sense of pervasive paranoia characteristic of Bayzai's films, which was partly connected to a wider political comment regarding surveillance.

In Mahmud Kalari's *Abr va Aftab* (*The Cloud and the Rising Sun*, 1999), a film cast and crew impatiently wait for the weather to clear in order to shoot the last scene of a film. When the main actor, an old man, receives the news that his wife has had a heart attack, he immediately leaves. The rest of the cast and crew, who cannot continue in his absence, follow the old man to Tehran. The film is a primal and moving tale that presents a warmly romantic image of death and the spirit.

The last half of the 1990s was a feverish time, a period in which paranoia became the norm. Kiarostami's films had always been considered non-political, though concerned with themes of life and death, but in this period a paranoid tone crept in. With *Taste of Cherry* and *Bad Ma ra Khahad Bord* (*The Wind Will Carry Us*, 1999), the theme of death and the intellectual was further developed.

In *Taste of Cherry* an apparently wealthy, educated man drives round the outskirts of Tehran on a bright, airy day, stopping various men and asking them to perform some kind of undisclosed favour in exchange for money. He is repeatedly rebuffed. Gradually, we learn that he is planning to commit suicide, and wants someone to bury him, although the audience is only given hints as to his reasons for wishing to kill himself. Eventually, he meets someone who can help him. *Taste of Cherry* is a complex and multilayered story. It can be seen as a film about the dilemma of the intellectual in Iran, or as an essay on Tehran at the end of a century – a city of refugees, unemployment, rapidly changing landscapes and silent despair. Its subtly observed details of Iranian life led journalists at Kiarostami's Cannes press conference to ask about the film's references to Kurds and Afghans, and to various wars in the region, while the audience enquired about geopolitics and class division. Yet it is also an optimistic fable about how a taxidermist, whose job is inseparable from death, gives a desperate man a taste for life.

Today, many Iranians in the cities live primarily as consumers in an advanced capitalist society, but when someone dies, an ancient set of customs is resurrected. Traditional Iranian funeral rites have never been discarded. They still mirror the old family values, human relations, beliefs about life and death, and even the view of martyrdom that was shaped during the war. Thus the funeral is an extremely useful device with which to depict in films the contradiction between old and modern Iran.

In *The Wind Will Carry Us*, Kiarostami looks at death from a new angle. Four men arrive in a village in Iranian Kurdistan, causing speculation amongst the villagers as to the purpose of their visit. When the strangers walk around the cemetery, the villagers think they might be looking for treasure. However, one of the visitors enquires after an ailing old lady who seems near to death. When she eventually dies, the women gather for the mourning ceremony. It becomes clear that the men have come to film it. As soon as they have their pictures, they leave the village for Tehran. Kiarostami provides some comic moments throughout the film, but in the cemetery the mood changes as he addresses the theme of death. *The Wind Will Carry Us* is a scathing portrait both of the media, and of a society that considers ceremony and appearance to be more important than simple human feelings.

In 2000, director Bahman Farman'ara returned to Iranian cinema after more than a decade's absence to make a film about Iranian burial ceremonies. Obsessed with his own mortality, he made *Bu-ye Kafur, Atr-e Yas* (*The Smell of Camphor, the Fragrance of Jasmine*, 2000). The film, which won the main

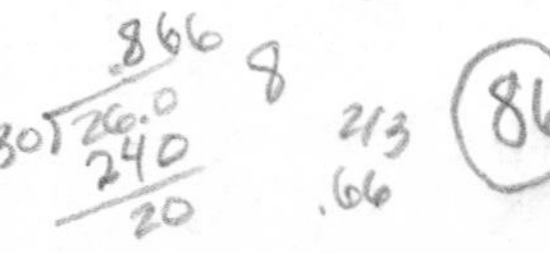

prize at the Tehran Fajr Film Festival in the same year, held up a mirror to society, covering past and present, life and death (symbolised by the camphor and jasmine of the title). The recent death of other film directors of his generation, including Sohrab Shahid-Sales and Ali Hatami, and his own heart condition, made him deeply aware of his own fragility, and he expressed his desperation through this film, which, though fictional, was essentially about his own funeral.

The film is structured into three acts: 'A Bad Day', 'Burial Ceremony' and 'Rebirth'. A filmmaker (played by Farman'ara himself) embarks on a train journey seeking answers to various questions such as what has happened to his burial plot, which he had bought years before, and why one of his close relatives has disappeared. With each character briefly encountered and every reminiscence during this voyage of death, we learn something new about the filmmaker – his failings and obsessions, the reasons why, despite his apparently successful career, he feels so alone. It is admittedly an uneven, verbose film, but it is packed with vivid imagery and political comment. The strand concerning the missing relative, a writer, makes reference to the death of a group of political writers who had been mysteriously murdered the year before.

Bayzai's thriller *Sag-Koshi* (*Killing Mad Dogs*, 2001) was made just after the turn of the millennium but is set in the post-revolutionary 1980s. The complex script, which shows how the Iranian intellectuals are under pressure, focuses on the writer Golcherhreh Kamali, played by Mozhdeh Shamsai. At the beginning of the film she returns from the provinces to Tehran to find that her husband is in hiding. He has been accused of embezzlement, framed by his partner, and asks her to pay back his debts. After a series of violent confrontations with the sleazy business partner – who kidnaps and almost rapes her – the intellectual heroine wins out.

Photographed in rich, dark colours that give the cityscape an almost shocking vividness, *Killing Mad Dogs* is an anxious portrait of human falsehood on a large scale. The audience is never sure who or what to believe since all the characters are monsters – the misogynist businessman, a corrupt lawyer, a ruthless prison guard, liars, swindlers, crooks – the rabid people of the title. A misanthropic atmosphere unlike that of any other Iranian thriller pervades this film. The woman's lonely confrontation with these characters gives the impression that she is too civilised for such a barbaric country, whose citizens pretend to be a spiritual people, while in reality they are in the clutch of a furiously destructive materialism.

A public sign seen at the beginning of the film symbolises the restrictions to freedom imposed by society: 'Women in Islamic dress only. Political discussion forbidden.' In the course of the film, the woman experiences an increasing sense of powerlessness, unable to accept a definition of herself imposed by an indecipherable male discourse. The task of the anti-intellectual ideology in this materialistic society is to mask the socioeconomic contradictions between the forces of production and consequent division of society into opposing class interests that are the driving force of contemporary Iran. Working against this, the young writer is an isolated individual who must confront those who are trying to ignore or destroy her. The question of the freedom of intellectuals in Iranian society and cinema after the Revolution seems more pressing than ever.

Women: off limits

Despite the silencing of women in Iranian cinema during the 1980s, three female directors – Rakhshan Bani-Etemad, Puran Darakhshandeh and Tahmineh Milani – were the torchbearers for their gender. Among them, Bani-Etemad achieved the most consistent body of work, gaining international recognition and winning numerous awards. She was one of the few documentary filmmakers who gradually moved into feature filmmaking. As a result, her films are often sympathetic portraits of actual people, and are frequently praised for their forceful and engaging approach to Iran's contemporary problems. It is worth noting, however, that though her films cannot be described as conventional since they express radical ideas and reach for complex and inaccessible truths, their thematic material is more groundbreaking than their more conventional cinematic syntax and form.

The importance of films such as *Kharej-e Mahdudeh* (*Off Limits*, 1988), *Zard-e Ghanari* (*Canary Yellow*, 1989) and *Pul-e Khareji* (*Foreign Currency*, 1990) lies largely in the fact that they weave a path between fiction and documentary, between the imagined and the actual.

FIG. 28 *May Lady (Banu-ye Ordibehesht)*, Rakhshan Bani-Etemad, 1998.

Nargess (1992), a daring film, tells of a complex, triangular relationship between a divorcee, her petty-thief lover, and a young, innocent woman. This was one of the first films after the Revolution to focus on sexual relationships, and played with another Iranian taboo: sex between an older woman and her younger lover. For this reason Bani-Etemad was forced to add a short scene establishing that the couple were originally married, but have resumed their relationship following their divorce. She effectively lampoons the tensions of the lower classes regarding such issues as employment, sex and law, and the melodramatic story acts as a metaphor for the moral decline of this class. Farima Farjami is outstanding as the sullen older woman coming to terms with the ageing process, a character who touches on many rewarding political and personal issues. A'tefeh Razavi also delivers a sensitive, complex performance as the simple, tortured bride who marries the young man with a dark past. The characters are so well drawn that the unfortunate fate of this demented trio seems perversely justified. Rejected by her ex-husband in favour of his young wife, the older woman throws herself in front of a moving truck.

In two films made after the election of Khatami, *Banu-ye Ordibehesht* (*May Lady*, 1998) and *Under the Skin of the City*, Bani-Etemad directly referred to political change and social tensions. Her cinematic style had become more bold and visually exciting, with a stronger tension between the aesthetic and documentary elements. The intellectual heroine of *May Lady*, Forough Kia, bears a striking resemblance, both physically and as regards her circumstances, to Bani-Etemad herself – she plays a divorced documentary filmmaker, commissioned to make a film about mothers from all walks of life. As the mother of a teenage son, she attracts much consternation, not least from the boy, when she becomes involved with a new man. This film acts as a magnifying glass on the 'moral', traditional social order that views with distaste a middle-class widow and mother embarking on a new relationship. All the difficulties that separate her from society are hurled into the story with an almost painful frankness. This drama about forbidden love and the battle against convention smashes the sentimental myth of family life in contemporary Iran.

In both *May Lady* and *Under the Skin of the City*, a tension is maintained through Bani-Etemad's disinclination to present the stories from a single, fixed viewpoint that would present a clear or coherent statement. She attempts a dissection of historical and present reality, but she rarely reaches the kind of rigid conclusions that one would expect from this forensic approach. Instead, the various events are presented from several social and economic angles, leaving any final resolution and interpretation to the viewer. The heroines are normal-looking women who wear make-up and regain the right to be attractive, as long as they preserve a plebian simplicity in their manner of dress. The woman in *May Lady* is granted a high social position, raised from the depths of passivity as the representative of a new social class that gained power through conviction in the rightness of its mission to create a more equitable world.

However, the standard female film personality in the 1990s, defined by Niki Karimi, Hedieh Tehrani and Mitra Hajar, evolved partially in response to what was perceived as the economic and sexual threat posed by educated non-traditional women. Niki Karimi personified this character in these years, the stereotype of the film heroine. Her two films with Dariush Mehrjui, *Sara* (1993) and *Pari* (1994) are considered the landmarks of her career in the mid-1990s. She appeared on screen as a melancholic mixture of woman and girl, often with the features of the femme fatale, but infused with suffering virtue. Most of Karimi's characters were prisoners of their social circumstances. Socially, this character comes from the middle classes: she is the wife of a yuppie (*The Bride*), or a bank manager (*Sara*), the sister of an actor (*Pari*) or is living abroad *Bu-ye Pirahan-e Yusof* (*The Scent of Yusof's Shirt*, Ebrahim Hatamikia, 1996).

This retrograde image of women in the 1990s reflected the official mood. Women were still technically second-class citizens, remaining the virtual property of men; girls could still be married off at the age of nine; wives were not permitted go out without their husbands' consent, and mothers had no right to child custody following a divorce. However, the aspect of social criticism in these films requires analysis. While women were seen in political terms as the simple, passive mass, the most significant and touching aspect of these films was in the woman's transition towards awareness. The subject of these tales is usually revelation, and in the course of these films the woman's life is usually transformed as she moves to a 'higher' level of understanding than her spouse. In *The Bride*, for example, the wife criticises her husband's materialism, while in *Sara* she rescues him from a fatal illness by secretly working day and night to earn money. In both films, her transition is provoked by her sense of social outrage. But the boundaries within cinema itself were strict, and the path from housewife to independent woman (*Sara*), from young student to intellectual (*Pari*), from past to future, could not easily be trodden. This type of heroine, with her initial poorly developed self-awareness, who was accustomed to allowing her fragile femininity to be trampled upon, is an indication of the lack of emancipation in patriarchal Iranian society. But the compassion of cinema audiences towards her plight, and her journey towards self-discovery were the first steps on the path to changing women's social standing. Karimi's appearance, with her classical, incised profile combined with the huge, bright, innocent eyes of a child embodied this paradox.

From 1998, women took advantage of the more relaxed climate to increase their visibility. President Khatami appointed the country's first female executive officer, Masumeh Ebtekar, as the head of the Environmental Bureau Organisation. In the same year, around 5000 women defied public segregation regulations to attend a welcome-home celebration for Iran's World Cup football squad. The trajectory of the heroine throughout the 1990s reflects this situation, as well as the atmosphere of risk that came with a new sense of licence. From the victim who had just woken up to a sense of her own position, she went on to become an attacker in a film like *Ghermez* (*Red*, Feridun Jeirani, 1998), in which a wife kills her husband, or a woman defined by her female friendship in *Dow Zan* (*Two Women*, Tahmineh Milani, 1999). This more aggressive, independent image appeared not just on screen, but also in posters and paintings.

In these daring new films, which also included *Hemlock*, about polygamy, and *Sweet Agony*, women came to the front line, no longer willing to play dead, demanding and sometimes winning modification of the discriminatory rules. Women had achieved new political muscle that those in power could no longer afford to ignore: opinion polls showed that more than 80 per cent of women, often disregarding their husband's preferences, had voted for Khatami in the presidential election.[91] If the female stars of the late 1990s and early 2000s are still defined more by type than the men, they are also more colourful and more central to the struggles of the period. For the first time in Iranian cinema, most commercial films now give higher billing to their women stars, such as Hedieh Tehrani and Niki Karimi, than they do to male actors.

Nim-e Penhan (*Hidden Half*, Tahmineh Milani, 2001) dealt with the theme of women's complex, interwoven intellectual and emotional lives, touching on many controversial issues. Karimi plays a housewife married to a judge on his way to see a woman prisoner who has been sentenced to death. To make him understand the woman's situation, she writes him a long letter detailing her own past. Back in the late 1970s/early 1980s during the *Enghelab-e*

Farhangi (Cultural Revolution), she had been a leftist college student linked to an all-female cell, who sported army jackets, images of Che Guevara and, in an ironic confusion of ideologies, of Gary Cooper. As an activist she handed out political notices, dodging the hardliners who would have arrested or even killed her for this act; it took place shortly before non-Islamic groups were subjugated by Islamic forces.

Milani depicts these hard times through the reminiscences of her heroine, a young woman torn between revolutionary political activism and romance. On one level the film is a personal melodrama of violence and love, but on another it portrays a climactic political period in contemporary Iranian history. For Milani this story is far more than the description of a single romance, or the life of one political revolutionary. This was the first time that Iranian cinema had illustrated this major event, when in 1980 all the universities had closed down for roughly four years. The film tells the story of a lost generation: the prisoners of political tensions who were powerless to escape. The young woman stands at a crossroads between two eras. Through the years of bloodshed, hardship and struggle, she has been too preoccupied with the necessities of survival to give much thought to the exact shape of post-revolutionary realities. There is a suggestion in *Hidden Half* of hostility towards the young revolutionary generation, and even scepticism as to the freedom achieved by this upheaval, when a huge challenge was made to the nation's traditional moral and social hierarchies, beliefs and myths, and a different mentality, way of life and ideals were put forward in their place.

Karimi's character in *Hezaran Zan Mesl-e Man* (*Thousands of Women Like Me*, Reza Karimi, 2000), a lawyer who walks out on her upwardly mobile husband, leaving him to fend for himself and their ill young son, deals with contemporary issues surrounding motherhood and divorce. Single women, widows, divorcees – or as they are referred to in Iranian society, 'unprotected', 'unsheltered', 'vulnerable' or 'deprived' women – were perhaps seen as the most problematic social groups in Iran after the Revolution. This is a perceptive film about a raw sore in contemporary Iran – the dissolution of the family unit as the price paid for the relative emancipation of women. When Karimi, as a career woman, comes to claim her child as a mother's prerogative, a nasty court battle ensues, ending in her attempt to kidnap her son. Her predictable failure in court demonstrates the weakness of women against the law.When the police catch her after a thrilling chase, it is not simply the vulnerability of women that is illustrated, but also the breakable nature of the individual in society.

The problem of women's custody rights has always been a controversial political issue in Iran. The campaign to improve these rights and protect children from separation from their mothers is ongoing. Iranian women have based their campaign on contradictions in state policy. On the one hand, the state defines women as mothers and considers motherhood the basis of their dignity and value in Islamic society. On the other, it refuses to grant them the right to keep and raise their children in the absence of the father. This implies that the Islamic nation's children cannot be entrusted to women. The fate of the children of war martyrs was seized upon as a politically sensitive issue by some Islamic women leaders to makes inroads into the issue.

The most controversial film on the theme of Iranian family law was *Divorce Iranian Style* (1998) by Kim Longinotto and Ziba Mir-Hosseini, a European production that focused on the the Family Law Courts in Tehran and also looked at universal issues surrounding women today. Although it was never screened officially in Iran and even the Fajr Film Festival would not show it, it became an underground cult hit, and travelled successfully all over the world. In the course of the film, we are shown the many reasons why women seek divorces in the first place: their husbands are usually unjustifiably distrusting, restrictive, deceitful, impotent, or violent. The main thrust of the film, however, was to show that these women are not just passive victims. The film also reveals the barriers that stand between Iranian women and their new ambitions: stalling tactics or silent treatment from their husbands and families, the empty gestures of reconciliation from the Court.

Even in commercial films the image of a new kind of woman was tested out. The traditional veiled face was dispensed with, instead appearing on screen heavy with make-up. The main tasks of these new heroines were not just to suffer from male jealousy or unfair laws but to rebel – if need be – against the very heart of the family. Hedieh Tehrani was the quintessence of this kind of woman in Iranian cinema. She became the most profitable star of Iranian cinema during 1998–2000, receiving more money even than

FIG. 29 Hedieh Tehrani, the quintessential new heroine of Iranian cinema at the turn of the twenty-first century.

the male stars. It seemed that both commerical films and audiences were ready to accept this new heroine.

Tehrani's peculiar, asymmetrical face with its indifferent expression was an important aspect in formulating the new type – or lack of it. The camera found an exciting individuality in her features, rejecting as uninteresting the earlier bland countenances that expressed no sense of mystery, and concentrating instead on uniqueness, enigma, the secrets of the inner life that existed behind the external facade. For the first time in post-revolutionary Iranian cinema, women could be elusive, unreadable and resistant to the presence of men. A combination of light and shadow emphasised this mystery, and the formal lighting of the studio portrait was abandoned.

The closer women on screen came to claiming their rights and freedom, the more strident was the film's message that these characters live in a world with many unanswered questions regarding women's autonomy. But women are always punished for demanding independence in these films. Men in Iranian cinema are still not allowed to touch women sexually but they can slap them, since this is seen as an expression of love, usually when directed towards city-bred women. This savagery, essentially a reaction of inadequacy in relation to a woman's urban sophistication and independence, often comes across as a sadomasochistic gesture.

This theme lurks behind the relationships in films like *Two Women* or *Red*. The couples torture and punish each other. If the men love the women, it is a sadomasochistic kind of love. The women must eventually choose between violence and loneliness. In *Two Women*, the husband has sought out a woman who will make life miserable for him. Far from wanting a real modern woman, he desires a child-woman, resulting in the decision of Karimi's character to leave him. In *Red*, Tehrani plays a mother who asks her cynical husband for a divorce; when he refuses she resorts to killing him. She becomes the perfect expression of Iranian cinema's ambivalence towards the new women in Iranian society: a mixture of idealism and misogyny.

These films reveal a glacial view of a society that is political and social rather than moral and psychological, a cry for collective rather than individual deliverance. The dark endings of *Red* and *Two Women*, as well as of *Hemlock* and many other films in which women make a counter-attack against men, show that their problems are too deep for resolution. The attack is on the unrealistic image that men have constructed and fallen in love with. The heroine's bravado is presented as an unsophisticated, naive attempt to preserve inner freedom and independence, but is in fact a cover for the deep inner wounds and defencelessness of women. When Tehrani stands over her dying husband at the end of *Red*, she gazes blankly into space, seeing and feeling nothing. Despite her crime, the audience sympathises with this woman whom the law has been unable to save from destruction.

The 1990s had, however, advanced the image of womanhood from a passive cipher to a more fully formed, moulded character with clear convictions. The audience was encouraged to see her as an equal, in contrast to earlier periods when the camera had either looked down on her from above, or up at her from below. This was no beauty on a pedestal, but a strong, ordinary woman, emphasised in Tehrani's case by her prominent features. She was a 'healthy' beauty. The young mother of Iranian folklore, the ideal of femininity, played a considerable role in the creation of this image.

Ruzi keh Zan Shodam (*The Day I Became a Woman*, 2000) by Marzieh Meshkini is perhaps the quintessential film about contemporary femininity. It is an allegorical work that explicitly examines feminist issues in a culture moving towards change yet tied to ancient conventions. In three interconnected stories, the film explores the struggle of a female, in three stages of life, whose desires conflict with societal expectations. The first is about a girl who wakes up on her ninth birthday, wholly unprepared for the fact that her life will never be the same, since she is now considered a woman by Islam and her culture. Prohibited from playing with boys, including her best friend, this is her first inkling that her new status is in fact a lesser one. In one lyrical sequence, she attempts to enjoy a last moment of happiness with her friend. In the second section, a young woman fights to be allowed to compete in a cycle race. The final section displays a dreamlike, tragicomic surrealism as an elderly woman looks back on a wasted life without passion or desire. As the three sequences link, yielding a testimony to the bounded choices of Iranian women, the film closes.

In search of the future

Since the mid-1990s, Iranian cinema has become an important element in world cinema. It has lost its inferiority complex and gained self-confidence and assurance. Iranian cinema has at last become a culture.

The battle between commercial and intellectual films has been exacerbated since the Khatami era, and the problem of genre is now a central concern for contemporary Iranian filmmakers. While the new Iranian cinema has rehabilitated experimental cinema and the auteur, most contemporary Iranian films are socio-psychological dramas that largely praise the dominant values of the day, sometimes making excursions into the past and only occasionally incorporating elements of realism. Important issues are raised on-screen in

a predictable, unchallenging manner, and the values of the counterculture are invoked only through caricature, with considerable energy focused on the most unappealing facets of youthful disaffection. If Iranian cinema is to remain a credible representation of life, it must take into account the new mores of the counterculture.

There has been much discussion about the state of cinema in Iran since 1998. This has led to the general conclusion that both branches of the cinematic tree, popular and experimental, must be developed, and that it will do no harm if the two become entangled. Iranian filmmakers have founded international festivals in an attempt to stimulate development in each area. At the same time, the issue of self-financing has been raised, in an industry that has up to now received government subsidy for many aspects of filmmaking, from raw materials to post-production and editing facilities.

In 1999, Parviz Kimiavi, the director of *Mongols*, returned to filmmaking after twenty years of silence with *Iran Sara-ye Man Ast* (*Iran Is My Land*, 1999). This film took a fresh approach to the subject of censorship in Iran through a study of different historical periods. A young provincial writer who has compiled a book of classical Persian poems is seeking the authorities' permission for publication. On his way to Tehran, his car breaks down, and he wanders into the desert, to embark on a voyage through space and time, meeting the five great classical poets, Ferdowsi, Omar Khayyam, Sa'di, Rumi, and Hafiz. Each offer advice and insights into love, tolerance, women, politics and freedom.

It is impossible not to be enthusiastic about a daring film like Jafar Panahi's *Dayereh* (*Circle*, 1999). This dextrous drama covers one long night in the lives of half a dozen women, each of whom has been imprisoned, or may soon be, for such crimes as riding in a car with a man who is not her husband. The film was banned in Iran for its references to prostitution but won the Golden Lion at the Venice Film Festival. Critics, both in Iran and abroad, greeted *Circle* as a sign of the renewal of more inventive themes and styles in Iranian cinema, as testimony to its greater freedom. When three of the women are released from prison on temporary leave they decide to run away. Their need for money and proper identification papers leads them to desperate measures. Another woman, who is unmarried, escapes in order to seek an abortion and is banished from her father's house by the violent threats of her brothers. At the end of the film the first and last women featured are shown back in the same prison, with the implication that the fate of women is an inescapable circle of imprisonment. Their world is one of constant surveillance, bureaucracy and inequality. But this stifling atmosphere cannot extinguish women's spirit, strength and courage.

9 2000–2005

September 11th and the Taliban

Within a mere 18 minutes, on 11 September 2001, two hijacked airliners slammed into New York's World Trade Center towers, drastically altering both the skyline and the world. The world's spirit changed on this day, and the changes seemed be permanent. The attack had a profound effect upon people across the world: one of shock, outrage and hostility. Once again the Middle East came under the spotlight and this time the intelligence experts focused on one name: Osama Bin Laden, the man who had planned, monitored and executed the attacks.

Who would have believed that Al-Qaida, which emerged from the heart of the Taliban regime in Afghanistan, would change the history of the world? Perhaps Iranians, as neighbours of the Afghans, felt more keenly the harsh realities of that troubled land, realities which had always been tied up with and yet covered over by religious rhetoric. Certainly Iranian filmmakers were amongst the first to travel to Afghanistan after September 11th, with the intention of making films that would unveil the realities of a country so little known to the rest of the world.

In 1989, Soviet troops had left Afghanistan, and a civil war had taken place. Fundamentalists had come to power (those fighting with the Soviets, the mujahedin, had been mostly fundamentalists) and this fundamentalism had been an enormous problem in Iran since 1979. As the war drew to a close, the increasingly radical Bin Laden formed Al-Qaida ('the Base' in Arabic and Persian), an organization of ex-mujahedin and other supporters channelling fighters and funds to the Afghan resistance. The Koran School camps, mostly based in Pakistan, which had the total support of Saudi Arabia and the United States and which were funded in part by the Saudis, created the Taliban, an army of fundamentalists. Most Talibs (meaning 'religious students') were young zealots and graduates of these religious schools. In these cloistered environments, boys grew up completely segregated from women, including female family members.

The Afghans surrendered themselves to this army, which had supposedly come to bring peace and order. From 1994 the Taliban began to emerge as a viable political force, vowing to restore order and enforce strict Islamic law (an enforcement which was welcomed by the people at the time). They captured Kabul in 1996 and imposed a harsh system of law. Mullah Muhammad Omar was named Supreme and established one of the worst human rights records in the world. The regime systematically repressed all sectors of the population and denied the rights of the individual.

The distressing number of Afghan refugees over the following years reveals the effect of the Taliban on Afghanistan. At least 6 million Afghans fled their country over two decades. According to statistics from the International Red Cross, around 1.4 million Afghans are currently living in Iran, although the actual figure is believed by the Statistics Bureau of Iran to border on 3 million. Although not officially assimilated into Iranian society, the Afghans in Iran have become the mainstay of a black-market economy, exploited and appreciated in equal measure.

The image of a country as represented to the world through the media is made up of a combination of facts about that country and imaginary or selective notions that the people of the world have of that place. The general world perception of Afghanistan was based on its reputation as one of the main producers of opium and on prejudiced notions, particularly within the Middle East, of Afghans being 'cold-blooded' and cruel. Thus the Afghans received little or no share in the world news. When the Taliban blew up two giant Buddha statues – one thought to be the tallest of its kind in the world – in defiance of international efforts to save them, the world media suddenly turned its eyes towards the situation in Afghanistan. The Iranian filmmaker Mohsen Makhmalbaf summed up the situation in a letter to the United Nations:

> The statue of Buddha was not demolished by anybody; it collapsed out of shame. Out of shame for the world's ignorance towards Afghanistan. It collapsed knowing its greatness was to no avail.[92]

The crusade on women

In its drive to restore twelfth-century fundamentalism, Afghanistan's ruling Taliban launched the country's greatest assault on womanhood in nigh on a millennium. Prior to the rise of the Taliban, women in Afghanistan were protected under law and increasingly afforded rights in Afghan society. There was a mood of tolerance and openness as the country began moving toward democracy. Women were making important contributions to national development. In 1977, they comprised over 15 per cent of Afghanistan's highest legislative body. Before the Taliban ban on female employment, 70 per cent of teachers in Kabul, Afghanistan's capital, were women, as were 50 per cent of civil servants and university students, and 40 per cent of doctors.

Under Taliban control the Afghan women disappeared under the burka (a gown that covers the entire body), the symbol of this new enslavement. The Taliban effected the 'ethnic cleansing' from one country of an entire gender: 10 million women were denied education, work and hospital care. The Taliban implemented the closing of hospitals to women, so that sick and dying women were dumped into a derelict clinic without running water.

It became illegal for women to wear makeup, nail polish or jewellery; to pluck their eyebrows; to cut their hair short; to wear colourful or stylish clothes, sheer stockings, white socks or shoes, or high-heeled shoes; to walk loudly, talk loudly or to laugh in public. In fact the government didn't believe women should go out at all: 'Women, you should not step outside your residence', reads one of the Taliban dictates. If a woman did venture out, it was ruled, it should be for an essential, government-sanctioned purpose, and she should wear the all-enveloping burka.

In 1998 30,000 men and boys poured into the dilapidated Olympic sports stadium in Kabul. Street hawkers peddled nuts, biscuits and tea to the waiting crowd. They were there to see a young woman receive a hundred lashes.

She had been arrested for walking with a man who was not a relative, a sufficient crime for her to be found guilty of adultery. Many Afghan women were executed during this period – the Taliban regime opened a new chapter in the history of cruelty to women in the Middle East.

In 2003 Babak Payami, an Iranian director who grew up in Afghanistan, made the film *Silence between Two Thoughts*, about the execution of a very young woman in Afghanistan. An executioner is ordered to kill three people in a small town, and as the camera pans 360 degrees around a courtyard in an an eight-minute opening sequence we see a man, his head wrapped in a scarf, slowly taking aim with his rifle and firing. We hear bodies fall. After killing the first two, a local cleric tells him to stop. He believes that killing the third, a young woman, would send her soul to heaven. Rather than 'save' her in this way, he therefore tells the executioner to marry and 'deflower' the girl so that she will go to hell instead. The title refers to that dawning moment in which the main character realizes he should abandon fundamentalism for truth. The story revolves around the inner doubt of the executioner and gradually the main theme becomes clear: blind faith and how it is exploited for the purposes of brutality and absurdity; how weakness – religious, ideological, nationalistic – contributes to such cruelty.

The minimalist approach gives the film the feel of being deeply realistic and artistically beautiful at the same time, bringing out the sharp edges of personality, the colourful culture and the struggle for life and truth in the middle of this parched and literally godforsaken desert. The female character – without even saying anything – is opinionated and resolved. When she does speak she is calmly radical.

When Nelofar Pazira, an Afghan woman whose family fled to Canada, heard from a friend living under Taliban rule in Kandahar that she was thinking of committing suicide, she asked Iranian filmmaker Mohsen Makhmalbaf to accompany her into Afghanistan to find her friend. Makhmalbaf made *Kandahar* (2001) a lightly fictionalized film about this journey, after the collapse of the Taliban. When it premiered at the Cannes Film Festival, few critics thought it more than a curiosity. But after September 11 all that changed, and George W. Bush – a man whose attention span rarely stretches to subtitled films – requested a special screening in order to gain a better understanding of Afghan culture.

The film was about a woman called Nafas (literally 'breath'), an exiled Afghan journalist who flies to the Afghanistan–Iran border to find her sister. But the film was also the story of a people's devastation and a country's destruction. Recording her thoughts on a portable tape-recorder, Nafas reveals that she is going to the city of Kandahar where her sister, unable to bear Taliban rule, has threatened to commit suicide at the eclipse in three days. Kandahar, the base of Taliban government, was a city full of violence and death – yet this lonely young woman still attempts to reach it. Beginning a journey of fear and agony, she goes to a refugee camp and meets tribal families. An old man, Tabib Sahib, agrees to take her across the border but on the way they are robbed by bandits. A young boy proceeds to guide her and, when she falls ill and he consults Tabib Sahib, discovers that he speaks English. The old man confesses to the woman that he is not in fact a medical doctor as he has said but an American Muslim missionary who had come to Afghanistan with the idea that he would find God by fighting in the Afghan–Soviet war. All of the characters are looking for someone or something that they will never find.

Filmed in the barren Iran–Afghan border region with non-professional actors, *Kandahar* was a road movie which blurred the boundaries between reality and fiction. The popularity of the road movie in Iran since *Where is the Friend's House?* owes much to its potential for romanticised alienation, as well as for delineating the different aspects of a nation's culture. *Kandahar* was a hymn to the doomed people, and a warning that once you enter the open hinterlands between cities and villages, you're on your own, like the lonesome woman who travelled against all the odds through this ferocious and unknown territory.

Road movies provide a ready space for exploration of the tensions and heartbreaks of the particular historical moment during which it is produced. Key moments in the history of the road movie tend to come at periods of upheaval and dislocation. In *Kandahar*, set in the deserts of decaying Afghanistan, the road appears as a specifically and violently anti-female territory and the film addresses sociopolitical issues. Around the travellers lurk menace, spontaneous mayhem and dead-end fatalism, like the city of Kandahar itself, in which the Taliban are everywhere and in which they arrest the woman at the end of the film, leaving us to wonder what happened to her. The anguish of that lonely woman was a parable for the state of Afghanistan. Makhmalbaf's concern for her, and for the Afghan people, merged in this film with his interest in post-revolutionary Islamic codes and rules in Iran and other Muslim countries.

In *Kandahar* we see the woman's face every time she lifts the burka. All the characters she meets on the road want to see her face, like the young boy, who insists on seeing her before he guides her through the desert. The contradiction between her face – an innocent beautiful face – and the hidden body under the burka, like a faceless statue, exposed the contradiction of freedom and subjugation. On her journey the woman meets various people who manifest different aspects of Afghan society and, metaphorically, of any conservative society. An old man presents a traditional tribal morality; the young boy displays the limited intake of the same; the black American fails to fight the Russians and, more gallingly, to find God in Afghanistan, symbolically failing to find God in the Middle East.

What followed the public release of *Kandahar* was a shocking moment in Iranian cinema. US prosecutors claimed that HasanTantai, who played the role of Tahib Sabib, the American Muslim doctor who helps the lonely woman, was an American fugitive wanted for killing an Iranian dissident 21 years previously. The *Guardian* wrote,

> An actor in the acclaimed Iranian film *Kandahar* is an Islamic terrorist responsible for the assassination of a political dissident, it has been alleged. Officials in the US say the man credited in the film as HasanTantai is actually David Belfield, prime suspect in the murder of former Iranian diplomat Ali Akbar Tabatabai. Tabatabai, a fierce critic of the Ayatollah Khomeini, was shot three times outside his home in Washington DC in July 1980. Belfield left the US for Iran immediately after the killing. According to Maryland state attorney Doug Gansler, the American-born Muslim was operating under orders from the Ayatollah's regime. 'We are very confident that the man who appears in the film is indeed David Belfield,' says Gansler. 'He's an assassin and he's a terrorist.' Asked for a response, the film's director, Mohsen Makhmalbaf, insisted: 'I never ask those who act in my films what they've done before.'[93]

The piece goes on to say that HasanTantai had indeed admitted that he had taken on several assumed several identities over the previous decades, but also pointed out that 'this is not an uncommon phenomenon among

Americans of my generation, the 60s generation.' Tabatabai's brother, the article continues,

> is now demanding that *Kandahar* be banned. 'Considering that our nation is now mobilized to counter international terrorism [the prospect of] a fugitive for 21 years coming back to the US glamorized as a movie star is, to say the least, unsettling,' says 71-year-old Muhammad Tabatabai. 'Not seeing the movie is not any major cultural loss to anyone. It should be stopped.'[94]

The film was not, however, banned.

Female Iranian directors in Afghanistan

A few months after 9/11 the French film producer Alain Brigand invited eleven renowned international directors and actors to each create a film lasting eleven minutes, nine seconds and one frame, based around September 11th and its consequences and looking towards their own cultures. The young Iranian filmmaker Samira Makhmalbaf was among them.

11'09"01, directed by Youssef Chahine, Amos Gitai, Alejandro González Iñárritu, Shohei Imamura, Claude Lelouch, Ken Loach, Samira Makhmalbaf, Mira Nair, Idrissa Ouedraogo and Sean Penn was a collection of shorts by people who had already attracted hostility for daring to offer different responses to this tragic event. The thought-provoking results, made with complete freedom of expression, testify to the resonance of the event across the globe. The film was an extraordinary response to the catastrophic events in New York City that had shaken the world on 11 September 2001.

The first segment, by Samira Makhmalbaf, centered on an Afghan village just after September 11th. The film opens with Afghan refugee children in Iran desperately making bricks from mud, in order to build shelters against expected retaliatory bombing by the USA. 'Hurry', urge their elders, 'the United States wants to bomb us, we must build shelters.' A teacher, who asks them if they've heard the really big news, tells them, 'You can't stop atom bombs with bricks.' As she tries to explain to them what has happened, the Afghan schoolchildren have difficulty even understanding what a tower is. Exasperated, the teacher leads the children to a towering chimney and prompts them to imagine the two towers, so that they can begin to fathom the magnitude of the tragedy. When in class she asks them for a moment of silence for the victims of 9/11, they ignore her as they discuss God and what God might or might not do. This episode was a look at how children – whom we always think of as 'innocent' – can be naive to the point of dangerousness, shrugging off the attacks halfway around the world as an act of God, while they work to build bomb bunkers.

Samira Makhmalbaf journeyed to Afghanistan in the months following the war, as a million refugees poured back into Kabul and the surrounding areas. What she discovered was the desperate plight of the people, who had no homes to return to and little food. On the aftermath of the fall of the Taliban in Afghanistan, she made *Five in the Afternoon* (2003) (the title comes from a sorrowful Lorca poem about bullfighting), and recruited residents of Kabul to take lead and minor roles in the film. The documentary-style film received a rapturous reception on its Cannes debut. The film focuses on the treatment of women and the failure of the West to avert a humanitarian crisis. It follows the character Noghreh, an independent 23-year-old woman who dreams of becoming President. But her fundamentalist father cannot abide women showing their faces and cannot understand the liberalization of his country. The film showed how, despite the Taliban having left, their ideas were still anchored in peoples' minds, in their traditions and culture.

Hana Makhmalbaf's *Lezzat-e Divanegi* (*Joy of Madness*, 2003) a documentary following the trials her sister Samira endured whilst preparing to shoot *Five in the Afternoon*, was about the climate of fear in Afghanistan and revealed the long shadow of the Taliban over women in the country, who were frightened to appear in front of the camera. Marzieh Meshkini, who is married to Mohsen Makhmalbaf, also made *Stray Dogs* (2003) in Afghanistan. She traveled there to find suitable locations, one day visiting a prison in Kabul, where she met the children of female inmates who were leading the lives of prisoners beside their mothers. They had no homes outside the prison, staying there with their mothers at nights and being let out in the mornings to earn a living. It was around these children's lives that the story took shape. For Meshkini, the Taliban were the the embodiment of a medieval outlook in the contemporary world and, after their defeat, Afghanistan had reawakened into a new age.

Iranian filmmaker Yasamin Maleknasr also took a journey across Afghanistan from Herat to Balkh, becoming the first woman filmmaker to have travelled these distances since the fall of the Taliban. Her film *Hagigat-e Gomshodeh (The Lost Truth*, 2003) reveals that, despite the turmoil and suffering they have endured, the women, men and children she encounters have held on heroically to their hopes for the future. Maleknasr's survey was diverse, ranging from rural families who dream of steady employment and peace to proud female medical students who aspire to serve their country.

The film includes a frank debate about Taliban restraint with one of the country's only women judges, describing the regime's senseless destruction of countless films and works of art. The camera captured subtle facial expressions, as well as the beautiful landscape and architecture, and painted a lucid portrait of both the Afghan people and their country. *The Lost Truth* was a tribute to a people in search of peace and determined to rebuild their nation.

Osama, I want to live

Osama (2003) by Saddiq Barmak, based on a true story, was the first Afghani feature film since the fall of the Taliban. The winner of the Golden Globe for best foreign-language film, it is a heartbreaking depiction of life in Afghanistan under the brutal Taliban regime. By showing these horrific events, *Osama* stood out as a strident protest, and as a clear lesson about the dangers of fanaticism. Barmak received assistance in the making of *Osama* – financial as well as in finding international funding for the project – from Mohsen Makhmalbaf. The similarities between *Osama* and any other number of Iranian films produced during the 1980s and 1990s are apparent. Yet it is to Makhmalbaf's and Kiarostami's films that *Osama* owes the greatest debt. The spare images of the ruined Kabul cityscape and the moments of surreal, dreamlike spectacle were very similar to those of a film such as *Kandahar*. The influence and parallels are clear, but the note of overt, unambiguous anger was new, and for this author Barmak's film was vastly superior to Makhmalbaf's.

Like Majid Majidi's *Baran* but infinitely more astringent, the story hinges on a girl (12-year-old non-professional actress Marina Golbahari) having to masquerade as a boy in order to find work in a world based on fundamentalist rules and laws. Once again childhood and adolescence play the major role. Representations of childhood, tied to representations of the family, serve as windows on to the sociopolitical landscape. The child becomes a figure through which to portray and investigate social concerns and shifting notions of the family, sexuality, normality and abnormality. Increasingly in Iranian filmmaking, as we have seen, childhood has become a realm in which intense and moving questions can be asked about the psyche, sexuality and responsibility, and, in *Osama*, about religion.

The Osama of the film's title is a girl, disguised as boy, trying anything to survive in Taliban-ruled Afghanistan. With her father killed in 'the Kabul war' and her uncle in 'the Russian war' responsibility for supporting the family falls to the girl. However, due to the law forbidding any woman from leaving her home without a male relative in supervision, she is forced to find a way – any way – to earn a living, in order to save her mother and grandmother.

Osama was prefaced with a quotation from Nelson Mandela: 'I can't forget, but I will forgive.' The film begins as if seen through the eyes of a Western news journalist, who is recording a mass rally organized by women, carrying placards and all wearing blue burkas, demanding the right to work. The journalist is later sentenced to death, and the story concerns the regime's many offences, distinctively against women.

The most breathtaking scene is the girl's witnessing of the teaching of the ablution ritual in the boy's school, which she is forced to attend at the risk of revealing her true identity. In this scene we learn that Afghanistan masculinity (as is the case all over the world, but in this case literally) is a 'performance' based upon certain codes and conventions. When officials discover that she is a girl, a death sentence is passed on her by a religious court. As she unknowingly waits her turn, a decrepit mullah obtains the girl's pardon from the leading cleric in order to take this 12-year-old as his latest wife.

The film relays a succession of virtually unrelieved horrors against and humiliations of women. Barmak represents the Taliban movement as merciless and primitive, the sworn enemy of everything modern. The cleric/judge and the lecherous mullah are cynical in the one case, hypocritical in the other. *Osama* sends an extremely powerful message against fanaticism of all kinds. Not only does it condemn the Taliban but any of us who follow despotism, absolutism and dictatorship.

Young Osama's endeavours to hide her identity are fraught with her own uncertainty – she is not sure how to behave, since the boys' routines and culture are so wholly other to her own. The film depicts the crisis of identity in Middle Eastern Muslim countries. The girl is never convincing as a boy at school, though she does her best to act 'tough', climbing trees even though she's afraid, enduring the taunts of boys who find her girlish. Her face, haunted and grim, offers a simple, resonant, immutable truth. In a dream, she is in prison: the camera pans across the bars to reveal women in blue burkas bowed down in horror and submission. The utter impossibility of this simple child's game is unforgettable.

The 'far from home' films

Since the beginning of 2000, the most scrutinized aspect of Afghanistan in Iranian cinema has been the theme of being 'far from home'. Such films explore the problems of the Afghanistan people through the use of children, who define the sense of rejection, the Afghani people's invisibility, and their physical or psychological wounds.

About 2 million people – around 10 per cent of Afghanistan's population – died during the Taliban regime as a result of poverty, famine, war and homelessness. Many children lost their parents: those who had no chance of emigrating to other countries and could not be housed in orphanages had to live on the streets. In Kabul, the number of street children rose from an estimated 28,000 to 60,000 in 2004 alone. This city, once a symbol of modernity for Afghanistan, is now in ruins. The land mines also maimed or killed an average of 25 people a day after the invasion of Afghanistan by the USA. Two-thirds of these were children. It was predominantly children who herded animals, or searched for fuel or scrap metal to sell in order to help support their families.

The 'far from home' films tackled a number of issues, firstly, the Afghans' refugee dilemma in Iran, including the troubled acceptance of refugees and their children into Iranian society. Second, films on this theme looked at the illegal employment of Afghans and the often attendant issue of 'black market job syndrome'. Third, they focused on the chaotic situation of Afghans in the refugee camps.

Delbaran (2002) by Abolfazl Jalili tackled the effects of the war in Afghanistan through episodes from the life of an Afghan boy working in a truckstop just inside the Iranian border. On the Afghan border, Jalili had by chance come across a teenage Afghan refugee and decided to integrate his story into the film, where he features as the lead character. The imagery is minimalistic and, by abandoning dialogue, music and even the bare basics of storytelling, offers an atmospheric portrayal of this remote border town, whilst never doing more than hinting at the wider tensions that were producing such misery. The episodic nature of this film – which is composed of details, close-ups and snatches of action – captured the effect that the war had on individuals.

Everyone in this film is estranged from each other, and indeed from themselves, trapped in the barren, empty landscape and forced to find human connection in only the most basic, often antagonistic ways. The story is purposefully filled with redundant shots and contains a refreshing portrait of a young man trying to find a place for himself during a chaotic period. Far from dwelling on the tragic circumstances, Jalili looks for moments of humour and triumph and, with a poetic approach, captures the grittiness of the boy's life. Although the war hovers in the background of the film, there are no scenes of tanks or soldiers. Instead Jalili captures the details, dwelling on the scarce liquids that sustain life in this desolate desert – water, petrol, tea, soup, medicine. And the repetitive mechanical failures echo the inability of the Iranians to cope with the influx of refugees over the border during the Taliban civil war.

Baran (2001) by Majid Majidi was a glimpse at the situation of Afghan refugees living in Iran over the past three decades. Baran (Zahra Bahrami), whose name means 'rain', is a teenage Afghan girl who can only find the necessary work under camouflage as a boy. Latif (Hossein Abedini), a young labourer, does everything in his power to sabotage his rival until the day he discovers she is not a boy but an Afghan girl. He develops a bond with this powerless, almost hopeless child and becomes her protector. Through the speechless girl he becomes increasingly fascinated by her history. *Baran* is an allegory about the need to change one's attitudes to refugees, to racism and to sexism.

Set in the vast Afghan refugee community in northern Iran, *Baran* has a vivid visual impact, with its pristine silver light, the snow on the ground and a weak sun low over the city. Majidi narrates his story as much by simply observing the behaviour of his characters, which are played almost entirely by non-professional actors, as through plot and dialogue. He made the film in order to draw attention to the plight of Afghan refugees in Iran, who were at the time the largest population of refugees anywhere in the world. (The film was made just before September 11th; the American bombing campaign increased the number of refugees.) The ending of *Baran* is lyrical yet harsh: the Afghan girl disappears; she and her family, it is said, have returned to Afghanistan, yet Latif is in love with her – perhaps will love her for ever. In hindsight this ending lends a sad irony to the director's stated desire to show that 'love can conquer all borders'. Indeed his faith in the cumulative power of small, courageous steps and the idea that love will provide a way of understanding the Afghan people and their difficulties contrasts strongly with their actual situation in the face of hunger and homelessness.

Majidi's *Pa Berehneh ta Herat* (*Barefoot to Herat*, 2002) was shot during two trips to Western Afghanistan. During the first he visited two refugee camps, one in a Taliban-controlled area and another a small camp situated in an area held by the Northern Alliance (a foreign-supported group fighting the Taliban). This trip came just after a series of American attacks on the Taliban forces, when people were fleeing from the air raids on Kandahar, Herat and other cities and villages. The second trip was to the city of Herat itself, now freed from the Taliban, and to the hunger stricken camp of Maslakh (literally and ironically meaning 'slaughterhouse'), one of the largest in the world. With the Afghans fleeing to take refuge in the ill-equipped camps, the film witnessed the struggle of families who had lost everything and who were attempting to secure for themselves a minimal life. Faced with cold, hunger and death, Afghan children still tried to learn, to play and to enjoy whatever life offered them. In the aftermath of the fall of the Taliban, the film captured the reactions of those living in Herat, who expressed their memories and their hopes. Forgotten in the nearby camp, 150,000 displaced

Afghans could barely survive, and hunger and hopelessness prevailed. Yet amid the overwhelming poverty and chaos, the daily quest for survival, the desire for joy, for beauty and for music was still alive.

Majidi interviewed peasants and soldiers, men and women, youngsters and the elderly, and brought a humanistic view to the children's extraordinary joy and optimism in the face of the emotional and physical turmoil of war. *Barefoot to Herat* was a roar for support and a poem to life. Majidi made *Olimpic dar Camp* (*Olympics in Camp* 2003) with the same spirit. Here kids in an Afghan refugee camp gather bullet-shells, turning the battlefield into a playing field for eternal friendship, in the hope of a future with no war and no violence.

The people without a homeland

> The reasons for the entire region derive from the borders. In Europe, despite the different cultures and languages, they have a single currency. We Kurds are one community with one language, but we are divided between Iran, Iraq, Turkey and Syria.
>
> Bahman Ghobadi[95]

The Kurds are a nation without a state, probably the largest stateless people in the world, comprising over 30 million people. They live in an area called Kurdistan, a mountainous area southeast of Turkey, northeast of Syria, north of Iraq and west of Iran. Many have fled poverty and oppression under the dictatorships of Iraqi, Iranian and Turkish rulers to different parts of the world. Today, the majority of Kurds, some 15 to 20 million, live in Turkey, which refuses to recognize their existence and cultural rights. As part of an ultra-nationalist policy, the Kurds are submitted to intense assimilation, deportation and dispersion and to the systematic elimination of their dissident intellectual elites. Since June 1991, in a territory as big as Switzerland, 3.5 to 5 million Iraqi Kurds have lived independently in a region between Iran, Iraq and Turkey, where they were beyond the control of Saddam Hossein's regime. They have a parliament, three universities, schools, television stations, and over 120 newspapers and magazines in Kurdish. Furthermore, 10 million Kurds, the victims of ethnic and religious discrimination, live in

Iran. The 1.5 million Kurds living in Syria have no collective linguistic or cultural rights. To complete the picture, mention must also be made of the Kurds from the former Soviet Union, said to number some 500,000.

The Kurds always had very limited resources. Their armed struggle for autonomy has ended each time in defeat, with the increased oppression of Kurdish civilians. This is the nature of war. If you lose, you lose in a big way, and your condition will be worse than it was before. This has happened to the Kurds several times. Every small improvement or change has been abolished after each lost war. The other difficulty in the struggle for liberation of the Kurds is that for decades they have relied on the regimes of Iran and Iraq, with the Kurds from Iran receiving help from Iraq and the Kurds from Iraq receiving help from Iran.

Saddam Hossein's Iraqi regime forcibly displaced and killed millions of Kurds and, ironically, whilst the world was keen to punish Saddam for his crimes, few seemed interested in helping the Kurdish victims. Even the right to establish a Kurdish Red Cross or to receive international aid from the Red Cross has been denied. The Iraqi regime argued that since Kurdistan was not a country, they could not help them. The impact of this policy has brought Kurds further pain, especially over the past decade.

In 1988, the destruction of Kurdistan and the mass killing of the Kurds by the Iraqi regime were well-known facts, but because the regime never allowed anybody, including officials, to record the details of Saddam Hossein's reign, these were understandably not documented, at least not in the west. During the war over Kuwait in 1990, the Iraqi regime's repression of 'its own' people, in particular the use of chemical weapons against the Kurds, became an important part of the ideological justification for the 'just war' to restore Kuwait. During the unsuccessful Kurdish uprising of March 1991, the Kurds captured huge quantities of Iraqi government records held in the secret police buildings in the major towns and cities. Genocide in Iraq and the Bureaucracy of Repression were however documented in the Iraqi regime's policy against the Kurds.

Lakposhtha ham Parvaz Mikonand (*Turtles Can Fly*, 2004) was set in Bahman Ghobadi's native Kurdistan on the eve of the American invasion of Iraq on 20 March 2003. Set in a Kurdish refugee camp town on the Turkish border of Iraq, the film opens in the days before the invasion. Under an

FIG. 30 *Turtles Can Fly (Lakposhtha ham Parvaz Mikonand)*, Bahman Ghobadi, 2004.

ice-blue sky, in primitive surroundings made of tents and barbed wire, a boy nicknamed Satellite (played by Soran Ebrahim) commandeers an army of children to work for the town, clearing the fields of mines. He assigns a motley gang of refugee children, many of whom have lost limbs because of the landmines, to various jobs in the rugged countryside, which is littered with landmines, spent shells, and wrecked and rusted vehicles.

The children collect enough landmines to trade with or sell to an arms dealer in exchange for a satellite dish, which will allow them to receive news about what is going to happen in Iraq when the USA invades. The UN representative in the village also offers to pay the children for recovered landmines – which he says will not be re-armed – but the arms dealer pays more. The landmines the children collect could explode at any moment;

the best ones, says the ironic Satellite, were 'made in America'. Satellite's essential stratagem often seems like a parody of the global conflict raging around him, when he makes clear that 'those who work with me aren't allowed to work with him', it is tempting to see an ironic side-glance at George W. Bush's post-September 11th statement that, 'either you are with us or you are with the terrorists'.

Newly arrived in the camp are a refugee girl called Agrin (Avaz Latif) and her armless brother Hengov (Hirsh Feyssal), along with a small blind child, the product of Agrin's rape by Iraqi soldiers. When Satellite falls for this unlikely sad-faced orphan the world changes for him. *Turtles Can Fly* is not just a political film and it sometimes seems more clearly like a love story between an energetic teenager and a survivor of the war. Ghobadi has dedicated *Turtles Can Fly* to 'all the innocent children in the world – the casualties of the policies of dictators and fascists'. The familial savagery is spotlighted in the life of the young girl Agrin who, despite an ensemble cast, emerges as Ghobadi's central character. Sympathetic throughout and portrayed like an angel, she nonetheless tries to get rid of her child – her brother forced her to keep the boy and this only fuels the self-loathing she feels because of the rape. The girl's crushed soul forms one extreme and Satellite's optimism, symbolized by the colorfully adorned bicycle he pushes down the muddy roads, is the other.

The devastation of this land and its inhabitants is revealed in the film in the matter-of-fact perspective of the children and is displayed in poignant details which reveal its unbearable nature. The exquisitely haunting mountains play a backdrop to violence and tragedy; at the same time the full hearts and humour of the children remain an undeniable force. In one telling scene, American helicopters fly over the refugee camp. The villagers and refugees have fled to a hillside where they are trying to look like trees so that they will not be bombed. The Americans drop leaflets saying, 'We will make this country a paradise. We are here to take away your problems. We are the best in the world.'

There is therefore, in the children's relationships, light amidst the darkness. There is in *Turtles Can Fly* a deep compassion and, above all, a wicked sense of humour. Ghobadi said,

> This is Kurdish life. This is how the people are. They express their love; they laugh a lot. So when I wanted to reflect what was going on in Iraq, I had to bring a sense of humour into it, because this is how the Kurds survive their hardships.[96]

Turtles Can Fly is a story of oppression. The turtles of the title remind us of the generations of migration and genocide whose burden clings to the Kurds like the keratinous armour of the turtle. While state-sponsored oppression and the Kurdish diaspora form the inspiration for Ghobadi's films, more insidious forces are to be found in each of his carefully constructed plots: the twin evils of tradition and family (in Ghobadi's films the parents are generally absent and the children alone in a cruel and frightening world), both in direct opposition to individual identity.

Cinema's unique capacity for stimulating dialogue about ourselves has been acknowledged from the outset of this book. The films discussed have affected the way we visualize not just the past, but also the present. I have throughout juxtaposed the films themselves with their contemporary historical situations and subjects, looking at them in relation to the two provocative terms 'politics' and 'Iran'. Iranian filmmakers have had their say about the past and present. They have spoken eloquently and sometimes foolishly. Sometimes their fabrications have fascinated us; sometimes they have have gone unnoticed.

Particularly in an international climate of growing pessimism and doubt, I have come to dismiss the old idea that films can be thought of as pure entertainment or art – or occasionally as both. I believe that films reflect the currents and attitudes of society, of the world and its political dimensions, and I have come to accept that most films have a bitter political content, whether conscious or unconscious, hidden or overt. Yet it remains difficult to accept that cinema does not still exist in a sublime state of innocence, untouched by the world and its politics.

Notes

1. I have assumed that readers will not necessarily have seen the films discussed and have accordingly given some indication of content. The English translation, director and date of the film are provided after each original Persian title and are henceforth referred to in English (where there is no translation, the title of the film is a character's name). Where films do not have an 'official' English title under which films have been shown outside Iran, I have directly translated from the Persian. Dates for films are often hard to ascertain because the year of completion, year of registration and year of public release may not always coincide. Where possible, the date given for each film is that of the year of completion. For Iranian newspapers and magazines, dates according to the Western calendar are provided.
2. Mozzafar al-Din Shah, 'The Travels of His Grace, Mozzafar al-Din Shah', 1900, in Ketabkhaneh-ye Majlis (the Library of Parliament), Roshdie Publications, Tehran, 1984.
3. Shi'ism is a major branch of Islam that considers Ali – the son-in-law and kinsman of Muhammad – and his descendants to be Muhammad's true successors. The concept of matrydom is crucial to Shi'a thought, and has had an enormous impact on Iranian art and culture.
4. *Taraghi* 864, 1958.
5. *Sur Esrafil* 26, 1908.
6. *Etella'at*, December 1926.
7. *Etella'at*, 4 January 1930.
8. *Setare-ye Jahan* 426, 1930.
9. *Aiene Iran*, 12 October 1930.
10. *Etella'at*, 24 November 1928.
11. *Etella'at*, 17 January 1930.
12. *Etella'at*, 5 August 1935.
13. Hamid Mowlana, 'Journalism in Iran: a History and Interpretation', doctoral dissertation, Northwestern University, Chicago, 1963.
14. *Etella'at*, 22 July 1935.

15. *Iran*, 22 November 1933.
16. *Iran*, 2 July 1934.
17. Most famously by Edward Said in *Orientalism*, Vintage, New York, 1979.
18. Quoted in Parvin Paidar, *Women and Patriarchal Process in Twentieth-Century Iran*, Cambridge University Press, Cambridge MA, 1995.
19. *Etella'at*, 13 October 1934.
20. Quoted in Nikkie Keddie, *Religion and Politics in Iran*, Yale University Press, New Haven, 1983.
21. *Hollywood*, 5 May 1945.
22. *Hollywood*, 1 July 1943.
23. *Hollywood*, December 1944.
24. *Pravda*, 25 September 1945.
25. See Pari Sheikholeslami, *Zanan-e Rooznamenegar va Andishmand Iran* (*Women Journalists and Free-thinkers of Iran*), Chapkhaneh Mazgraphic, Tehran, 1972.
26. Arthur C. Millspaugh, *The American Task in Persia*, Century, New York, 1925.
27. Ibid.
28. Arthur C. Millspaugh, *Americans in Persia*, Brookings Institution, Washington DC, 1946.
29. Ibid.
30. See Ali Banuzzi, *Iranian National Character: A Critique of Some Western Perspectives*, Princeton University Press, Princeton NJ, 1974.
31. Willam S. Hass, *Iran*, Colombia University Press, New York, 1946.
32. *Iran*, ed. Herbert H. Vreeland, Human Relations Area Files, New Haven CT, 1957.
33. *Setare-ye Cinema* 45, 1955.
34. *Setare-ye Cinema* 91, 1956.
35. *Setare-ye Cinema* 32, 1955.
36. *Setare-ye Cinema*, 18 March 1954.
37. *Setare-ye Cinema*, 16 June 1959.
38. *Peik-e Cinema*, 30 December 1954.
39. *Ferdowsi*, 6 December 1954.
40. *Monsieur Beaucaire* (George Marshal, 1946); *The Bride Wore Boots* (Irving Pichel, 1946); *Unconquered* (Cecil B. DeMille, 1947); *Joan of Arc* (Victor Fleming, 1948); *Desert Hawk* (Frederick de Cordova, 1950); *Christopher Columbus* (David Macdonald, 1949); *Samson and Delilah* (Lee Philips, 1948); *Silver Queen* (Lloyd Bacon, 1942); *The Accused* (William Dieterle, 1948).
41. *Jahan-e Cinema*, 31 January 1952.
42. *Setare-ye Cinema* 56, 1955.
43. *Post Tehran Cinemaie*, 28 January 1958.

44. See Karin Van Nieuwakaesk, *A Trade Like Any Trade: Female Singers and Dancers in Egypt*, University of Texas Press, Austin, 1995.
45. *Setare-ye Cinema* 494, 1965.
46. *Setare-ye Cinema* 332, 1962.
47. *Setare-ye Cinema*, October 1958.
48. See *Film Magazine* 92, 1990.
49. *Ercan*, February 1979.
50. In an interview, Kimiai stated: 'I chose *Deers* as the title, because a deer has a beautiful horn and an ugly foot. But it is its horn that traps it, and its ugly foot that sets it free.'
51. See Robert Graham, *The Iranian Illusion of Power*, Croom Helm, London, 1978.
52. Ibid.
53. Oriana Fallaci, *Interview with History*, Houghton-Mifflin, Boston MA, 1977.
54. Ibid.
55. Ibid.
56. *Sight and Sound*, Spring 1974.
57. *Films and Filming*, March 1977.
58. See *Time*, December 1979.
59. See Asef Bayat, *Street Politics: Poor People's Movements in Iran*, Colombia University Press, New York, 1997.
60. See *Kayhan*, 6 January 1979.
61. See *Islam's Artistic Perspectives* (*Negahi beh Falsafe-ye Honaraz Didgah-e Eslam*) and *Art Waiting for Promises* (*Honar dar Entezar-e Moeood*).
62. *Jomhouri-e Eslami*, November 1980.
63. *Ettela'at*, November 1981.
64. *Ettela'at Haftegi* 2080, March 1981.
65. *Etella'at Haftegi* 2087, April 1982.
66. *Kayhan*, June 1981.
67. *Ettela'at*, November 1981.
68. *Ettela'at*, December 1981.
69. *Ettela'at*, June 1980.
70. *Kayhan*, June 1980.
71. See *Kayhan*, July 1980.
72. *Kayhan*, 30 May 1982
73. *Jomhuri-e Eslami*, 13 June 1982
74. *Jomhuri-e Eslami*, 10 June 1982.
75. Ibid.
76. *Etella'at-e Haftegi*, 23 June 1982.
77. *Time*, 3 December 1979.
78. Other films outlawed during this period were: 1980: *Seem-e Khardar* (*Barbed Wire*,

Mehdi Madanian), *Khashm-e Elahi* (*Divine Wrath*, Aziz Rafi'i), *Ghiam* (*Rebellion*, Reza Safai), *Mosafer-e Shab* (*Night Rider*, Mansur Tehrani), 1936 (Muhammad Reza Bozorgnia and Hassan Gholizadeh); 1981: *Afioun: Tab-e Marg* (*Opium: Death Fever*, Aman Manteghi and Dariush Kushan), *Peikar Tarash* (*Sculptures*, Muhammad Reza Moma'jed), *Jadeh* (*Highway*, Muhammad-Ali Sajadi); 1982: *Efrit* (*Demon*, Farshid Falaknazi, *Haji Washington* (Ali Hatami); 1983: *Fasl-e Khakestari* (*The Grey Season*, Seyyed Muhammad Shahram Shobeiri); 1984: *Hamase-ye Mehran* (*Legend of Mehran*, Hamid Taherian).

79. *Sight & Sound*, April 1997.
80. *International Herald Tribune*, 16 February 2001.
81. See Matthew Bernstein and Gaylyn Studlar, *Visions of the East*, I.B. Tauris, London, 1997.
82. *Blockbuster Video Guide*, 2000.
83. *Elle*, May 1998.
84. *Sight & Sound*, February 1997.
85. Godfrey Cheshire, *Projection*, Faber & Faber, London, 1998.
86. *Time*, 5 January 1998.
87. *Newsweek*, 27 April 1998.
88. *Elle*, May 1998.
89. *Guardian*, 11 December 1998; *Newsweek*, 26 October 1998; *New York Times*, 30 September 1998; *Time Out*, 16–30 December 1998.
90. *Newsweek*, 26 October 1998.
91. *Time*, 27 July 1998.
92. Letter dated 25 January 2002.
93. *Guardian*, 2 January, 2002.
94. Ibid.
95. *Sight & Sound*, February 2005.
96. *Daily Telegraph*, 28 March 2005.

Index